Table of Contents

Getting Started

Welcome to the official Level Two Apple Pro Training course for Final Cut Pro X.

This book is an in-depth journey into the advanced editing techniques and effects of Final Cut Pro X. It uses diverse footage ranging from the feature film *SuperGirl Rocks* to the music video *One Night in Jordan* (based on a live concert performance by internationally renowned artist Zade Dirani). It also explores creating promotional spots and show bumpers to demonstrate application features and practical techniques you'll use daily in your editing projects.

Whether you've been editing for years or are just beginning to work in film and video, this book will enhance your knowledge of Final Cut Pro X while it enhances your editing skills. So let's get started!

The Methodology

This book takes a hands-on approach to using the software. It's divided into projects—based on footage on the accompanying DVD—that teach you advanced techniques as you work through the lessons. Every exercise is designed to get you editing and creating effects professionally in Final Cut Pro as quickly as possible.

Each lesson builds on previous lessons to guide you through the application's functions and capabilities. However, if you're already familiar with Final Cut Pro, you can go directly to a specific section and focus on that topic because every lesson is self-contained.

Course Structure

This book is designed to improve your skills both as an editor and as a Final Cut Pro user. You'll begin by learning editing techniques designed to streamline your workflow and allow you to effectively perform complex editing tasks. Then you'll focus on sound editing and multicamera footage. Next, you'll explore the world of effects, covering such diverse topics as compositing, filters, keyframing, compound clips, titling, and speed changes. Finally, you'll finish your studies by learning a variety of techniques for color correcting clips, balancing scenes, and creating deliverables using Compressor.

The lessons are grouped into the following categories:

▶   Advanced Editing: Lessons 1–6

▶   Advanced Compositing and Effects: Lessons 7–9

▶   Finishing Techniques: Lessons 10–14

In addition to the exercises, some lessons include project tasks that provide an opportunity to practice what you've learned. Throughout the book, other valuable sections will guide you in evaluating your project before moving to the next editing stage.

Downloading Final Cut Pro X

Final Cut Pro X is available as a download from the Mac App Store. Because installation can begin immediately after purchase, you should read the Apple best practices (http://support.apple.com/kb/HT4722) *prior* to installation to ensure the best performance of the application. The exercises in this book are based on Final Cut Pro version 10.0.3. If you have an earlier version of Final Cut Pro X, update your software or some exercises may not work as described.

Using the DVD Book Files

The Apple Pro Training Series: Final Cut Pro X Advanced Editing DVDs (included with the printed book) contains the project files and media you'll use for each lesson. After you transfer the files to your hard drive, each lesson will instruct you in the use of the project and media files.

> **NOTE** ▶ If you purchased this title as an eBook, you will find a URL to download the files on the "Where Are the Lesson Files" page located at the end of the eBook.

Installing the Final Cut Pro X Lesson Files

On the DVDs, you'll find three files: APTS FCP X ADV Part 1.sparseimage, APTS FCP X ADV Part 2.sparseimage, and APTS FCP X ADV Part 3.sparseimage. These disk image files function like virtual disks. You will use their contents for the exercises in the book. Specific instructions in the lessons will explain which disk image to load.

1   Insert the Apple Pro Training Series: Final Cut Pro X Advanced Editing, Disc One DVD into your DVD drive.

   Depending on which version of OS X you're using and the Finder preferences, you may not see the DVD on your desktop. If you don't see the DVD, take a quick look in a Finder window to see all the mounted volumes (such as hard disks or DVDs) that are available.

2   In the Dock, click the Finder icon.

3   In the Finder window, select the APTS FCP X ADV DVD listed in the left sidebar under Devices.

4   With the DVD selected, drag the three disk images from the DVD to your desktop to copy them.

   Alternatively, you may drag the disk images to any locally connected storage device such as an external hard disk. Whichever destination you choose, Final Cut Pro must have access to the disk image files, and you must have read and write privileges. In addition, the storage device must have at least 23 GB of free space available.

5   After the disk image files are copied, eject the DVD.

6   Insert the second disc, Apple Pro Training Series: Final Cut Pro X Advanced Editing, Disc Two, into your DVD drive, and repeat steps 2 through 5.

Before you begin a section in this book, you must mount the corresponding disk image to give Final Cut Pro access to the necessary project and media files.

7   On your desktop (or the location you chose for the files), double-click an APTS FCP X ADV disk image file to mount the disk images.

A virtual disk labeled APTS FCP X ADV Part 1 (or Part 2 or Part 3) appears under Devices in the Finder window's sidebar.

NOTE ▸ Depending on which version of OS X you use and the Finder's preferences, you may not see the APTS FCP X disk on your Desktop.

Each lesson will identify the disk image and the files to use for that lesson's exercises. You should not alter the contents of the Final Cut Events or Final Cut Projects folders on a APTS FCP X ADV virtual disk.

Using Final Cut Pro on a Portable

Some of the desktop Mac keystrokes identified in this book differ from the keystrokes used with a MacBook Pro. Specifically, you'll sometimes need to hold down the Function key (fn) when pressing the Left and Right Arrow keys to access the Home and End keys, respectively.

About the Footage

Footage from eight diverse projects is used throughout this book—ranging from a feature film and a documentary to a concert video and various broadcast promos. Together, they represent a real-world sampling of the types of projects and media formats you'll likely encounter as a working video editor. Although the lesson exercises instruct you to edit the footage in a particular way, you can use any part of this footage to practice your own editing methods. Techniques you've learned using one set of clips in a lesson can be practiced using a different set of clips to create a new project.

NOTE ▸ Due to copyright restrictions, you cannot use this footage for any purpose outside this book or upload any version of the files in this book to YouTube or any other public or private video sharing site.

System Requirements

Before using *Apple Pro Training Series: Final Cut Pro X Advanced Editing,* you should have a working knowledge of your Macintosh and its OS X operating system. Make sure that you know how to use the mouse; standard menus and commands; and how to open, save, and close files. If you need to review these techniques, see the printed or online documentation for your system.

To review the basic system requirements for Final Cut Pro X, refer to the technical specifications at www.apple.com/finalcutpro/specs/.

About the Apple Pro Training Series

Apple Pro Training Series: Final Cut Pro X Advanced Editing is both a self-paced learning tool and the official curriculum of the Apple Pro Training and Certification Program.

Developed by experts in the field and certified by Apple, the series is used by Apple Authorized Training Centers worldwide and offers complete training in all Apple Pro products. The lessons are designed to let you learn at your own pace. Each lesson concludes with review questions and answers summarizing what you learned, which can be used to help you prepare for the Apple Certification Exam.

For a complete list of Apple Pro Training Series books, see the page at the back of this book, or visit www.peachpit.com/apts.

Apple Pro Certification Program

The Apple Pro Training and Certification Programs are designed to keep you at the forefront of Apple digital media technology while giving you a competitive edge in today's ever-changing job market. Whether you're an editor, graphic designer, sound designer, special effects artist, student, or teacher, these training tools are meant to help you expand your skills.

Upon completing the course material in this book, you can earn Apple certification. Certification is offered in all pro applications, including Aperture, Final Cut Pro, Motion, and Logic Pro. Certification gives you official recognition of your knowledge of Apple professional applications while allowing you to market yourself to employers and clients as a skilled user of Apple products.

Apple offers three levels of certification: Apple Certified Associate, Apple Certified Pro—Level One, and Apple Certified Pro—Level Two. Certification exams do not require class attendance. Students who prefer to learn on their own or who already have the necessary skill set in the chosen application may take an exam for a fee.

Apple Certified Associate status validates entry-level skills in a specific application. Unlike an Apple Certified Pro exam, you can take Associate exams online from the comfort of your own home or office. Apple Certified Associate status is appropriate for students, for someone who is preparing for a first job out of school or a college-level program, or for anyone interested in validating entry-level credentials. Instructions on how to take the exam are included later in this book. For details on what the exam covers, please visit http://training.apple.com/certification/proapps.

An Apple Certified Pro is a user who has reached the highest skill level in the use and operation of Apple Pro Applications as attested to by Apple. Students earn certification by passing the online certification exam administered only at Apple Authorized Training Centers (AATCs). Apple Certified Pro status is appropriate for industry professionals.

For those who prefer to learn in an instructor-led setting, training courses are taught by Apple Certified Trainers at AATCs worldwide. The courses use the Apple Pro Training Series books as their curriculum and balance concepts and lectures with hands-on labs and exercises. AATCs are carefully selected to meet Apple's highest standards in all areas, including facilities, instructors, course delivery, and infrastructure. The goal of the program is to offer Apple customers, from beginners to the most seasoned professionals, the highest-quality training experience.

For more information, please see the page at the back of this book, or to find an Authorized Training Center near you, visit training.apple.com.

Resources

Apple Pro Training Series: Final Cut Pro X Advanced Editing is not intended as a comprehensive reference manual, nor does it replace the documentation created for the application. For comprehensive information about program features, refer to these resources:

▶   Final Cut Pro Help—Accessed through the Final Cut Pro Help menu, the Reference Guide contains a complete description of all features. You can also access Help at http://help.apple.com/helplibrary/category/videoediting.

▶   For a list of other resources, please visit the Apple website at www.apple.com/finalcutpro/resources/.

▶   For details on the Apple Training and Certification programs, please visit http://training.apple.com.

Advanced Editing

1

Time   This lesson takes approximately 120 minutes to complete.

Goals   Understand metadata and how to generate it

Incorporate auto-generated and user-generated metadata

Filter the Event Browser based on metadata

Create custom metadata views

Batch rename clips in a nondestructive way

Organizing Your Media

Good editing begins with good organization. No matter how skilled you may be at juxtaposing images, finding a scene's rhythm, or making your cuts invisible, you still need to find the right footage when you need it. And that means effectively cataloging your clips and adding enough *metadata* (information about the content of the clips) to ensure that everything is always at your fingertips.

Final Cut Pro X has an expansive and extendable metadata architecture that allows you to categorize, organize, manage, and otherwise prepare your source media with precision, ease, and tremendous flexibility.

Final Cut Pro X automatically detects a wide range of metadata from the source clips. Camera type, format, image settings, and other data are passed directly from the camera. You can also instruct Final Cut Pro to detect additional information such as areas that are very shaky (and require stabilization); human faces that appear in the frame; and the number of human subjects and their distances from the camera.

For each clip, you can enter information such as scene number, camera roll, or camera angle; and create custom fields to identify character name, shot type, interview style, or other information that might be useful for your project.

You can search for and sort by all of this information when looking to find a particular shot. You can also create custom layouts to view this data at a glance, enabling you to easily see the information most important for any given project.

Finally, you can use some of this information (as well as a variety of other metadata) to automatically rename your clips, turning that filename into a basic identifier to quickly supply essential information and ultimately speed your editing workflow.

Using Hands-Free Metadata

Much of the metadata associated with your clips is generated automatically—either imported directly from the camera or determined by analyzing the clip contents.

Adding this information to your Event (for searching, sorting, filtering, and so on) requires no manual work on your part—no selecting, no typing, no thinking. It's just there when you need it. This metadata falls into two categories: source media metadata and auto-analysis metadata.

The two types are acquired in different ways and are generally stored in separate places. Source media metadata is present whether you want it or not. Auto-analysis data requires you to make a one-time request, either during import or at any later point.

Viewing Source Media Metadata

Source media metadata includes the basic information about your clips, such as duration, frame size, frame rate, compression type, data rate, and so on. It also may include information about the brand and model of your camera, lens used, focal length, ISO setting, date and time of the recording, and any other data your camera stores with the source clips.

All of this information is visible in the Info Inspector.

1   In the Finder, double-click the APTS FCP X ADV Part 1.sparseimage disk image to mount it.

2   In Final Cut Pro X, in the Event Library, click the disclosure triangle for the APTS FCP X ADV Part 1 mounted drive, and then select the *Lesson_01* Event.

If you want to match the settings displayed in the preceding figure, from the Event Library Action pop-up menu, choose:

▶ Group Events by Date > Don't Group Events by Date

▶ Group Clips By > None

▶ Arrange Clips By > Name

▶ Arrange Clips By > Ascending

3   In the Event Browser, click **Shot_01** to select it.

4   In the toolbar, click the Inspector button to display the Inspector.

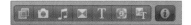

5   Click the Info button to open the Info pane of the Inspector (if it's not already open).

6 From the Metadata View pop-up menu, choose Extended View. The Info Inspector updates to show the extended view.

7 Scroll down in the Inspector to view the various data fields.

Fields such as Media Start, Media End, Media Duration, Frame Size, Video Frame Rate, Codecs, and so on contain hard-coded data gathered from the inherent properties of the file or using information passed from the camera to Final Cut Pro during the import process.

8 In the Event Browser, click **Shot_02**. The Inspector automatically updates to show the metadata for that clip.

Notice that this clip has a different video codec and frame size. That's because this clip was transcoded from the original camera file to a file format optimized for editing.

For the most part, source media metadata isn't used on a day-to-day basis during editing. However, this information can be useful to compare different footage types or to understand the exact nature of your source files (such as the number of native audio channels in a clip, or its frame rate).

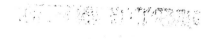

Using Auto-Analysis Metadata

A second category of metadata consists of information that Final Cut Pro can identify automatically during import (or later, if you choose to analyze your clips after importing them). Final Cut Pro can examine every frame and locate useful information to speed your editing workflow.

Final Cut Pro performs two main types of analysis to identify visual mistakes the software can correct (such as shaky camerawork or rolling shutter artifacts), and to detect human faces. Facial detection not only attempts to identify when a human face is in the shot, but also how many people appear, and how close their faces are to the camera.

Auto-analysis can be performed during the import process (regardless of how you import files into your Event) by choosing the appropriate options in the Import Settings window, or it can be performed after clips are already imported.

> **NOTE** ▶ Analysis settings appear in different places, depending on whether you use the "Import from Camera" or Import Files windows. When dragging a clip from the Finder into Final Cut Pro X, the settings in the Import pane of Final Cut Pro X Preferences determine if analysis is performed.

The advantage to performing analysis on import is that all your files are scanned. By the time you are ready to edit, this data is already added to your clips.

The advantage to delaying analysis until after your clips are imported is that you can select specific clips for this time-consuming task, thereby avoiding analysis of clips you'll never use. Post-import analysis also allows you to choose the specific type of analysis for specific clips. (You don't need to analyze scenic vistas for human faces, or search for shaky camerawork in interview clips shot with a rock-steady tripod.)

Finding People

In this exercise, you'll analyze specific clips for specific types of information, beginning with facial recognition.

1   Control-click (or right-click) Shot_02, and from the shortcut menu, choose Analyze and Fix.

2   In the "Analyze and Fix" sheet, select "Find people" and "Create Smart Collections after analysis." Click OK.

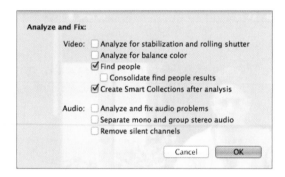

NOTE ▸ You could also select "Consolidate find people results" to group any Find People keywords into two-minute sections. This avoids too many short keyworded sections in shots with much variability across a range of footage. For the purpose of this exercise, leave this setting deselected.

Final Cut Pro examines the clips for human faces, and if it finds any, automatically creates a Smart Collection associated with the types of faces it finds. The analysis is performed in the background, so you can continue your work without waiting for the results.

NOTE ▸ If you skim or play other clips during analysis, the background processing will automatically pause. This helps keep the application fully responsive, but ultimately delays the analysis.

You can monitor the progress of the background analysis to the left of the current timecode in the middle of the toolbar.

Background Process button

3   Click the Background Process button to open the Background Tasks window.

4   Click the disclosure triangle to expand the "Transcoding and Analysis" section and see the progress of the current task.

When the analysis is complete, you'll notice several things: A purple keyword bar covers the duration of the clip to represent the areas marked with *analysis keywords*, and the Event Library now contains a folder called People. Inside that folder are two new Smart Collections: *Medium Shot* and *One Person*.

Auto-analysis represents the data it collects with these special keywords. Analysis keywords are different from user-generated keywords (which are covered later in this lesson). You cannot modify analysis keywords, and they appear in a different color than user-generated ones.

5   In the Event Library, select the *Medium Shot* Smart Collection.

The Smart Collection contains the one clip that contains that keyword. As you ana-lyze more clips from this event, any additional clips with that keyword will automati-cally appear in that collection.

Although it may seem like magic, the analysis simply examines the pixels of your clips looking for human faces. It can be fooled, both by pixels that look similar to a face, and by the presence of people in the frame who are not facing the camera.

6   In the Event Library, select *Lesson_01* to view all the clips.

7   In the Event Browser, select Shot_03, and choose Modify > Analyze and Fix to open the "Analyze and Fix" sheet. The settings remain the same as in step 2.

8   Click OK to begin the analysis.

9   When the analysis is finished, observe the clip in the Event Browser.

Purple line indicates keyword location

The purple line representing the analysis keyword is only present for the second half of the clip. Even though people appear in the first half, none of their faces are clearly visible, so the analysis ignores them.

10 Click the List View button to switch the Event Browser to list view. In list view, clips with keywords have disclosure triangles beside their names.

List View button

11 Click the Shot_03 disclosure triangle to view the keywords assigned to that clip.

In this case, two keywords were added: *One Person* and *Wide Shot*. Final Cut Pro recognized one face, and based on the relative size of the face in the frame determined that the person was far from the camera.

12 Click the *One Person* keyword. The keyworded area is selected in the filmstrip.

TIP ► You can also click the purple line directly in the filmstrip to select the keyworded area.

If you skim the marked section of the clip, you'll see there are obviously two or more people in the shot; however, Final Cut Pro marked it as *One Person* because only a single face is clearly visible.

As keywords are added to clips, those keyworded sections are added automatically to the Smart Collections associated with those keywords.

13 In the Event Library, click the *One Person* Smart Collection. The Smart Collection contains the keyworded area of the clip (as well as the previously marked clip).

Removing Analysis Keywords

If you find that analysis keywords are not accurate, you may choose to remove them to avoid later confusion.

1 In the Event Library, click the formatting icon to view all the clips in that Event.

2 In the Event Browser, select **Shot_03**, and choose Mark > Remove All Analysis Keywords, or press Control-Option-0, to remove the analysis keywords from the clip.

> **NOTE** ▶ You can manually add more accurate keywords to better identify this clip, as you'll learn later in this lesson.

3 In the Event Library, click the *Wide Shot* Smart Collection.

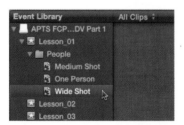

Another clip still appears in the *One Person* Smart Collection, but removing the analysis keywords from **Shot_03** emptied the *Wide Shot* Smart Collection.

If further analysis tags other clips with this keyword, they will be added to the Smart Collection. However you can also tidy your Event Library by deleting the empty collection.

4 Select the *Wide Shot* Smart Collection, and press Command-Delete to remove it.

Creating Additional People Keywords

To add to the keywords already created, other people-related keywords may be created depending on the specifics of the shot. If two faces are visible, Final Cut Pro will assign a *Two Persons* keyword. If more than two faces appear, Final Cut Pro will assign a *Group* keyword.

Also, in addition to *Wide Shot* and *Medium Shot* keywords, close-ups will garner a *Close Up Shot* keyword.

1   Select the *Lesson 01* Event. In the Event Browser, Control-click Shot_04, and from the shortcut menu, choose Analyze and Fix.

2   Leave the settings as they are, and click OK to begin analysis.

3   When the analysis is complete, click the disclosure triangle beside the clip's name to observe the analysis keywords that were automatically assigned.

NOTE ▸ Also notice the new Smart Collections added to the People folder in the Event Library.

Finding Shaky Camerawork

Auto-analysis can also identify clip areas where the camera is excessively shaky, or when clips display *rolling shutter* artifacts (an undesirable visual distortion caused when CMOS camera sensors pan quickly across vertical lines).

1 In the Event Browser, Control-click Shot_05, and from the shortcut menu, choose "Analyze and Fix."

2 In the "Analyze and Fix" sheet, select "Analyze for stabilization and rolling shutter," and deselect "Find people." (Leave "Create Smart Collections after analysis" enabled.)

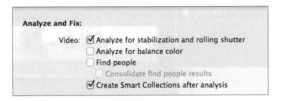

3 Click OK to begin the analysis.

4 When the analysis is completed, observe the clip in the Event Browser.

A few small areas are marked with the purple analysis keyword indicator near the beginning of the shot, and one longer section is marked at the very end.

5 Click the second purple bar to select that marked area.

6   Press / (slash) to play the selected range. This is clearly not an area of smooth camerawork.

NOTE ► To stabilize the shaky shot, you must first add the clip to a project, and then adjust the appropriate settings in the Video Inspector.

A new folder and Smart Collections were added to the Event Library for *Excessive Shake* and *Steady Shot*. Each of the shaky sections appears in the *Excessive Shake* Smart Collection. Clips that are not shaky appear in the *Steady Shot* collection.

NOTE ► Clips that are not yet analyzed also appear in the *Steady Shot* Smart Collection, so if you're analyzing clips on an individual basis (as in this lesson), the list in the *Steady Shot* collection may be inaccurate.

Entering Metadata Manually

In addition to all that automatically generated metadata, you can also manually add additional data about your clips. This information is sometimes visible in the Inspector, and sometimes visible as keywords in the Event Library and Event Browser.

Creating Clip-Based Metadata

Some metadata are stored on a clip-by-clip basis. These primarily include logging information such as general notes, the scene name/number, take number, camera reel, and so on. But you can also add custom data fields.

1   In the Event Browser, select Shot_01.

2   If the Inspector is not currently visible, press Command-4.

3   From the Metadata View pop-up, make sure Extended View is chosen.

4   In the Inspector, in the Notes field, type *Walks right to left*.

5   In the Scene field, type *Nazret Farmer*.

6   Click the clip name in the Event Browser to confirm the selection, and deselect the clip.

   NOTE ▶ If this were one of multiple takes or multiple camera angles, you might also have entered a value in the Take or Camera Angle fields.

Entering Data for Multiple Clips

You can simultaneously enter data for more than one clip at a time, which is much quicker than entering data to individual clips. Doing so has the added benefit of ensuring that the entered data are identical across the various clips.

1   In the Event Browser, Shift-click Shot_06, Shot_07, and Shot_08 to select them. The Inspector shows multiple values for the source media metadata fields, but the user-editable fields remain available for text entry.

2   In the Scene field in the Inspector, type *Injera Making*, which adds the data to all three clips.

3   In the Event Browser, click any one of the clips to confirm the text entry, and then deselect the group of clips.

Creating Custom Metadata Fields

You can also create custom fields to identify information that may be especially important for your particular Event.

> **NOTE ▸** Once added, custom metadata fields are visible across all the Events on your system. Hide or show them by creating custom metadata views, as described later in this lesson.

1   Select any clip in the Event Browser, and from the Inspector Action pop-up menu, choose Add Custom Metadata Field.

2   In the Name field, type *Region*, and in the Description field, type *Shooting location of scene.*

3   Click OK to create the new field and add it to the current view.

> **TIP ▸** Hover your pointer over a field in the Inspector to see that field's description (as shown in the figure).

4   Scroll to the bottom of the Inspector to see the new field.

5   In the Event Browser, Shift-click `Shot_06`, `Shot_07`, and `Shot_08`, and in the Region field, type *Tigray*.

6   In the Event Browser, select `Shot_01` and `Shot_02`, and in the Region field, type *Oromia*.

Organizing Clip-Based Metadata

As you use custom metadata fields more frequently, you'll probably want to modify the Inspector's layout to display frequently used fields near the top of the window.

You can customize the built-in views and even create your own views featuring just those fields you care about most. Doing so quickly increases the usefulness of the Inspector and the metadata displayed within it.

Switching Between Metadata Views

Final Cut Pro X has seven default views, each containing a different set of metadata useful for various types of clips. You can switch between the views on-the-fly.

1   In the Event Browser, select `Shot_08`.

2   In the Inspector, from the Metadata View pop-up menu, choose Basic View. The basic view hides the Scene, Take, and Camera Angle fields; moves the Camera Name field to the bottom; and otherwise simplifies the view to show a small subset of essential information about your clips.

   Other views show data useful for specific media types.

3   From the Metadata View pop-up menu, choose EXIF View. This view displays data that many still-photo cameras use to document the camera settings. You can use this view with a video clip, but it is much more useful when applied to a still photograph.

4   In the Event Browser, select `Shot_09 (still image)`. The EXIF view updates to show the camera data for the image.

5   Scroll through the Inspector to view the various data fields available in this view.

There's also a view to display metadata commonly associated with music files.

6   In the Event Browser, select **Shot_10 (audio only)**.

7   In the Inspector, from the Metadata View pop-up, choose Audio View. Scroll through the Inspector to see which fields are filled in.

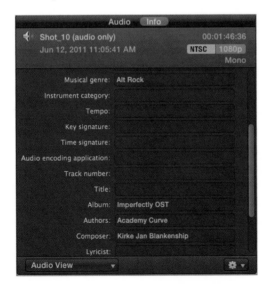

NOTE ▶ Metadata can be added to audio clips in a program such as iTunes.

Customizing Metadata Views

The fields in many of these views cannot be edited within Final Cut Pro. The information is stored in the media files on the disk. However, as you add more of your own editable fields, you can modify the layouts and even create your own views.

1   In the Event Browser, select Shot_01.

2   In the Inspector, from the Metadata View pop-up menu, choose General View. This view shows a standard collection of commonly used metadata fields.

3   From the Metadata View pop-up menu, choose Edit Metadata View to open the Metadata Views window.

This window shows all the possible metadata fields and allows you to decide which fields are visible in a view.

The list on the left shows the available views. The General View is currently selected. In the list in the center of the window, checkmarks indicate fields that are displayed in the Inspector for the selected view.

4   In the search field in the upper right, type *date*. The list of parameters is filtered to show only fields containing the word *date*.

5   From the Properties pop-up menu, choose Camera Properties. The list is filtered to show only camera-generated data including the word *date*.

6   Select the Shooting Date Start property. That field will now appear in the Inspector when the general view is selected.

NOTE ▸ The Inspector won't update until you close the Metadata Views window.

7   In the search field, click the Reset button (X) to clear the text filter.

8   From the Properties pop-up menu, choose Custom Properties. The filtered list shows just the Region field you created earlier.

NOTE ▶ When you create a custom field, it is added to the currently selected view. Because you created the Region field while looking at the extended view, the field is enabled in that view, but disabled in the other views.

9   Select the Region field checkbox to add the field to the current view.

10   Control-click the Region field, and choose Edit Custom Metadata Field from the shortcut menu.

The sheet opens at the top of the window, allowing you to modify the field's name or description. In this example you are not required to make any changes.

11   Click OK to close the sheet without making any changes.

TIP ▶ To delete a custom metadata field, Control-click it in the Metadata Views window, and choose Delete Custom Metadata Field from the shortcut menu.

Next, you'll hide the fields you're not using so that the view contains only the most useful information.

12   From the Properties menu, choose Selected Properties. The window updates to show only the active fields in the selected view.

NOTE ▶ Some active fields will only appear in the Inspector when appropriate media types (video, still, or audio) are selected.

13   Deselect the Camera Angle and Codecs fields.

14 Click OK.

The Metadata Views window closes, and the Inspector updates to show the new collection of fields you have selected.

Managing Metadata Views

The changes you made in the previous exercise were helpful, but you were modifying one of the default views. This modified view might confuse another editor who is used to the default set of fields in the general view. To avoid any confusion, you can convert this modified view into a custom view and restore the general view to its default settings.

1 In the Inspector, from the Metadata View pop-up menu, choose Save Metadata View As to open the Save As sheet.

2 Type *awesome new view* into the Name field, and click OK.

The custom view you created now has a unique name; but at the moment, it's also a duplicate of the general view you previously modified.

3 From the Metadata View pop-up menu, choose Edit Metadata View to open the Metadata Views window.

4 In the left column, select General View.

5 From the Action pop-up menu, choose Restore Metadata View to Default.

The general view is reset to contain its default fields.

NOTE ▸ The Action pop-up menu also allows you to create new custom views or delete custom views. You cannot delete the default views.

6   Click OK to close the window.

TIP ▸ You can also delete fields from a particular view without opening the Metadata Views window. Control-click a field in the Inspector, and from the shortcut menu, choose Remove From *[view name]*.

Using Intraclip-Based Metadata

You're probably already using the last category of metadata quite often: *Rating* clips as Favorites or Rejects, and adding custom keywords using the Keyword Editor and its associated shortcuts.

These methods of identifying the contents of your clips are intuitive and user-friendly, but they're also incredibly powerful and constitute a significant part of Final Cut Pro X metadata.

NOTE ▸ If you're already familiar with rating clips as Favorites or Rejects, you may skip this section.

Rating Clips

Any clip or portion of a clip can be rated as a Favorite or a Reject. You can create ratings in a variety of ways.

In this exercise, you'll identify the portion of the clip you would use if you were going to edit the clip into a project. Because clip selections are discarded every time you deselect a clip, you can apply a Favorite rating to create a selection that sticks around.

Contrarily, you can use the Reject rating to identify a portion of the clip you want to avoid using when it comes time to edit the clip into a project.

1   In the Event Browser, select **Shot_11**. In this shot, a farmer is unwrapping an ear of corn.

2   Play the clip by pressing L. At about 14 seconds, you begin to see the corn kernels. Press I to mark a start point there.

3   Keep playing the clip, and when the ear is fully unwrapped (at around 23 seconds), press O to mark the end of the selection.

4   Mark the selected area as a Favorite by clicking the Favorite button in the toolbar, or by pressing F. A green bar appears in the filmstrip to indicate the rated area.

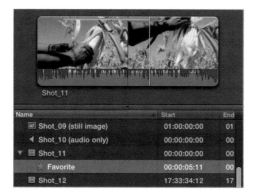

TIP ▶ To match the preceding figure, deselect the clip (click outside of the filmstrip in the Event Browser) to make it easier to see the green Favorite bar.

5   Press Option-I to change the start point to the beginning of the clip.

An end point is automatically chosen for you, but you can ignore that and set your own.

6   Play forward until you hear the cinematographer say, "OK," (at around 1:15); and press O to set an end point at that point.

7   Mark this area as a Reject by clicking the Reject button in the toolbar, or pressing the Delete key.

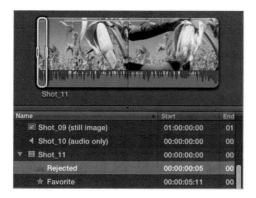

A red bar appears in the filmstrip to indicate the rejected area.

Filtering by Rating

Final Cut Pro allows you to restrict the Event Browser view to clips of certain ratings, which you might do to hide rejected footage or to limit the view to just those clip areas that have not yet been viewed.

1   From the Filter pop-up menu in the upper-left corner of the Event Browser, choose Hide Rejected, or press Control-H.

The portion of **Shot_11** you rejected is hidden.

> **NOTE ▸** If you have rejected areas in the middle of a clip and choose to hide rejected clips, the remaining clip may be split into multiple instances, each with the same clip name.

2   From the Filter pop-up menu, choose Rejected, or press Control-Delete.

The Event Browser updates to show only the Rejected clip. You can also choose to view only Favorites, or clips without any rating or keywords.

3   From the Filter pop-up menu, choose All Clips, or press Control-C.

The view returns to showing all clips, and the Rejected or Favorite areas are indicated by red and green lines in the filmstrip.

> **TIP ▸** You can also view Favorite and Rejected sections by expanding the disclosure triangle to the left of the name of a rated clip when in list view.

Adding Keywords

Identifying your most (or least) favorite parts of clips is helpful, but it can be a bit of an all-or-nothing approach. In many cases, you will want to add much more descriptive or elaborate identifiers using keywords.

In this exercise, you'll mark the specific ranges of a clip so that later—when you're ready to edit it into a project—you'll have easy access to the most useful sections of the clip.

1   In the Event Browser, select Shot_12 and play it. This shot shows a shepherd leading his oxen down the road.

2   Play the clip until the oxen clear the frame and you have a clear *full shot* of the shepherd (around 17:33;53:00). Press I to set a start point at that point.

3   Play forward until just before the camera pans away from the shepherd (at around 17:34:03:00), and press O to mark the end of the selection.

4   In the toolbar, click the Keywords button, or press Command-K, to open the Keyword Editor.

5   Type *Full shot shepherd*, and press Return to apply the keyword to the selected section of the clip.

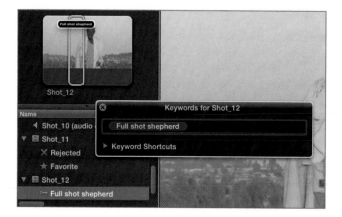

A Keyword Collection is also added to the Event in the Event Library. If you later mark any other bits of your footage with the same keyword, that new section will appear inside the Keyword Collection alongside this clip.

Because grouping clips using identical keywords can be very helpful, creating multiple simple keywords instead of a single complex keyword is often best.

For example, rather than marking this area with one *Full shot shepherd* keyword, you could label it with two keywords, *Full shot* and *Shepherd*. This approach makes it easier to later identify and locate any clip that contains a shepherd (even in close-ups or medium shots); as well as any full shots, even if they're of firemen, musicians, or anteaters. Let's make this change.

6   With Shot_12 still selected, in the Keyword Editor, click the keyword item (the words *Full shot shepherd*), and press Delete. The keyword is deleted and vanishes with a "poof."

TIP You can also press Control-0 at any point to delete all keywords from a selected clip.

7   In the Keyword Editor, type *Full Shot*, and press Return. Then type *Shepherd*, and press Return.

TIP Final Cut Pro will try to auto-complete your text entry to match the keyword you previously used. Just press Delete when the word *shepherd* appears to create the *Full Shot* keyword.

Both individual keywords are added to the marked section of the clip.

8   Click the disclosure triangle next to the Keyword Shortcuts section to expand the Keyword Editor.

Click to expand Keyword Editor

As you create keywords, they are automatically assigned to shortcut keys. The three keywords you created are assigned to the first three shortcut slots.

You're very unlikely to use the *Full shot shepherd* keyword in the future, so you certainly don't need it assigned to a shortcut.

9   Click the *Full shot shepherd* keyword in the Control-1 shortcut slot, and press Delete to remove it from the slot.

Next, you'll identify a different section of the clip, and mark it with a different keyword.

10 Play the clip forward to around 17:34:10:00. At that point, the shot focuses on a group of women and children walking down the road.

11 Press I to mark the start of a selection. The end of the media is automatically marked as the end of the selection.

12 In the Keyword Editor, type *women*, and press Return. Then type *children*, and press Return. The two keywords are applied to this section of the clip and also added to the next two available shortcut slots in the Keyword Editor.

When keywords are assigned to shortcut slots, you can easily apply them to other clips, even without having the Keyword Editor open.

13 In the Event Browser, select Shot_04.

14 Close the Keyword Editor.

> **NOTE ▶** If you've used the Keyword Editor prior to beginning this lesson, the short-cuts in your Keyword Editor may not match those listed here.

15 Press Control-4 to add the *children* keyword to Shot_04. This technique allows you to very quickly add common keywords to your footage.

16 In the Event Library, click the *children* Keyword Collection. The footage containing that keyword appears in the collection.

Organizing Keywords

As you create more keywords, the Keyword Collections in the Event Library can create a bit of a mess, which can make finding what you need a bit harder.

To manage all the Keyword Collections, you can create folders in which to group Keyword Collections and Smart Collections.

NOTE ▶ Folders cannot contain individual clips. They can hold only collections.

You already have two folders in your Event: the People folder, and the Stabilization folder created automatically to hold the analysis keywords you generated earlier in the lesson.

In this exercise, you'll create a folder to group the new keywords you added in the previous section.

1   In the Event Library, select the *Lesson_01* Event, and choose File > New Folder, or press Command-Shift-N. A new, untitled folder appears within the Event, and its name is automatically highlighted so you can immediately name it.

2   Type *Humanfolk* to give the folder a unique name.

3   Drag the *children* collection, the *women* collection, and the *Shepherd* collection into the Humanfolk folder.

Notice that a *Full shot shepherd* Keyword Collection still appears in the Event, even though you earlier deleted the one use of that keyword. Keyword collections are never automatically deleted. Even if they contain no clips, they remain in case you later assign their namesake keyword.

However, in this case, you don't want that unused collection cluttering your Event Library. Let's get rid of it.

4   Select the *Full shot shepherd* collection, and press Command-Delete to delete the collection.

NOTE ▶ Be careful when deleting Keyword Collections! Deleting a Keyword Collection automatically deletes any instance of that keyword in the Event.

Adding Markers

You have one more device to add metadata to your clips: markers. These are indicators associated with a specific frame within a shot. Markers can be used in the Event Browser and in the Timeline when you're editing projects. For the purpose of this exercise, you'll add markers in the Event Browser.

1   In the Event Library, select `Shot_06`. This shot shows a woman making an Ethiopian staple bread called injera. The bread is made by pouring a thin, fermented teff-based batter onto a hot griddle.

2   Play the clip until the batter is pouring onto the griddle (approximately 17:46:08:00).

3   Press M to add a marker to the clip at that frame.

4   Press M again to open the Marker window.

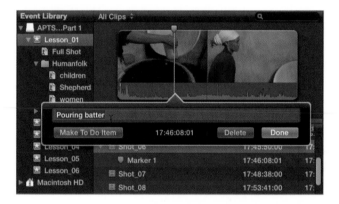

5   In the Marker window, type *Pouring batter*, and press Return, or click Done.

6   Play forward in the clip until the woman lowers the lid over the griddle (at approximately 17:46:38:00).

7   Press Option-M to add a new marker at that point, and to open the Marker window.

8   Type *Close griddle*, and press Return, or click Done.

9   Select Shot_07 and add similar markers (*Pouring batter* at 17:49:13:00 and *Close griddle* at 17:49:39:00).

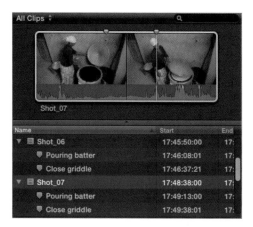

You can add as many markers as you like. They'll make it easier to quickly line up the similar action in multiple angles when the time comes to edit the shots together.

Filtering Clips

The main reason you enter all this metadata is to help you quickly find the precise clip you're looking for when you need it. Rather than scrolling through large lists of clips, metadata allow you to instantly hone in on the right shot.

One of the most powerful ways to do this is to utilize the built-in filtering capabilities of the Final Cut Pro Event Browser. You can filter clips based on almost any combination of metadata, regardless of where they are stored. For example, using the metadata in this project, you could search for *Favorite* shots of *shepherds* in *Tigray* from *Reel 04* that were imported at least three months ago.

Searching for Text

Before you combine all the types of metadata, you'll start off with some simple search examples. To start, you'll search for some text to find the specific clips you might need for editing this footage into a real-world project.

The text you search for can appear in the name of the clip, in the Notes field in the Inspector, or in the marker text.

1   In the Event Library, select the *Lesson_01* Event.

2   In the search field of the Event Browser, type *02*. The Event Browser is instantly filtered to show two clips: Shot_02 (which has the number *02* in its name), and Shot_07
(which has the number *02* in the Take field in the Inspector).

3   Click the Reset button (X) to clear the search field.

4   In the search field, type *walks*. The Event Browser updates to show the clip containing
the word *Walks* in the Notes field in the Inspector.

NOTE ▶ This text was entered earlier in this lesson. If you didn't complete the earlier
part of this lesson, this search won't work.

5   Click the Reset button (X) to clear the search field.

6   Type *batter* in the search field. The two clips with markers containing that word
appear in the Event Browser.

7   Click the disclosure triangle to reveal the relevant markers.

This method allows you to very quickly find clips and markers based on their names.

NOTE ▶ You can automatically rename your clips in a variety of ways based on other metadata in the project. For details, see the "Renaming Clips" section later in this lesson.

Searching for Metadata

You can search for any of the metadata stored in your Event, including metadata displayed in the Inspector and data stored as ratings and keywords. Furthermore, you can specify the terms of the search, omit criteria, limit criteria, and so much more. You can take advantage of all this mega-metadata power in the Filter window.

1   To open the Filter window, do one of the following:

▶   In the search field, click the magnifying glass icon.

Click to open Filter window

▶   Press Command-F.

▶   Choose Edit > Find.

By default the Filter window contains the same text that was in the search field, but you now have the option to be much more specific in your search.

2   From the Includes pop-up menu, choose Does Not Include.

The Event Browser instantly updates, now displaying all the clips that do not include the current search term.

3   Click the Add Rule (+) button, and choose Ratings to add a Ratings search term to the window.

Now, you are searching for clips that are Favorites and also that *do not include* the search term *batter*.

4   In the upper-left corner, choose Any from the pop-up menu.

You are now searching for any clip that is a favorite *OR* does not have the search term.

5   From the Does Not Include pop-up menu, choose Includes.

The Event Browser updates to show clips that have a Favorite rating or include the text search term *batter*. This includes the two clips with the *batter* markers plus the one shot with a Favorite rating.

6   Deselect the checkbox to the left of the Text search term.

The text is now excluded from the search, and the Event Browser immediately reflects the change by showing only those clips that meet this new criteria.

7   Click the Add Rule (+) button, and choose Media Type to add a Media search term to the Filter window.

8   Set the Media Type pop-up to Stills.

The still image is added to the find results in the Event Browser.

9   Click the Remove (–) button to the right of the Media Type search term.

Click to remove filter criterion

The Media item is deleted from the view, and the Browser updates accordingly.

10 Click the Add Rule (+) button, and choose Keywords.

The Keywords search term is added to the filter list. Each of the keywords in the project appears with a checkbox next to it. Select or deselect the specific keywords to show or hide those keywords in the list.

11 From the Checkmark pop-up menu, choose Uncheck All. Then select the *children* checkbox.

Only shots with the *children* keyword (or Favorites) appear in the Event Browser.

12 Click the Remove (–) button to the right of the Keywords search term.

13 Click the Add Rule button, and choose People.

The People search term appears in the list and works exactly like the Keywords search term. You can select specific keywords and choose whether to search for all or any of the selected terms.

Choosing Include All locates clips that contain all the criteria. If you selected both Group and Close Up Shot, only clips that have the *Group* keyword *AND* the *Close Up Shot* keyword would appear in the Event Browser.

Choosing Include Any locates clips that have either the *Group* keyword *OR* the *Close Up Shot* keyword. Generally this search will yield more results than choosing All.

14 Click the Remove (–) button to the right of the People search term.

15 Click the Add Rule (+) button, and choose Format Info.

This search term allows you to search the metadata fields that appear in the Inspector.

16 Click the Reel pop-up menu, and type *AF-100_10* to add clips from that reel to the search results.

You can search for specific text in the Reel, Scene, Take, Camera Angle, or Camera Name fields; or you can search for specific information about the number of audio tracks, frame size, frame rate, and audio sample rate.

17 Set the pop-up menu to Scene, and type *Injera* in the search field to find clips containing that search term.

You can add even more criteria, searching based on date or role.

Creating Smart Collections

Once you create a complex search filter, you can save the search as a Smart Collection. Not only does this allow you to return to it at a later date, but because it's a *Smart* Collection, if any clips qualify for the search terms they are automatically added to the collection. (Or if they no longer qualify, they're removed.) So if you add (or remove) keywords, markers, or other metadata, that information is automatically evaluated to see if the affected clips meet the search criteria for your saved Smart Collection. Clips that match show up in the Smart Collection, and clips that don't do not.

1 In the Filter window, click New Smart Collection.

The Smart Collection is added to the Event Library, and the name is highlighted so you can immediately add a memorable name.

2   Type *Favorites & Injera*, and press Return to name the Smart Collection.

3   Select the *Lesson_01* Event, clear the search field, and in the Event Browser, select **Shot_04**.

4   Press F to mark the clip as a Favorite.

5   In the Event Library, click the *Favorites & Injera* collection.

Shot_04 now appears in the list.

Clearing the Filter Window

Unless you create a Smart Collection, search terms continue to filter an Event even when you close the Filter window.

NOTE ▶ Various icons in the search field represent the types of search terms.

To clear the filter, you must manually delete or disable the various items in the filter window, or you can clear the whole search at once.

1   In the search field, click the Reset button (X) to clear the search criteria.

Click to clear filters

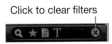

2   Note that the browser updates to reflect the filter removal.

Renaming Clips

Another benefit of the embedded metadata in Final Cut Pro is the ability to nondestructively rename clips using a wide range of criteria. You can rename clips using the data in the Scene and Take fields, the date and time the clip was created, the original filename created by the camera, or any number of custom metadata combinations.

1   In the Event Browser, Shift-click **Shot_06**, **Shot_07**, and **Shot_08** to select them.

2   In the Inspector, from the Action pop-up menu, choose Apply Custom Name > Original Name from Camera.

The clips are renamed based on the name provided by the camera.

3   From the Action pop-up menu, choose Apply Custom Name > Scene/Shot/Take/Angle.

The clips are renamed based on the information in the Scene, Take, and Angle fields.

NOTE ▶ These clips don't have any data in the Angle field, so that info is ignored.

Creating Custom Naming Options

In addition to switching between the preset naming options, you can create custom naming schemes.

1 From the Inspector Action pop-up menu, choose Apply Custom Name > Edit to open the Naming Presets window.

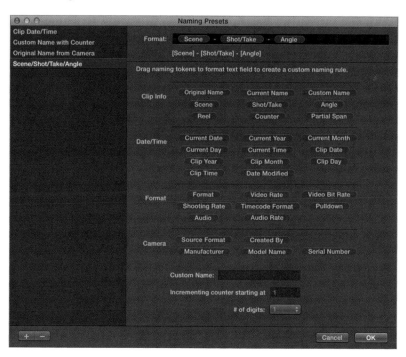

In this window, you can modify any of the existing naming presets, or create new ones by stringing together naming "tokens" based on the metadata associated with the clips.

2   Click various items in the list on the left and observe how the tokens are represented in the Format field on the right. Each name comprises a collection of the tokens from the underlying categories. A preview of the name appears beneath the Format field.

3   Click the Add (+) button to create a new naming scheme. A new Untitled item is added to the list on the left, highlighted and ready for you to give it a custom name.

Click to add a new naming scheme

> **TIP** ▶ You can drag naming presets to rearrange their order in the list and they will appear in the new order in the Inspector Action pop-up menu.

4   Name the new naming scheme *Camera/Project/Number*.

> **TIP** ▶ You can also open the window with a new scheme already created by choosing Apply Custom Name > New from the Inspector Action pop-up menu.

5   In the Format field, select the Current Name token, and press Delete.

6   Drag the Manufacturer token from the Camera section into the Format field.

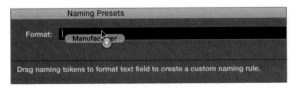

7   In the Format field, type a hyphen (–) and a space.

NOTE ▶ You can add any characters you want, but remember these will be the same for every clip.

8 Drag the Custom Name token from the Clip Info section into the Format field. When using the Custom Name token, type the name you want in the Custom Name field near the bottom of the window.

9 In the Custom Name field, type *Ethiopia*.

10 In the Format field, type another hyphen (−) and space after the Custom Name token.

11 Drag the Counter token from the Clip Info section into the Format field. When you use a counter, you can specify the number of digits and starting number at the bottom of the window.

12 Leave the "Incrementing counter starting at" field set to 1, and set "# of digits" to 2.

13 Click OK to close the window.

14 With the three clips still selected in the Event Browser, from the Inspector Action pop-up menu, choose Apply Custom Name > Camera/Project/Number.

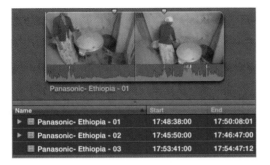

The custom name is applied to the clips. At any point you can switch between any of the naming schemes or create new ones.

Lesson Review

1. Where is metadata viewed in the Final Cut Pro interface?
2. What clip characteristics can auto-analysis detect?
3. Where are analysis keywords displayed?
4. Can you enter metadata for more than one clip at a time?
5. How can you enter metadata that doesn't fit in one of the preexisting data fields?
6. Can you modify one of the existing Inspector views?
7. Where can you control which data fields are visible in metadata views?
8. Can you attach multiple keywords to the same clip selection?
9. Can you search for clips based on text entered in the Notes field in the Inspector?
10. If you set the Filter window to All, will the results find clips that meet any one of the listed search terms?
11. Can you search for multiple people keywords (analysis keywords) at the same time?
12. True or false: Renaming clips using the Apply Custom Naming command always permanently replaces the existing name.

Answers

1. In the Info Inspector, in the Event Library, and in the Event Browser
2. Shaky camerawork, rolling shutter artifacts, and people
3. In the Event Library as Keyword Collections, and in the Event Browser when in list view
4. You can enter clip-based metadata (fields in the Inspector) for all selected clips.

5. Create a custom metadata field using the Action pop-up menu in the Inspector.

6. Yes. You can modify any of the existing views or create custom views.

7. Turn off or on specific fields in the Metadata Views window.

8. Yes. You can add as many keywords to the same clip selection as you like.

9. Yes. Text searches find clips containing the search term in the marker text, or in the Name, Notes, or Scene fields.

10. No. All locates only those clips that contain all the search terms.

11. Yes

12. False

Keyboard Shortcuts

/ (slash)	Play selected range
Control-0	Delete all marker text, or in the Name, Notes, or Scene from a selected clip
Control-Option-0	Remove analysis keywords from a clip
Delete	Mark a selected area of a clip as a Reject
Command-Delete	Delete a collection
Control-Delete	Show only Rejected clips
Control-C	Show all clips
F	Mark a selected area of a clip as a Favorite
Command-F	Open the Filter window
Control-H	Hide Rejected clips
I	Create a start point
Command-K	Open the Keyword Editor
L	Play a clip
M	Create a marker
Option-M	Create a marker and open the Marker window
Command-Shift-N	Create a new folder in Event
O	Create an end point

2

Time

Goals

This lesson takes approximately 75 minutes to complete.

Review basics of editing clips into a project

Master edit types

Learn advanced techniques such as project-defined, backtimed, and audio-only or video-only edits

Utilize secondary storylines to group connected clips

Apply transitions to connected clips

Use compound clips to group clips across layers

Navigate into compound clips and make additional changes

Break storylines and compound clips into their constituent components

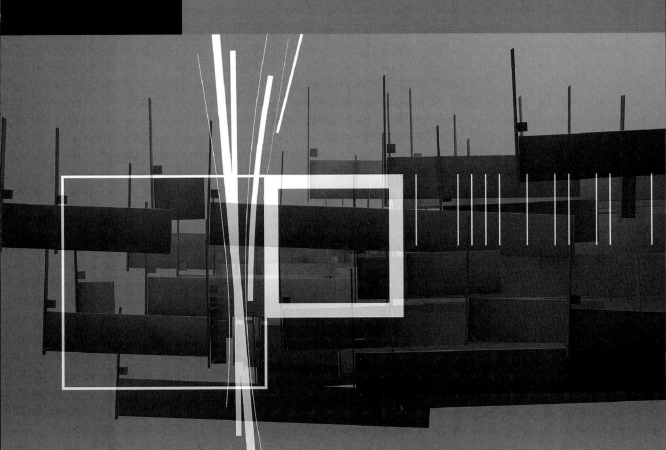

Lesson 2
Advanced Editing Techniques

Once you master the basics of Final Cut Pro X, you'll find that variations of its myriad edit styles can accommodate every situation. When the end point of the edit is more important than the starting point, you can *backtime* your cuts; or when the clip placement in the project is paramount, you can use *project-defined edits*. By using *multiple storylines*, you can create collections of *b-roll* or *cutaway* shots that can be moved and manipulated as a group. *Compound clips* allow you to treat a multilayer segment as a single item.

All of these techniques elevate your editing prowess, speed your work, ensure that you cut more accurately, and help you improve your storytelling effectiveness.

Reviewing Editing Basics

Before we get into the advanced topics, let's briefly review some of the fundamental aspects of editing clips in Final Cut Pro X.

TIP ▸ If you're already very confident in your knowledge, feel free to skip ahead to the "Modifying Edits" section and begin work with *Project_2B*.

Adding Clips to a Project

One of the most fundamental aspects of the editing process is the *assembly*, when you first add your clips to a Timeline. Although nothing prevents you from adding clips in a random or imprecise manner, the more care you take when performing this basic assembly, the more time you'll save when the time comes to modify and finesse the project.

To accommodate this, Final Cut Pro has many ways to add clips to your project, each one tailored to various situations you may encounter. In the following exercise, you'll use different edit types to construct a basic project.

Appending Clips

The least destructive way to add a clip to a project is to use the append edit. Appending always adds the new clip to the end of the project.

Unlike other edit types, append isn't affected by clips already placed in the project, whether a selection is active in the project, or where the project playhead is located, which makes the append edit very reliable and consistent. But it does have correspondingly limited use.

1   In the Project Library, open the Lesson 02 folder and double-click *Project 2A* to open this empty project into the Timeline.

2   In the Event Library, select the *Lesson_02* Event.

3   In the Event Library, click **Shot_01** and press the Spacebar to watch the clip.

4   Watch the clip a second time, and just before the camera move begins (at approximately 16:54:06:00), press I to set a start point.

5   Press O to set an end point as the woman walks back through the kitchen, right after she coughs (at approximately 43:00).

6   To add the selected range of the clip to the project, click the Append button, or press E.

Append button

TIP When adding the first clip to a project, you get the same results whether you choose append, insert, or overwrite.

7 In the Event Browser, select **Shot_02**.

This shot has a Favorite section marked, which saves you the task of manually choosing the desired start and end points.

8 Click the green favorite bar in the clip preview area, or click the disclosure triangle to the left of the clip name, and click the Favorite item to select the desired range of the clip.

9 Click the Append button or press E.

The selected range of the second clip is added to the end of the project.

Inserting Clips

Sometimes you may want to add a clip between two existing clips. You could manually rearrange the clips after adding them to the Timeline, but adding the clip to the correct location in the first place is far more efficient.

> **TIP** You can also use an insert edit to split an existing clip by adding a new clip in the middle and moving the downstream footage farther to the right.

1 In the Event Browser, select Shot_03.

2 Select the section of the clip marked as a Favorite, as you did in the previous exercise.

3 In the Timeline, position the playhead between the two clips.

> **TIP** Press Up Arrow to navigate exactly to the previous edit point, or press Down Arrow to navigate exactly to the next edit. Using these keyboard shortcuts (instead of skimming or dragging the playhead) ensures that the playhead is placed precisely between the two clips and you don't erroneously split an existing clip, which can result in an unwanted two- to three-frame flash.

4 Click the Insert button, or press W, to insert the clip between Shot_1 and Shot_2.

Insert button

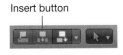

> **TIP** > You can deliberately split an existing clip by positioning the project playhead in the middle of a clip prior to performing the insert edit.

Overwriting Clips

Overwriting clips allows you to align the matching timing of similar shots and cover an existing clip with a new clip. This edit is most frequently used for narrative cutting when editors frequently lay in a *master shot*, and then bit by bit overwrite it with the *coverage* (other angles).

1 Skim or play the project from the beginning, and find the point after the woman grabs the potholders and reaches into the oven (at approximately 17:10). Click to place the playhead on that frame.

2 In the Event Browser, select Shot_04 and select the Favorite section.

3   Press / (slash) to play the selected area. This close-up provides much more emotion than the long shot from over her shoulder.

4   Choose Edit > Overwrite, or press D.

Shot_04 is edited into the project, covering the portion of Shot_01 beginning where you positioned the playhead and continuing for five seconds (the duration of the marked section of Shot_04).

5   Play the project to see how your edit is shaping up.

Replacing Clips

You can also cover an existing clip by *replacing* it with another clip. Replacing a clip exchanges the existing clip in the project with one from the Event Browser.

You can control the timing of the replace edit in one of three ways: You can replace a shot using the marked area in the Event Browser (thus changing the duration of the shot in the Timeline). You can retain the timing of the shot in the Timeline and replace its contents by cutting off the new clip when it reaches the end of the selection in the Timeline—regardless of the duration of the marked area in the Event Browser. This method is called Replace from Start.

> NOTE ▸ Alternatively you can Replace from End, in which the clip in the Timeline retains its length but the end point in the Event Browser is lined up with the end point in the Timeline. For more about this type of edit, see the "Backtiming Edits" section in this lesson.

1   In the Event Browser, play Shot_05.

This shot is similar to **Shot_03** that you inserted earlier, but its framing is a bit tighter and the smoke coming off the chicken is more pronounced.

2   In the preview area, click the green bar to select the Favorite range. Observe that the selected section of the clip in the Event Browser is 4:15 seconds long, whereas **Shot_03** in the Timeline is 3:00 seconds.

Duration of selection in Event Browser   Duration of selection in Timeline

3   Drag the selected range of the clip from the Event Browser onto **Shot_03**, but do not release the mouse button. When a white highlight appears around the clip, release the mouse button.

A drop-down menu appears listing the replace edit options.

4   Choose Replace. `Shot_05` replaces `Shot_03` in the Timeline, thereby increasing the
    overall duration of the project.

5   Play the project to see how the new shot fits. Unfortunately, the new clip duplicates
    the action where she puts the dish down in `Shot_03`.

6   Press Command-Z to undo the replace edit.

7   Repeat step 3, but this time, choose Replace from Start.

    The shot is once again replaced, but is limited to the 3:00 duration based on the clip it
    replaced.

8   Play the project to verify that the overlapping action is gone and the edit is much
    smoother.

Modifying Edits

Now that you've refamiliarized yourself with the most common edit types, you'll learn
how to control those edits in various ways to dramatically increase your versatility and
flexibility as an editor.

> **NOTE ▸** If you chose to skip the "Reviewing Editing Basics" section, open *Project_2B*
> to proceed with the following exercises.

Using Project-Defined Edits

One powerful way to control how edits occur is by specifying both a starting and an ending point in the project itself.

You've previously specified start and end points in the Event Browser and positioned the
project playhead to determine where that selection was edited into the project. But at
times it's more important that you cover a specific range in the project, and it's less critical
to identify the exact frames of the source clip that are used.

For example, imagine a mistake in the clip in which a light stand is visible for three seconds. No problem; you can cut away to another shot during that section, but you want to make absolutely sure that you cover those entire three seconds. Using ordinary edits, you'd have to manually ensure that the selection in the Event Browser is exactly the right length, which means you'd have to measure twice (once to figure out how long the bad section is, and once again when marking the source clip selection). Using a project-defined edit, you can just make the selection in the project and let Final Cut Pro X make the selection in the Event Browser.

1　Play the project all the way to the end.

2　Play the project again, and press I to set a start point right after the woman says, "It said two hours," and the man comes into frame, but before he starts talking (at about 50:00).

3　Press O when the man starts walking toward her (at 1:06:00) to mark a selection that is approximately 16 seconds long.

4   In the Event Browser, select `Shot_06`.

5   Play or skim until just before the man says, "Yeah, well, we'll just go back out" (at approximately 18:31:37:00). Leave the playhead at that frame.

6 Press D to overwrite the clip into the project.

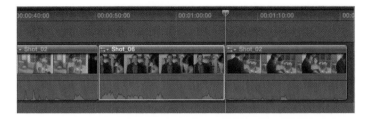

The clip is added, beginning at the selected frame and filling the selected range in the Timeline with the footage from the source clip.

TIP ▶ You can mark a start point in the source clip, and the project selection will override the selected duration in the clip.

Backtiming Edits

So far, you've made edits based on the *starting point* of the source clip. This is great for many situations because it ensures a smooth edit. But occasionally you'll want to base the timing of the edit based on the source clip's *ending point*.

In such a case, you ensure that the end of the new clip fits smoothly into the project by aligning the end of the source clip in the Event Browser with the playhead in the Timeline. This procedure is called *backtiming*.

NOTE ▶ Backtiming is most commonly performed as an overwrite edit, but you can also backtime a connect edit or a replace edit by choosing Replace from End.

1 In the Event Browser, select **Shot_07** and select the Favorite section.

2 Press / (slash) to play the selection.

The selection ends precisely after the man disables the alarm. It's most important in this case that turning off the alarm corresponds to a specific moment in the project; you want it to occur precisely before she turns on the lights.

3 Play the project, and stop the playhead precisely at 25:00, an instant before she turns on the room lights.

If you performed an overwrite edit at this point, the new clip would begin, and the section in the project where the woman turns on the light would be covered. By backtiming the edit, you can force *the end of the clip* to line up with the playhead and instead overwrite the section leading up to that frame.

4 Press Shift-D to perform a backtimed overwrite edit that adds the clip to the project, ending at the playhead position.

5 Play the project to watch the result. The man disables the alarm and then the project cuts immediately to the woman turning on the light.

> **TIP** If you're confused about the usefulness of backtiming an edit, undo step 4, perform a regular overwrite edit (press D) and observe the different result.

Limiting Source Media

One very common modification to an edit is to limit it to add only the video or the audio to the project. This is how you add a video *cutaway* while still hearing the sound of an interview, or line up a sound effect from one clip with the picture from another different clip.

You can perform audio-only or video-only edits regardless of which edit type you use: append, overwrite, insert, replace, or connect.

1   In the toolbar, from the Source Media pop-up menu, choose Audio Only, or press Shift-3.

TIP ▸ You can also change source media settings by choosing Edit > Source Media and selecting one of the menu items.

The edit buttons turn green to show that the next edit will be an audio-only edit.

NOTE ▸ When you specify an edit as Video Only or Audio Only, that state remains persistent until you change it again.

2   In the Event Browser, play Shot_08. This shot contains the sound of the beeping smoke alarm. You want to add that sound to the existing project, while leaving all the existing audio intact. But first, you'll identify the portion of the project where you want to hear the alarm sound—from the beginning of the scene until the man disables the alarm.

3   In the Timeline, position the playhead at the very first frame of the project, and press I, to place a start point.

4   Find the frame where the man disables the alarm (at approximately 24:00), and press O to mark the end of the selection.

5   In the Event Browser, skim through Shot_08 until you find the last beep of the alarm
     sound (at approximately 31:04 , and press O.

6   Press Shift-Q to perform a backtimed connect edit.

     Connect edits add the clip above the primary storyline (for video) or below it (for
     audio), and are connected to the frame at the Timeline playhead position.

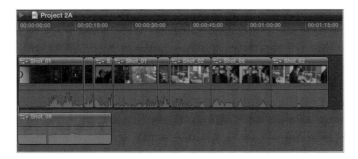

NOTE ▶ If you move or trim the clip to which a clip is connected, the connected clip
will automatically move with it. If you trim past the connection point, the connected
clip will automatically attach itself to the new clip.

7   Play the project to hear the results of your work. The alarm sound is added to the
     project, and ends precisely when the man presses the button on the device.

8   From the Source Media pop-up menu, choose All to prepare for the remainder of the
     lesson.

Combining Complex Edits

You can combine these techniques when the situation calls for it. For example, you just
performed an *audio-only, project-defined, backtimed, connect* edit. Pretty amazing, huh?

As you grow more proficient, you'll intuitively understand when you want to use these
tools and when to combine them, but don't despair if all those modifiers and possibilities
seem overwhelming. You can always do a simple edit and modify the other elements one
at a time after the fact.

Using Secondary Storylines

As you become more comfortable connecting clips to the primary storyline you may find yourself building a collection of connected clips you want to treat as a single item. For example, you might have a series of cutaways related to a particular interview, and you want to apply a single effect to the group; or you want to move this group, en masse, to another location in the project. In these situations, you would want to create a *secondary storyline*.

A secondary storyline allows you to combine a group of connected clips so they have a single connection line. This allows the whole group to be connected to a single frame in the primary storyline.

Creating Secondary Storylines

You can create a secondary storyline in several ways. The most common situation is to begin with existing connected clips.

1   Open the Project Browser, and double-click *Project_02C* to open it into the Timeline.

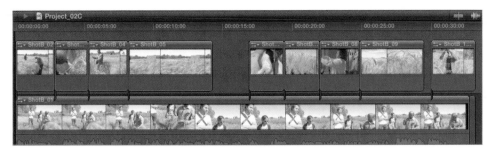

2   Play the project to get familiar with it. The primary storyline contains a single interview clip with several connected cutaway shots.

3   Drag a selection rectangle around the first four connected clips.

4   Choose Clip > Create Storyline, or press Command-G.

The clips are grouped into a new storyline. You can still adjust any of the individual clips; however, you also can manipulate the clips as a group.

5   Click the gray bar over the clips, and drag it to the right until it pushes **ShotB_06** out of the way. The entire storyline moves as a single unit.

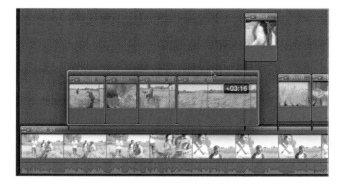

6   Drag the storyline back to the left until it lines up with the beginning of the project.

Applying Transitions to Connected Clips

When you create a storyline, it enables you to add transition effects (such as a cross-dissolve) between connected clips. Ordinarily, each connected clip is attached to a specific frame in the primary storyline, so even if two connected clips are adjacent (or overlapping), editing the clips to which they're attached could move them and change that relationship.

To apply a transition effect between two connected clips, they must share a single connection line so they can maintain their relative positions. In other words, they must be converted into a storyline.

Fortunately, when you add a transition effect to a connected clip, Final Cut Pro converts it into a storyline for you.

1   Select the four connected clips beginning at 17:00.

2   Choose Edit > Add Cross Dissolve, or press Command-T.

The clips are grouped into a secondary storyline, and cross dissolves are added to the beginning and end of each clip.

3   Play the project.

4   Stop the playhead just after the botanist says, "reducing," at around 15:10.

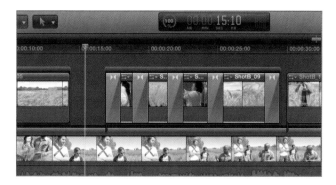

5   Drag the storyline to the left until it aligns with the playhead position.

> **TIP** To make this step easier, enable snapping (if it's not enabled) by pressing N, or clicking the Snapping button in the upper right of the Timeline.

Snapping button turns blue when enabled

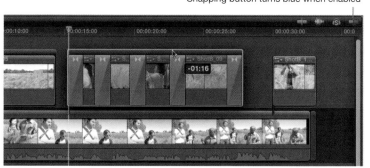

All the connected clips in the storyline and their cross dissolve effects move together to better align with the dialogue.

6   Play the project again to see your work.

You can use the same technique to create a fade-out on the last clip.

7   Select the end point of the last clip.

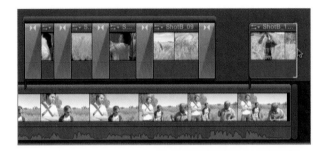

8   Press Command-T to add a cross dissolve effect.

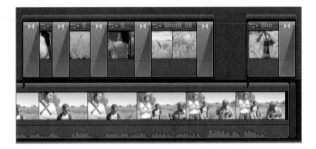

A secondary storyline is created containing that one clip, and the effect is added to its end.

9   Play the project.

Now the scene ends with a nice, clean fade-out.

Breaking Apart Storylines

Secondary storylines have many benefits, but sometimes you may want to remove a clip from a storyline, or convert a storyline back into connected clips.

1   Select the storyline that begins at 15:10.

2   Choose Clip > Break Apart Clip Items, or press Command-Shift-G. A warning appears to alert you that separating the clips will remove the transition effects.

3   Click Break Apart.

> **TIP**   If you don't want to be warned about this issue in the future, select the checkbox.

The clips return to their pre-storyline states.

You can also drag individual items out of an existing storyline.

4   Drag the third clip in the first secondary storyline (**ShotB_04**) out of that storyline, and place it above **ShotB_09**.

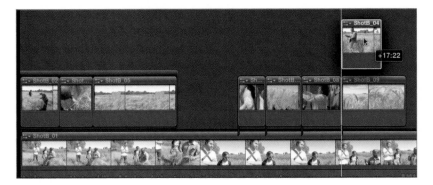

The clip is removed from the storyline, and the gap is automatically closed, unlike what would have occurred if the clips were connected clips, each one with its own connection line.

Let's look at the other behavior using the Position tool.

5   Press Command-Z to undo step 4.

6   From the Tools pop-up menu, choose the Position tool, or press P.

7   Repeat step 4 by dragging the clip out of the storyline and on top of **ShotB_09**.

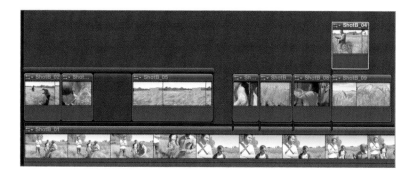

This time, a gap is left where the clip was. The storyline will maintain that gap unless you explicitly remove it, either by positioning another clip into the space, or by selecting and deleting the gap itself.

8   Press A to return to the Select tool to prepare for the next exercise.

Understanding Compound Clips

On occasion, you may want to group objects that span multiple layers or storylines. For example, you might want to collapse all the connected clips into the primary storyline to tidy up an overly complex Timeline; or you might align a title to a connected clip so the two objects always move together. Creating a compound clip will achieve both of these goals.

A compound clip can also be used when you want to apply a single effect to a group of shots all at once, or to group a collection of overlapping audio clips so they can be represented by a single bar in the Timeline.

A compound clip can even contain other compound clips. Best of all, creating compound clips (like everything in Final Cut Pro X) is nondestructive. You can continue to edit the contents of the compound clip after creating it, or even break it apart into its constituent clips.

Creating Compound Clips

You can create compound clips at any point during the editing process. In this exercise, you'll create multiple compound clips and navigate in and out of them.

1   Drag a selection rectangle around the five connected clips beginning at 15:10.

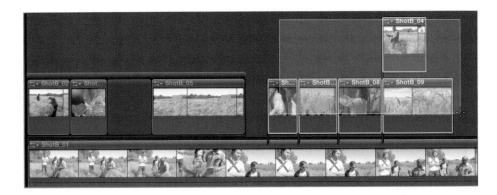

2   Choose File > New Compound Clip, or press Option-G.

The group of five clips is combined and represented by a single bar in the Timeline.

NOTE ▸ Compound clips can also be created in the Event Browser, allowing you to create a single object containing multiple source clips. This happens automatically when you apply the Synchronize Clips command.

3   Double-click the newly created compound clip.

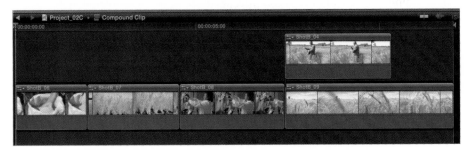

The Timeline updates to show the contents of the compound clip. You can edit these clips just like clips in any Timeline. Changes you make will be reflected in the parent project.

At any time, you can dive into, or step out of the compound clip using the Timeline History controls.

4   Click the Timeline history back arrow button, or press Command-[(left bracket).

Timeline history back button

NOTE ▸ You can see the name of the compound clip's parent project in the Timeline header bar.

The Timeline updates to show the entire project.

5   Select the compound clip.

6   Open the Effects Browser, scroll down, and double-click the Background Squares effect to apply it to the entire compound clip.

7   Play the project to see the result. To achieve a similar result without using a compound clip, you would have to apply the filter five separate times to each of the five clips.

Furthermore, this technique ensures that all the clips are filtered in exactly the same way. If you later want to change the filter, you'll only have to do so once for the entire compound clip.

Attaching Titles to Connected Clips

You can also use compound clips to connect a title to a connected clip (or in this exercise, a secondary storyline). Ordinarily titles can be connected only to the primary storyline, but by grouping a title and a connected clip into a compound clip, you can ensure that whenever you move, edit, or modify the connected clip, the title remains attached to it.

1   Position the playhead at approximately 9:00.

At this location you're going to add a title to identify the field seen in the cutaway shot.

2   Choose Edit > Connect Title > Basic Title, or press Control-T, to add a 10-second title to the project.

3   In the onscreen text controls, type *Oromia Province, 2011*, and drag the text to the lower-right corner of the screen.

To make the text more legible, you can change its size and color.

4   In the Text Inspector (press Command-4, if the Inspector is not open), change the Size to 80, the Face > Color to bright cyan/blue, and select the Drop Shadow checkbox. Reposition the text as necessary to keep it visible on the screen.

Canvas Zoom menu   On-screen navigation control

TIP ▶ When you're working with a small display, you can more easily see your title by zooming into the Canvas and using the onscreen navigation control to move within the frame.

The timing of the title is linked to the clip in the primary storyline; but in this case, you want to connect it to the clip in the secondary storyline.

5 Drag the right edge of the title to the left so it ends at approximately 13:00.

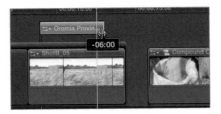

6 Select the title, as well as the secondary storyline below it.

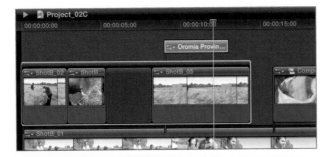

NOTE ▶ Be sure to select the storyline and not just the one clip beneath the title.

7 Press Option-G to create a new compound clip.

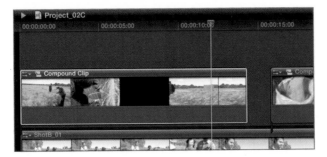

The title and the secondary storyline are combined into a compound clip. To change the title or any of the clips, double-click the compound clip to open a new Timeline displaying its component parts.

You can also incorporate clips from the primary storyline into compound clips.

8   Press Command-A to select all the items in the Timeline.

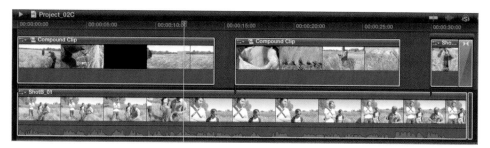

9   Press Option-G to combine them into a compound clip.

All the connected clips are collapsed into the primary storyline. You could now move this interview segment around within a larger program, and all the associated cutaways and titles would automatically move with it.

If at any time you want to remove the compound clip and return the Timeline to its previous state, you can easily do that as well.

10   Select the compound clip and choose Clip > Break Apart Clip Items, or press Command-Shift-G.

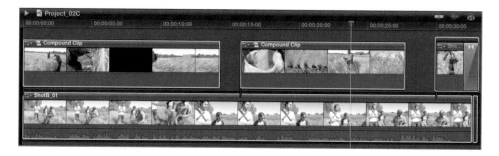

The compound clip is removed and the clips that were inside appear instead.

Lesson Review

1. What is the least destructive edit type?

2. Where in a project will an overwrite, insert, or connect edit begin?

3. What will be the duration of a clip after performing a Replace from Start edit?

4. What is a project-defined edit?

5. What is a backtimed edit?

6. How do you limit an edit to audio-only?

7. How many storylines can exist in a single Timeline?

8. Can storylines contain multiple layers?

9. Can clips within a storyline be edited?

10. How do you edit the clips inside a compound clip?

11. Can compound clips contain multiple layers?

Answers

1. The append edit is the least destructive.

2. At the current playhead (or skimmer) position

3. The same duration as the original clip in the project

4. An edit based on a range selection in the Timeline

5. An edit in which the end of the selection of the source clip is lined up with the play-head position in the project.

6. From the Source Media pop-up menu in the toolbar, choose Audio Only.

7. There is no limit to the number of storylines in a Timeline.

8. No, storylines must be flat.

9. Yes, clips in a storyline can be edited as any other clip in the Timeline.

10. Double-click the compound clip to open its own Timeline.

11. Yes

Keyboard Shortcuts

A	Choose Select tool
D	Perform overwrite edit
Shift-D	Perform backtimed overwrite edit
E	Perform append edit
Command-G	Create a storyline
Command-Shift-G	Break apart clip items
Option-G	Create a compound clip
N	Enable/disable snapping
P	Choose Position tool
Q	Perform connect edit
Shift-Q	Perform backtimed connect edit
Command-T	Add cross dissolve
Control-T	Create a basic title
W	Perform insert edit
Shift-3	Select only audio source media
Command-4	Open the Inspector
Down Arrow	Move playhead to next edit point
Command-[(left bracket)	Move back in Timeline history
Spacebar	Play clip
Up Arrow	Move playhead to previous edit point

3

Time

Goals

This lesson takes approximately 45 minutes to complete.

Learn what auditions are and when to use them

Create auditions in both the Event Browser and the Timeline

Navigate within auditions using the Audition window

Master the essential audition-related keyboard shortcuts

Use auditions to create duplicate versions to compare effects

Move effects to other audition clips

Lesson 3
Working with Auditions

One of the most unique and powerful innovations in Final Cut Pro X is auditions. This feature allows you to combine multiple shots in a single clip and swap between the different source footage on the fly during editing.

Auditions can help you compare and select between different takes of the same shot in a narrative project, sample different angles (such as a close-up and a wide shot) on a single action, and try out different B-roll ideas in a documentary environment. They can even be used to experiment with different filters or other effects on a single shot.

Auditions are powerful because they're so easy to implement and use. There's no CPU performance penalty, and they actually can make clip management easier and tidier than traditional editing methods.

The more comfortable you become with the audition workflow, the more you'll find yourself using it on nearly every shot in your project. You'll probably find unexpected and innovative uses for auditions well beyond the simple examples described in this lesson.

Creating Auditions

An audition is simply a group of clips treated as a single clip. Only one of the shots (the *pick*) displays when you play the clip, but you can switch between any of the *alternates* on the fly.

Auditions can be created in the Event Browser prior to being added to a project, or you can add alternates to any clip currently in a project, thereby creating an audition dynamically.

Creating Auditions in the Event Browser

When you have a group of related clips you want to compare in the context of the scene, you can group them into an audition in the Event Browser.

1   In the Event Library, select the *Romantic Night In* Keyword Collection in the *Lesson_03* event.

2   In the Event Browser, play each of the three clips.

These clips are three different performances of a particular line of dialogue. When you create an audition containing all three clips, you can delay the decision of which version to use.

NOTE ▶ Although this exercise represents one of the most common uses of the audition feature, you can audition any group of clips. They don't even have to be of the same subject. You could have five different "audience reaction" shots for a concert scene or a collection of different "fields of grain" for the documentary scene in Lesson 2.

3   Select the three clips, and choose Clip > Audition > Create, or press Command-Y. An audition clip is added to the event. Note that it has a different icon than the regular clips.

The name of the clip reflects the current pick. In this case, it assumed the name of the last of the clips selected when it was created.

Changing Picks

You can select a new active *pick* from among the *alternates* at any point in the Audition window.

1 In the Event Browser, select the **MCU Christina_02** audition clip.

2 Choose Clip > Audition > Open, or press Y. The Audition window opens displaying the contained clips. The current pick is marked with a star.

3   Press Left Arrow to view the alternate take.

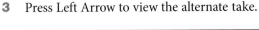

4   Press L or Shift-/ (slash) to play the alternate.

5   Press Left Arrow again and play the first clip.

6   Click Done (or press Return) to close the Audition window.

The active clip when you close the window becomes the new pick.

Editing with an Audition

Once you create an audition, you can edit it as if it were a regular clip.

1   In the Project Library, double-click Lesson 03 > Project 03 to open it into the Timeline.

2   Play the project, which is another version of the project you worked on in Lesson 2.

3   Position the playhead (or skimmer) to the moment just after the man says, "Eat some-where else," at around 50:10. This is a perfect time to add a shot of the woman and show how she's feeling about the fiasco.

4   Press D to overwrite the audition clip into the project.

5   Play over the section of the project containing the new clip. It fits well, but you can still change your mind and select one of the alternate clips at any time.

See how the different performances affect the feel of the whole scene. In some takes, the actor is patient, in others he's impatient. The choice of performance you make affects how the audience reads the other actor's response. Make no mistake: It's the editor who chooses how an actor's performance plays in each scene. This is why smart actors befriend the editors on their films.

6   In the Timeline, select the audition clip, and choose Clip > Audition > Next Pick, or press Control-Right Arrow.

The audition clip changes to show the new pick. Notice that this pick is shorter than the previous one. The Timeline automatically ripples to accommodate the new clip length.

7   Play over the section again to play the alternate in context.

Previewing Auditions

While these sample clips contain exaggeratedly distinct performances, in the real world, you'll frequently choose between picks that are very similar. To judge such clips accurately, you need to compare the alternate versions in context in rapid succession. The audition preview function enables this comparison.

1   With the audition clip selected in the Timeline, choose Clip > Audition > Preview, or press Command-Control-Y.

The Audition window opens, and the project begins playing a few seconds prior to the new clip and extends a few seconds afterward. Playback will continue to loop (regardless of the state of the global looping setting), allowing you to change picks and immediately see each clip in context.

TIP ▶ The duration of the pre-roll and post-roll are set in the Playback pane of Final Cut Pro Preferences.

2   Press Left or Right Arrow to select a new pick. When you choose a new pick, the preview begins over again at the beginning.

TIP ▶ You can also click the thumbnails in the Audition window to select a pick.

3   Watch each of the takes in context, switching between them by pressing the Right and Left Arrow keys.

NOTE ▶ Although the Audition window opens adjacent to the audition clip, feel free to move it anywhere on the screen.

4   Press Spacebar to stop the looping playback. Press Spacebar again to resume looping playback.

5   Settle on the middle clip (**MCU Christina_01**) and click Done, or press Return.

Creating Auditions in the Timeline

You can add new clips to any existing project clip to create a new audition clip. You can also choose whether the newly added clip is saved as an alternate (leaving the Timeline unaffected), or is selected as the current pick.

1   In the Event Library, select the *we'll come back* Keyword Collection in Lesson_03.

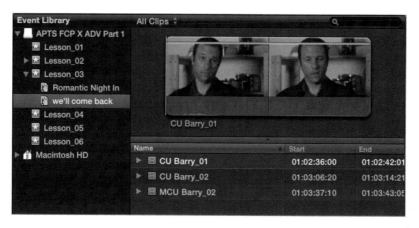

2 In the Event Browser, play each of the three shots, which are all alternate versions of the next line in the scene.

3 In the Timeline, drag the first clip, **CU Barry_01**, on top of the second instance of **Shot_06** (at approximately 52:23). When **Shot_06** turns white, release the mouse button. The Replace menu appears.

4 Choose "Replace and add to Audition." **CU Barry_01** replaces **Shot_06** in the Timeline, but **Shot_06** isn't deleted. Instead, the two clips are converted into an audition clip, and **Shot_06** is saved as an alternate.

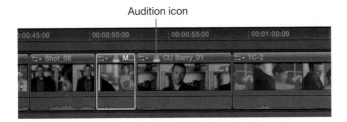

5 Select the **CU Barry_01** audition clip, and press Control-Right Arrow to make **Shot_06** appear in the Timeline.

6 Press Control-Right Arrow to once again to swap the two clips.

TIP ▶ When navigating the shots in an audition, if you get to the rightmost clip and press Control-Right Arrow again, the selections will loop around to the leftmost clip (and vice-versa).

You can add more clips to this audition. Doing so allows you to judge how differently the scene plays with a *close-up* or *medium close shot*, or how different performances will affect the rest of the shots in the scene. There is no right or wrong answer. Auditions allow you to trust your instincts and make the best choice for each situation.

7 In the Event Browser, select **CU Barry_02** and **MCU_Barry_02**.

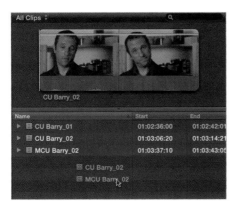

8 Drag the two clips onto **CU_Barry_01** in the Timeline, releasing the mouse button when that clip turns white.

9 In the Replace menu, choose "Add to Audition." Although nothing changed in the Timeline, the two shots were added to the audition as alternates.

NOTE ▶ If you choose "Add to Audition" prior to making a clip an audition, the Timeline clip is automatically converted into one.

10 In the Timeline, click the Audition icon to the left of the clip's name, or press Y to open the Audition window.

11 Press Spacebar to preview the audition, find the take you most prefer, and click Done or press Return.

Modifying Auditions

One of the best things about auditions is that creating them and leaving them in your project has no downside. No matter how many alternates you save, your project files don't get significantly bigger, playback doesn't require more RAM, and you experience no slowdown.

Still, you eventually may want to tidy your projects by removing alternates you're sure are out of the running that you don't intend to use.

1 Select the Shot_06 audition clip, and press Y to open the Audition window.

2 In the Audition window, select the rightmost clip.

3 Press Delete to remove this alternate from the audition.

4 Click Done, or press Return.

Finalizing an Audition

You can convert an audition back into a regular clip, or *finalize* it, using the current pick. Finalizing auditions, however, isn't required. You can safely output or share your project with auditions in it. Removing auditions from your project is strictly an organizational choice.

1 Select the MCU Christina_01 audition clip.

2 Choose Clip > Audition > Finalize Audition, or press Shift-Option-Y, to replace the audition with the single MCU Christina_01 clip.

Audition icon is gone

Using Auditions and Effects

Another common use of auditions is to sample different effects or effects settings on a single clip. In this scenario the audition contains multiple versions of the same clip, each with different effects applied.

Duplicating a Clip into an Audition

Let's say that you want to add a "look" to this project to make it more memorable. But before you choose to apply an effect to the whole project, you want to experiment with your options. Let's apply those options to a single clip and then use an audition to compare the results.

1   In the toolbar, click the Effects button, or press Command-5, to open the Effects Browser.

2   In the sidebar, select the Looks section.

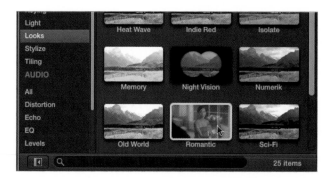

3   In the Timeline, select the last clip in the project, **1C-2**.

4   In the Effects Browser, double-click the Romantic effect to apply it to the selected clip. A blurred vignette is added to the edges of the clip, but on this clip, the result is very subtle.

TIP ▶ You can also drag the effect onto the clip in the Timeline, or onto an open Audition window.

5   Play or skim over the last clip in the project.

6   Open the Video Inspector, and increase the Amount slider in the Romantic effect to
    80 to increase the visibility of the effect.

This effect might work for the scene, but let's try some other options so we're sure to
choose the optimum effect.

7   With the same clip selected in the Timeline, choose Clip > Audition > Duplicate as
    Audition, or press Option-Y. The clip is converted into an audition clip, and a dupli-
    cate of the shot with the Romantic effect applied is saved as an alternate.

TIP ▶ You can also click the Duplicate button to duplicate the current pick in the
Audition window.

8   Press Y to open the Audition window. The Audition window shows two identical shots. At this point, switching between them would yield no noticeable result. Applying a new effect will change the appearance of the copy.

9   In the Effects Browser, double-click the Memory effect. The effect is applied, in addition to the Romantic effect, to the current pick.

10   Press Spacebar to preview the audition, and press the Left or Right Arrow to switch between the two versions.

Duplicate from Original

In the previous exercise, you duplicated a shot and added the copy as an alternate, so both shots were initially identical before you applied an effect. But on some occasions, you may want to add a duplicate to the audition without any effects applied to it.

In your current project, you have a copy of the clip with the Romantic effect, and one with Romantic and Memory effects added. But the version with both effects applied seems a little overwrought. What if you want to compare these versions with a version that has the Memory effect by itself?

1   With the audition clip selected in the Timeline and the Audition window still visible, choose Clip > Audition > Duplicate from Original. A new copy of the original clip appears in the Audition window with no filters applied.

2   In the Effects Browser, double-click the Memory effect to add it to the pick. The result is a more subtle effect that might be perfect for the scene.

3 Press Spacebar to preview the audition, and press Left or Right Arrow to switch between the three versions of the clip. Be sure to end on the version with the Memory effect applied.

Duplicating a Clip While Applying an Effect

There's yet another way to a duplicate a clip to create a new alternate with another effect applied to it.

1 In the Effects Browser, select the Glory effect.

2 Drag the effect over the audition clip in the Timeline and continue to hold down the mouse button.

3 Hold down the Control key and release the mouse button.

Four clips in the Audition window

A new alternate is created with both the Memory and the Glory effects applied.

NOTE ▸ Dragging an effect to the Audition window always applies the effect to the current pick.

Applying an Effect to All Picks

You might also want to add an effect to all the clips in the audition. In the current project, you still haven't chosen between the different looks, but have decided that whichever effect is chosen, it will need a vignette effect.

1   In the Effects Browser, select the Stylize category.

2   Scroll down to the bottom of the stack and find the Vignette effect.

3   Drag the effect onto the clip in the Timeline, but before releasing the mouse button, hold down the Option and Control keys. Release the mouse button to add the effect to all four clips in the audition.

4   Preview the audition and press Left or Right Arrow to switch between the four clips.

5   When you've chosen a favorite clip as the pick, press Return, or click Done.

Adding Effects to Other Clips

When you've finally chosen the perfect effect or combination of effects, you can copy the pick in the audition and choose Paste Effects to apply the effect to the rest of the project clips. You can also paste those effects as a duplicate, which turn all of the other project clips into auditions with the effect-altered clip added as the pick and the original clip retained as an alternate.

1   In the Timeline, select the last clip, and choose Edit > Copy, or press Command-C to copy the clip to the clipboard.

2   Select the rest of the clips in the project, excluding the last clip.

3   Choose Clip > Audition > Duplicate and Paste Effects, or press Command-Option-Y.

Each of the selected clips is converted into an audition, and the effects are applied to the pick, while leaving the original version as an alternate you can easily access using audition commands.

NOTE ▸ If any of the selected clips were already auditions, the added clip would simply be added to the audition, and selected as the current pick.

Lesson Review

1.   True or false: The more clips placed in an audition, the more computing power you need to process your project.

2.   True or false: Clips within an audition can be of different durations.

3.   When previewing an audition, where do you set the duration of the pre-roll and post-roll?

4.   Must the Audition window be open to change picks?

5.   Must the Audition window be open to delete alternates?

6.   How many of your auditions must be finalized before sharing a project?

7.   How do you add an effect to only the current pick?

8.   How do you add an effect to a newly created alternate?

9.   How do you add an effect to all picks in an audition?

Answers

1.   False. The number of clips in an audition has no impact on performance.

2.   True

3.   You set the duration of the pre-roll and post-roll in the Playback pane of Final Cut Pro Preferences.

4.   No, you can use keyboard shortcuts to change picks without opening the Audition window.

5.   Yes

6.   None. You can share or output a project with as many auditions as you like.

7.   Apply an effect by dragging it to a pick in the Timeline, or double-click the effect (just as you would for an ordinary clip) to apply it to the currently selected pick.

8.   Control-drag an effect onto a clip to create a new alternate with that effect applied to it.

9.   Option-Control-drag the effect onto an audition clip in the Timeline.

Keyboard Shortcuts

Y	Open Audition window
Command-Y	Create an audition clip
Command-Control-Y	Preview audition clip
Control-Right Arrow	Choose clip as the pick and place it in the Timeline

4

Time

Goals

This lesson takes approximately 85 minutes to complete.

Read and use the Audio meters

Fix overmodulated audio clips

Adjust and animate audio levels

Perform subframe audio adjustments

Apply audio fades and select fade shapes

Create audio pans in stereo and surround

Animate audio pan effects

Manage audio channels for multichannel clips

Break apart audio channels for independent editing

Lesson **4**

Working with Sound

It cannot be said often enough: Audio is more important than video. Audiences will tolerate shockingly poor quality video (see *Paranormal Activity*, *Cloverfield*, or *Blair Witch Project* for proof), but no one will sit through even three minutes on YouTube if the audio is hard to hear. You can always close your eyes, but closing your ears is far more difficult. And while the images carry the basic information of a scene, the sound invariably carries the emotional content. If seeing is believing, then hearing is feeling.

Fortunately, Final Cut Pro X contains an impressive number of ways to improve your video's sound. It has tools to set the audio levels to a uniform, accurate volume; multiple methods to create audio fades and four fade styles; intuitive controls for panning sound between speakers, in both stereo and surround sound environments; and much more.

NOTE ▶ *Apple Pro Training Series: Final Cut Pro X* by Diana Weynand (Peachpit Press) described the automatic audio enhancements you can apply to your clips to remove background noise, adjust levels, and remove silent audio channels. This lesson picks up where those lessons left off and delves into a more manual approach to improving your sound.

Setting Sound Levels

One of the most basic and fundamental aspects of good audio is ensuring that the volume level is consistent across your project. If one scene is too loud and the next is too soft, it's very hard for viewers to stay engaged in your program. And if the overall level is too quiet or too loud, other problems arise such as increased background noise or distortion.

Understanding Audio Meters

Final Cut Pro has highly accurate, easy-to-read Audio meters to monitor audio levels and ensure that they are correct and uniform. Tiny meters are always visible to the right of the current timecode in the center of the toolbar, but you can also display large meters with a single click.

1   In the Project Library, double-click the *Sound editing* project inside the Lesson_04 folder in the APTS FCP X ADV Part 1 disk.

The project opens into the Timeline.

2   Click the tiny Audio meters in the toolbar, or press Command-Shift-8 to display large Audio meters to the right of the Timeline.

 —— Audio meters

3   Drag the left edge of the meters to make them bigger or smaller and view more or less detail.

Drag separator bar

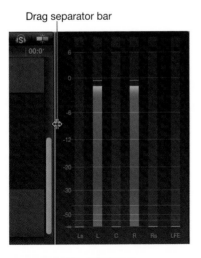

NOTE ▶ The meters show the number of channels in the current project. Surround projects show six meters (L, R, C, LS, RS, and LFE); stereo projects show two meters (L and R).

4 Play the first few clips of the project and watch the Audio meters.

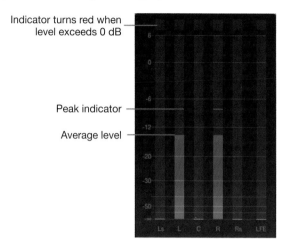

Indicator turns red when level exceeds 0 dB

Peak indicator

Average level

The meters display the average and peak levels, and alert you if your audio ever hits 0 db.

You can determine the average level by watching the bouncing bars. This is not going to provide a precise value, but watching the meters can give you a good sense of the overall volume of the clip. In this project, the average level for the first clip is around –24 dB. The second clip averages at around –9 dB, and the third clip is even louder, and reaches 0 dB at about 27 seconds.

The peak level is indicated by the thin white line that lingers (for a second or two) as the clips play. That line shows the loudest level reached over the last section of playback and can be especially helpful if the audio has a very brief peak that's much louder than the average level (such as you'll hear in clip 2 around 15:00).

▶ **How Loud Is Too Loud?**

There is no hard and fast rule about what defines a proper audio level. Whatever level you choose, your viewer can always adjust the volume of the playback device to make the overall sound louder or quieter.

However, if your levels are low, she will have to turn the playback volume up very loud, which can expose background noise and lower the overall sound quality. On the other hand, if your levels are high, your listener will have to turn the volume down, which can make quiet passages nearly inaudible. Furthermore, when sounds are too loud in a high-level clip, the sound can distort, making an unpleasant grating sound and rendering the audio unintelligible, even if the volume is decreased.

High- and low-level audio problems may be exaggerated when your video is converted to play on other platforms. So, a project that sounds OK during editing can reveal problems when you upload the result to YouTube or burn the video to a Blu-ray disk. Also, lower-quality speakers (such as the built-in speaker on a cell phone or a consumer television) can magnify problems that aren't apparent when monitoring your project on studio-quality speakers or headphones.

Because of this, a general guideline is that you want your levels as loud as possible, as long as they *never* touch 0 dB (at which point they *overmodulate* and distortion occurs).

NOTE ▶ Never, never let the audio hit 0 dB!

Also, audio is *additive*, so if you play a sound effect, ambiance, and music along with your main dialogue, the volumes of each item are added together, pushing the final result ever closer to that dreaded 0 dB. Most audio mixers set the dialogue, interview, or narration to an average audio level of –12 dB, which allows plenty of room for adding sound effects, music, and other elements without risking overmodulating. This average audio level also provides a little *headroom* if you want to make a specific sound deliberately louder than the dialogue (such as a music swell or explosion).

To this last point, sound mixers working on theatrical films typically set the average dialogue levels even lower (–24 dB or –31 dB). The theater turns up their (high-quality) speakers so that dialogue plays at a comfortable level, and when those explosions occur, they can be so loud they knock your socks off—without ever touching 0 dB!

However, beware of using this trick if your target platforms are computers, hand-held devices, or televisions without fancy sound systems. Those lower-quality speakers may not be able to reproduce so much *dynamic range* (variance between the loudest and quietest sounds), and your audio mixing artistry may come across as a muddy mess.

Fixing Overmodulated Audio

The warning indicator turns red if your audio level reaches 0 db. In this instance, you must turn down the audio below 0 dB or risk creating a distorted sound.

Excessive volume
warning indicator

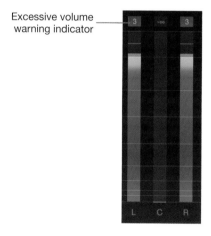

If you see this warning, do not ignore it!

NOTE ▸ If you don't see a number in the warning indicator, increase the width of the meters as described in the previous exercise.

The audio waveforms in the Timeline also indicate when a clip is too loud. When a part of the waveform is louder than −6 dB, it appears in yellow. If a part of the waveform is at 0 dB, it appears in red.

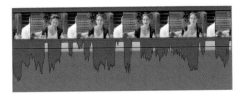

Fortunately, Final Cut Pro tells you how many decibels "over" 0 dB the peak is, making it very easy to fix the level. In **Shot_03**, the audio peaked at +3 dB.

> **TIP** ▸ When skimming is turned on, the excessive volume warning is dismissed as soon as you move your pointer. If you disable skimming (press S to turn skimming on and off), the indicator will stay active until you play the project again, enabling you to more easily see (and address) the offending audio level.

1 Select **Shot_03**, and choose Modify > Volume > Down (–1 dB), or press Control-- (minus).

2 Repeat step 1 three times to lower the level by 3 dB.

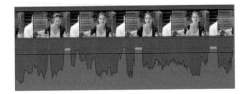

3 Play the project again.

The waveform no longer turns red. However, leaving that audio at such a high level might still cause problems if you later add any sound effects, music, or other clips. So lowering it even further is wise.

Unfortunately, lowering the whole clip will make the rest of the shot *too* quiet. To fix this, you'll need to utilize keyframes, as you'll learn to do in the next section.

> **NOTE** ▸ The figures in this lesson were captured with the "Show Reference waveforms" setting chosen. Reference waveforms factor out loudness and let you see the shape of the sound more clearly as it changes. (So, for example, the waveforms become smaller as the volume is decreased.) Choose this setting in the Editing pane of the Final Cut Pro Preferences window.

Setting Levels in the Timeline

You have many ways to adjust a clip's audio level. In addition to choosing the Modify menu item, you can adjust levels in the Timeline or in the Audio Inspector, or by using the keyboard. Each of these methods is best used in certain circumstances. To fix the problem in **Shot_03**, you will use the volume controls in the Timeline.

1   Click the Clip Appearance button, and set the clip appearance to the second icon from the left.

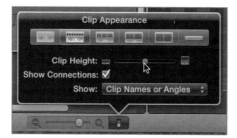

2   Drag the Clip Height slider to the middle to increase the clip heights.

TIP ▶ The Timeline doesn't update dynamically when you drag the slider, so for best results, drag and let go a few times to see the Timeline update until the clips are the size you desire.

3   Click outside the window to close the Clip Appearance window.

Making the audio portion of the clips larger makes it easier to see the waveforms and to make more precise adjustments to the volume control (the horizontal line across the audio waveform). In this case, you will return the volume to its default value, in preparation for lowering only the section that's too loud.

4   Position your pointer over the volume control for **Shot_03**, and when the pointer changes to the Adjust pointer, drag the line up until the volume reads 0 dB.

This adjustment raises the overall level, but now the middle part of the clip is too loud.

5   Play the project and press I just as she says "Uh…" at 25:00, and press O just after she says, "I'm enjoying that" at around 28:15. The area you want to attenuate is now marked as a selection.

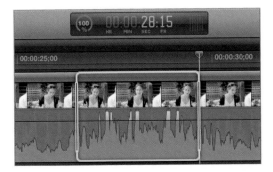

6   Position your pointer over the volume control within the selected area, and drag the line down to –7 dB. You may need to zoom in on the Timeline to more easily select the line within the selected range.

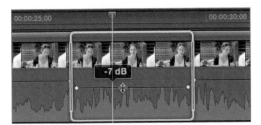

The level is lowered only in the selected section.

7   Play the clip to hear how the overall level is now far more uniform.

8   Press Command-Shift-A to deselect all.

Deselecting allows you to more clearly see that *keyframes* were automatically added to limit the volume change to the selected range.

When two keyframes are set to different values, Final Cut Pro automatically interpolates the audio levels between the two values, thereby animating the audio level.

Animating Audio Levels

To change audio levels over time, you can adjust the line between the keyframes, adjust specific keyframes, or add additional keyframes to make specific changes (such as removing a pop or cough, or adding an audio fade-in or fade-out). There is no limit to the number of keyframes you can add.

1   Drag the Timeline Zoom slider to the right to zoom in on the Timeline, or press Command-= (equal sign).

2   Position your pointer over the first keyframe, and then drag the keyframe to the left to create a slower fade effect.

NOTE ▶ You can drag a keyframe either vertically (to change its level), or horizontally (to change its location in time) but not both directions at the same time.

Changing the value of the first keyframe will affect the level of the clip prior to that keyframe, and changing the value of the last keyframe will affect the level of the clip from that point until the end of the clip.

3   Drag the line between the middle two keyframes down to –8 dB.

Both keyframes surrounding the line are moved proportionally.

4   Option-click the line twice to add new keyframes as shown in the following figure.

5   Drag the line segment between the two new keyframes up to –5 dB.

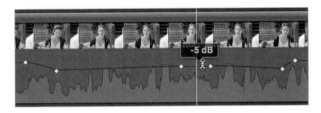

6   Play the clip to hear the results.

You may want to continue adding and adjusting keyframes to create an optimally smooth audio level.

Making Subframe Audio Adjustments

Audio clips recorded at a sampling rate of 48 kHz contain 2,000 samples for each frame of 24 fps video. That means you could conceivably add 2,000 audio keyframes in every single frame of video! Higher audio sample rates could have even more keyframes. Although no one is likely to add thousands of keyframes to a single video frame, having that kind of precision means you can fix miniscule errors such as clicks, pops, and extra sibilance.

1   With no clips selected, click the Current Timecode field, and type *14:16*. Press Return.

2   Press Shift-/ (slash) to play around that timecode.

You will hear a pop sound right as the woman says "green tomato jam."

3   Drag the Timeline Zoom slider all the way to the right to zoom all the way into the
Timeline.

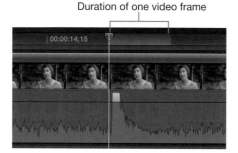

Duration of one video frame

You can see the waveform that represents the offending sound, but if you try to
remove it, you also risk removing some of the woman's voice. To avoid that, you
should adjust only the specific samples containing the sound.

The light gray bar in the Timeline ruler indicates the duration of one frame. As you
can see, audio keyframes can be edited with much greater precision than a single
video frame; but in fact, you can zoom in much farther for even more precision.

4   Make sure that View > Zoom To Samples (the default) is chosen.

If Zoom To Samples was not active, you'll notice that the Timeline Zoom slider sud-
denly has a little more room to the right.

5   Drag the Timeline Zoom slider farther to the right. The gray bar in the ruler, which
represents one frame, becomes larger as you zoom farther and farther into the
Timeline.

Duration of one video frame

At the farthest zoom point, each horizontal pixel on the screen represents an individual audio sample.

6   Option-click three times to add three keyframes around and on the unwanted noise.

7   Drag the middle keyframe all the way down to –96 dB.

The two surrounding keyframes limit the adjustment to the area between them.

8   Press Shift-/ (slash) to play around the area again. The offending noise is removed, and the woman's voice appears unaffected.

9   Press Shift-Z to zoom the Timeline back out to show all clips.

Setting Levels in the Inspector

You can also adjust audio levels for any selected clip in the Audio Inspector. One advantage to making changes here (as opposed to the Timeline) is that you can change clips that are in the Event Browser but not yet added to a project.

1   In the Event Library, open the *Lesson_04* Event, and in the Event Browser, click Shot_06 to select it.

2   If the Inspector is not visible, press Command-4 to open it.

3   In the Inspector, click the Audio button to open the Audio Inspector.

Dragging the Volume slider in the Audio Inspector has the same effect as adjusting the volume control in a waveform in the Timeline. For clips already placed in a project, both controls affect the same data.

4   In the Event Browser, click the green Favorite bar for **Shot_06** to select it.

5   Press E to append the clip to the end of the project.

6   In the Timeline, click **Shot_06**. The Inspector updates to show the audio level for the current playhead position of the selected clip.

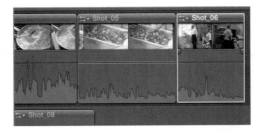

7   In the Inspector, drag the Volume slider down by 4 dB.

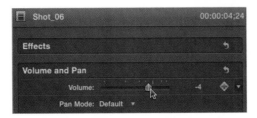

The volume control in the Timeline moves down by 4 dB.

8   Drag the volume control down to −5 dB. The Volume slider in the Inspector also updates.

You can also use the Inspector to change the level of multiple clips simultaneously.

9   In the Timeline, Shift-click **Shot_05** to add it to the selection.

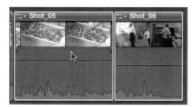

Now, both **Shot_05** and **Shot_06** are selected. The Audio Inspector no longer shows an indicator for the volume (since more than one clip can have more than one value) but you can still modify the clips' volume by a relative amount.

10 Position your pointer over the dashes to the right of the Volume slider and drag up or down to change the two clips' levels simultaneously.

TIP ▶ To see the resulting level for one of the selected clips, deselect both clips, and then select the one clip you want to observe.

Animating Levels in the Inspector
You can also add, modify, and navigate between audio keyframes within the Inspector.

1   In the Timeline, select **Shot_03**.

The Inspector updates to show the values for the selected clip at the current frame (either under the playhead or the skimmer, if enabled).

2   In the Timeline, drag the playhead and watch the Volume slider in the Inspector move as the existing keyframes affect the clip's volume.

Button turns orange when playhead/skimmer is over a keyframe

Keyframes are represented in the Inspector by the diamond-shaped Keyframe button to the right of the Volume slider. When the playhead is parked on a keyframe, the button turns orange.

NOTE ▶ The Keyframe button also turns orange (with a plus sign in the middle) when you position your pointer over a parameter—even if you're on a frame that doesn't yet have a keyframe assigned. This is the Add Keyframe button. It alerts you that if you click and make a change to the slider, a new keyframe will automatically be added. However, the Add Keyframe button looks very similar to the Keyframe button (especially on a high resolution screen), so it's easy to get confused. To be sure whether or not you're currently parked on a keyframe, move the pointer away from the Volume parameter.

You can navigate directly to keyframes by clicking the arrows on either side of the Keyframe button.

Previous keyframe

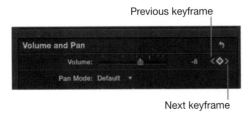

Next keyframe

3   Click the left arrow to jump to the first keyframe to the left of the current playhead position. Click the right arrow to jump to the first keyframe to the right of the current playhead position.

If no more keyframes exist either before or after the current playhead position, the appropriate arrow is dimmed.

NOTE ▶ Once a first keyframe is added to a clip, any changes you make to the Volume slider will automatically add a new keyframe at the current playhead position.

Deleting Keyframes

Keyframes can be deleted in the Inspector. To do so, the playhead must be positioned directly on that specific keyframe.

With the playhead parked on the keyframe, click the orange Delete Keyframe button.

Delete Keyframe button

The keyframe is removed. Final Cut Pro automatically recalibrates to interpolate the audio based on the remaining keyframes.

NOTE ▶ The X in the Keyframe button doesn't appear until you roll your mouse over it.

Resetting Audio Levels

The Inspector also contains an essential control: the Reset button. Clicking this button allows you to remove any keyframes or audio volume adjustments made to the selected clip, and restore the clip to its default volume.

1   In the Timeline, select Shot_03.

2   In the Inspector, click the Reset button for the Volume and Pan section.

Reset button

The volume (and pan) settings are restored to the default, removing any keyframes.

Setting Levels Using Keyboard Shortcuts

You have one more way to change audio levels: Select a clip (or portion of a clip) and press a keyboard shortcut to boost (raise) or *attenuate* (lower) the level by 1 dB.

These keyboard shortcuts are especially useful because they allow you to change the levels of a clip *while the video is playing back,* which means you can hear the changes dynamically, creating a more organic workflow.

1   In the Timeline, select Shot_01.

2   Play the project.

3   While the first clip is playing, press Control-= (equal sign) several times.

    Each time you press the keyboard command, the volume for the clip is boosted by 1 dB.

4   Press Control-- (minus sign) to lower the level by 1 dB.

Nudging Keyframes

When you have created audio keyframes, you can select an individual keyframe directly and move it up and down 1 dB at a time from the keyboard.

1   In the Timeline, Option-click the volume control for Shot_01 to add a keyframe.

2   Click the keyframe to select it. The keyframe turns orange.

3 Press Option-Up Arrow to increase or Option-Down Arrow to decrease the level of the selected keyframe.

> **TIP** ▶ You can also delete a selected keyframe in the Timeline by pressing the Delete key.

4 To deselect the keyframe, press Command-Shift-A or click anywhere outside the keyframe.

Creating Audio Fades

Nearly every audio clip should ideally have a small fade-in and fade-out applied to it. Tiny shifts in background sound levels can create subtle, but distracting clicks and knocks that can interfere with an otherwise flawless soundtrack.

Every audio clip in Final Cut Pro can easily be faded in and out without applying an effect, adding multiple keyframes, or performing any other elaborate manipulation. You can fade audio clips with a single gesture.

1 In the Timeline, position your pointer anywhere over **Shot_02**. Fade handles appear at the left and right edges of the waveform area.

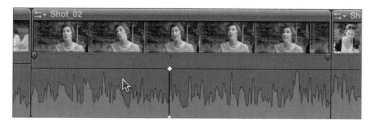

2 Drag the fade-in handle to the right to apply a fade-in effect to the clip.

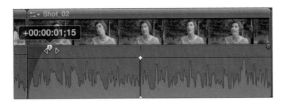

TIP ▶ Be careful not to drag the edge of the video area and perform a ripple trim instead of creating a fade effect. You can tell which effect you will get by the pointer that appears before you begin to drag.

3 Position your pointer over the right edge of the clip, and drag the fade-out handle to the left. The farther you drag, the longer (slower) the fade effect.

Fade effects are applied in addition to any adjustments made to the audio level parameter. The fade will always begin (or end) at complete silence, and fade up to the maximum level set by the level parameter.

Crossfading Between Audio Clips

Using fades, you can easily create a crossfade effect between two audio clips, as long as the clips overlap in the Timeline. For audio/video clips, you will first need to expand the audio to make the clips overlap; for connected audio clips, you can simply drag them into an overlapping position.

NOTE ▶ Applying a transition effect to adjacent video clips in the primary storyline automatically crossfades the audio in those two clips, but this exercise shows how to create an audio crossfade without using a video transition effect.

1 Double-click the audio waveforms for **Shot_02** and **Shot_03**. The audio is expanded, allowing you to manipulate it separately from the video.

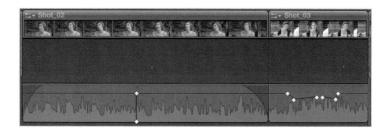

2   Drag the Audio start point of **Shot_03** to the left until it overlaps the fade at the end of
Shot_02.

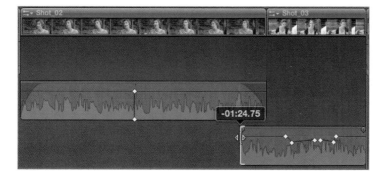

3   Drag the fade handle on the left edge of the **Shot_03** audio to add a fade that matches
the duration of the clips' overlap. The first clip fades out as the second fades in creating a crossfade effect.

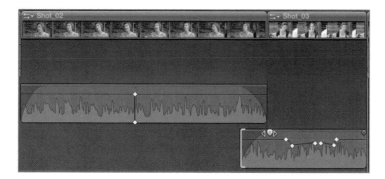

4   Select the two clips, and choose Clip > Collapse Audio/Video, or press Control-S. The
clips are collapsed, but the crossfade between the two shots remains.

TIP ▶ You can also collapse clips by double-clicking the audio waveform section or the gap between the audio and video.

Crossfading adjacent connected clips is even easier.

5   Select the edit between the two connected audio clips under Shot_04.

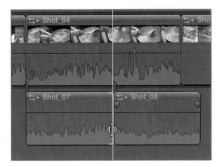

6   Press Command-T. The two clips are converted into a new storyline, and a crossfade effect is placed between the two items.

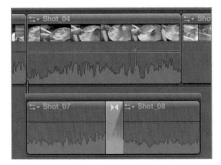

NOTE ▶ Connected clips can use transition effects only if they are embedded in a storyline, but Final Cut Pro takes care of that by automatically creating the storyline for you.

You can change the duration of the crossfade effect by dragging either edge of the gray transition icon.

7   Drag the left edge of the transition to the left to lengthen the duration of the overlap.

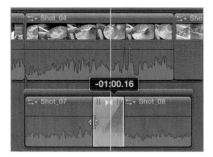

TIP ▶ You could also select the transition effect, press Control-D, and type a new duration.

Setting a Fade Shape

Final Cut Pro includes four fade shapes that perform different types of fade effects. It's up to you to decide which shape to use in any situation. There are no absolute rules because every clip will need a unique fade shape and length, but you can use the following descriptions to help you choose:

▶   *Linear*: Best for fades to or from silence on a clip with a relatively even waveform (such as a roomtone or ambiance track). Should not be used for crossfades, as a volume dip may be heard at the middle of the fade.

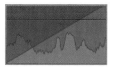

▶   *S-curve*: The default shape for crossfades. It is an all-purpose shape that creates an ease-in at the beginning and an ease-out effect at the end of the fade.

► *+3 dB:* The default shape for single fades. It is also known as *a fast-fade*, or when used as a crossfade, an *equal power* fade. This shape is ideal for crossfading between two clips of constant volume (such as roomtone, ambiances, and some music). The slight boost in the middle of the fade compensates for audio's naturally nonlinear response curve and creates a transition that is heard as a constant level across the edit.

When used for a fade-in, it creates what sounds like a uniform volume increase over the course of the fade. When used for a fade-out, the result is a seeming acceleration of the attenuation. This shape works well on dialogue or other clips when there's only room for a very short fade.

► *–3 dB*: Also known as a *slow-fade.* For a fade-in, it creates a slower, more gradual volume increase. It's often used for fading in clips with noticeable background noise or when there's room for a longer fade.

For a fade-out, the attenuation is accelerated at first, followed by a more gradual decrease in volume. When used on a longer fade, the slow-fade works well to make sounds disappear more subtly or organically.

1   Position your pointer over **Shot_02**. The fade handles appear.

2   Control-click (or right-click) the Fade In handle to open the Fade Shape pop-up menu.

3   Choose –3 dB.

4   Play the project to hear the fade-in.

5   Set the fade shape to +3 dB, and play the project again. The difference is subtle but audible.

> NOTE ▶ You may need to listen with headphones to hear the subtle difference (especially in a classroom environment).

You can also set the fade shape for crossfade effects.

6   Select the crossfade effect between the two connected clips.

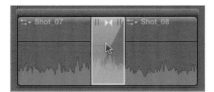

7   If the Inspector is not visible, press Command-4 to open it.

8   In the Audio Crossfade section of the Inspector, set both the Fade In Type and the Fade Out Type to +3 dB. The crossfade is now set as an equal power crossfade.

NOTE ▶ There's no reason you can't mix and match the fade types based on the specific clips you're fading.

9   Play the project and listen to the fade.

10   Experiment with the other fade types and try to hear the difference between them.

Panning Audio

One of the best ways to add dimension to your sound design is to take advantage of the fact that most audiences will be hearing your movie through multiple speakers. Surround sound enables you to spread the audio across several speakers that surround your audience; but even *stereo* projects enable you to choose the locations of sounds. You'd be very surprised to know how many editors simply leave all their audio mixed to the center, or worse, they leave it in the sometimes haphazard arrangement determined by the original sound recording.

Exercise restraint and subtlety when *panning* clips. In the real world, sound reflections and reverberations cause most sounds to come from a relatively neutral point of origin. If too much of your sound comes exclusively from a single speaker, the unnatural result might pull your viewer out of the story instead of drawing him in.

Still, appropriate panning is a great tool in your sound design arsenal, and Final Cut Pro X makes it easy to craft rich sound environments in both stereo and surround sound.

Choosing a Panning Environment

By default, all clips are imported with the audio placement information that was provided by the camera or audio recording device. Final Cut Pro examines such metadata and applies appropriate settings to your clips.

Although some devices record in full surround sound, they are extremely rare. Even stereo recording is not the norm, at least not on professional productions.

NOTE ▶ Many consumer-level camcorders will record stereo or surround audio using multiple microphones; but because the mics are mounted so close together on the top of the camera, they typically record nearly identical content on all channels.

Nearly every professional camera records (at least) two channels of audio, but those channels are typically used to record two different signals, such as the signals from two separate lavaliere microphones, or a built-in camera mic and an attached shotgun microphone controlled by a boom operator.

New projects in Final Cut Pro default to surround sound, and allow you to move sounds to any of five channels (though you can also just use the left and right stereo channels and ignore the others).

> **NOTE** ▸ Technically, six channels are included in a five-channel surround mix: In addition to the left, center, right, left surround and right surround channels, an additional channel is dedicated to low-frequency effects (LFE) such as explosions, rumbling trains, and Barry White vocals.

If you do want to mix in surround sound, you must have a surround-monitoring environment in your editing suite, which requires third-party hardware connected via PCIe, FireWire, USB, or HDMI.

Fortunately, all Macs can monitor in stereo. If you want to mix your audio only for a stereo sound environment, you can change the project from surround to stereo.

1   Activate the project by clicking anywhere in the Timeline pane (or by selecting the *Lesson_04* project in the Project Library). Choose File > Project Properties, or press Command-J. The Project Library opens (if the Timeline was showing) and the Inspector displays the Project Properties pane.

Modify Project Properties button

2   In the lower-right corner of the Inspector, click the Modify Project Properties button.

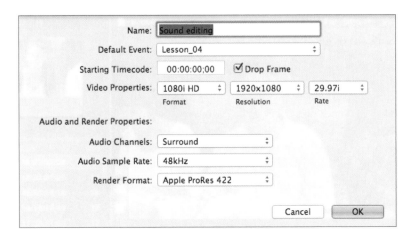

3   In the Audio and Render Properties section, set Audio Channels to Stereo, and click OK.

TIP You can tell at a glance whether a project is stereo or surround in two places: in the summary at the top of the Project Properties pane, and by noting how many meters appear in the Audio Meters section (stereo projects have two meters, surround projects have six meters).

> **NOTE** ▸ It is possible to have a mono project if imported from iMovie. Such projects can be converted to stereo (or surround) by following the same steps just described

Using Stereo Panning

In the Audio pane of the Inspector, you can assign which speakers will emit the sound of a clip. Panning between the left and right speakers can be done quickly and easily, and is very intuitive.

> **NOTE** ▸ Although editing a stereo clip into a surround project or a surround clip into a stereo project is possible, the final output will be based on the settings in the project. As a result, a surround clip edited into a stereo project will play out of only the left and right channels regardless of the panning you applied to the clip.

1   In the Project Library, double-click the *Sound editing* project in the Lesson_04 folder to open the Timeline.

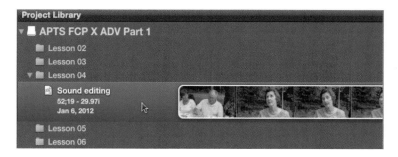

2   In the Timeline, select **Shot_01**, and in the Inspector, click the Audio button to open the Audio Inspector.

3   In the Volume and Pan settings, set Pan Mode to Stereo Left/Right.

4   Drag the Pan Amount slider all the way to the left.

5   Play the project and note that the sound from the first clip is heard only in the left speaker.

6   In the Inspector, drag the Pan Amount slider all the way to the right and play the project again. Now the audio for the first clip comes out of the right speaker.

Animating Pan Effects

You can use keyframes to change pan settings while a sound plays, which can be very effective to create naturalistic sounds for moving objects within a scene.

1   Move the playhead to the very beginning of Shot_02.

2   In the Inspector, set Pan Mode to Stereo Left/Right, and then drag the Pan Amount slider about halfway toward the left (to about –50), and click the Keyframe button to add a keyframe.

3   In the Timeline, move the playhead to 20:00.

4   In the Inspector, drag the Pan Amount slider halfway to the right (to around +50). A keyframe is automatically added because you've changed the value on a new frame in time.

5   Play the project and listen to the subtle audio shift from left to right.

Panning in the Timeline

You can also view and modify audio pan settings in the Timeline.

1   Select the clip in the Timeline, and choose Clip > Show Audio Animation, or press Control-A. The Audio Animation Editor appears below the clip in the Timeline. White diamonds represent the keyframes so you can see when they occur.

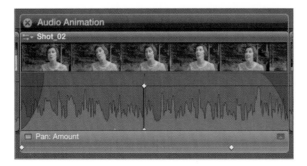

2   Drag the second keyframe to the left (to approximately 1:00:19:00), and play the project. Moving the keyframe to the left makes the panning animation happen more quickly.

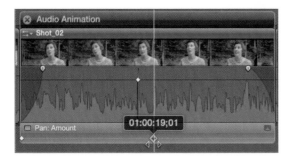

NOTE ▶ A numerical field shows the timecode for the individual clip, not the project timecode.

You can also change the pan value directly in the Timeline.

3   Double-click the keyframe area, or click the disclosure button in the upper-right corner of the Audio Animation Editor. The Pan graph expands showing the keyframes' relative values in addition to their positions in time.

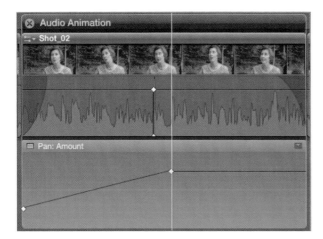

4   Drag the first keyframe all the way to the bottom of the graph.

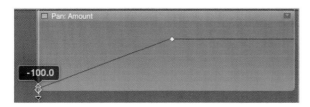

This sets the audio in the clip to begin exclusively in the left speaker. Dragging toward the top of the graph would pan it to the right speaker.

5   Option-click the black line in the Pan animation graph twice to add two new keyframes.

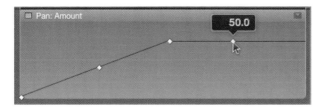

6 Drag the third keyframe down to create a plateau in the middle of the graph. This stops the panning action for the duration between the two keyframes.

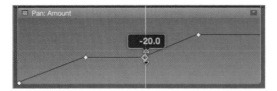

7 Play the project to hear the results of your work.

8 Click the close button.

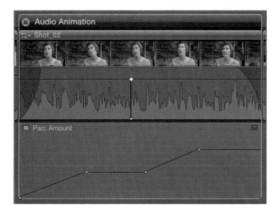

The Audio Animation Editor closes, but the keyframes and settings you modified remain applied to the clip.

Performing Surround Panning

Just as you can set stereo panning, you can make similar changes to clip audio in a surround project. To hear the surround panning, you must set your project's audio channels to surround.

> **TIP** If you do not have a surround-monitoring system attached to your editing system, you will not be able to hear the results of the adjustments in this lesson. Although you can perform the steps, Final Cut Pro will down mix to stereo outputs.

1 Press Command-J to open Project Properties.

2 In the lower-right corner of the Inspector, click the Modify Project Properties button.

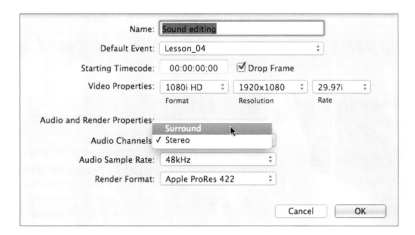

3 In the Audio and Render Properties section, set Audio Channels to Surround, and click OK.

4 Double-click the project to reopen it, and select **Shot_03**.

5 In the Inspector, click the Audio button to open the Audio Inspector.

6   Set Pan Mode to Create Space, and then click the disclosure triangle to reveal the
    Surround Panner, if necessary. The Surround Panner graphically represents the five
    surround speakers (left, center, right, left surround, and right surround).

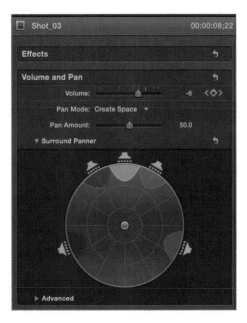

7   Drag the center handle around the Surround Panner.

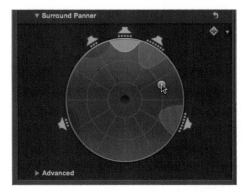

As you drag toward each of the speakers, the colored shapes expand and contract to
represent how much sound will emit from that speaker. (The bigger the shape, the
more sound will come out.)

8   Play the project and experiment with different positions to hear the result.

Keyframing Surround Sound

You can animate surround panning using one of two methods: by keyframing the Surround Panner itself, or by choosing one of the preset panning modes and keyframing the Pan Amount slider.

1   Position the Timeline playhead to the first frame of **Shot_03**, and then drag the Surround Panner handle to the left-rear speaker (at around 8 o'clock).

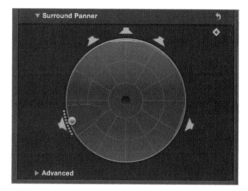

2   Click the Keyframe button.

3   Move the Timeline playhead forward by two seconds (to 25:18), and drag the Surround Panner handle to the right-front speaker (at around 1 o'clock). A second keyframe is automatically assigned.

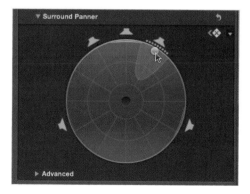

4   Play the project across **Shot_03**. The audio moves from the left-rear speaker to the right-front speaker over the course of the clip.

You can add as many keyframes as you like to create complex animations of your sound in the surround audio space.

Using Preset Pan Methods

You can also employ one of the preset panning settings and keyframe the Pan Amount slider.

1   Select Shot_04 and position the playhead at the first frame of that clip.

2   In the Inspector, set Pan Mode to Circle, which allows you to animate your sound to move in a circle around the listener, utilizing all five speakers.

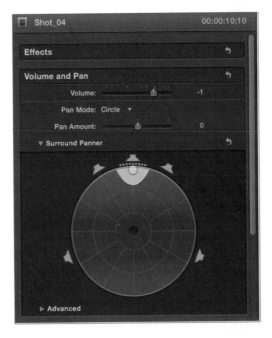

3   Drag the Pan Amount slider from left to right and observe the movement that occurs in the Surround Panner.

Using Pan Mode allows you to animate the Pan Amount slider to create surround sound animations based on a preset type of effect (which is arguably simpler than animating the entire Surround Panner).

4   Drag the Pan Amount slider all the way to the left to set the sound to come out of the rear speakers only.

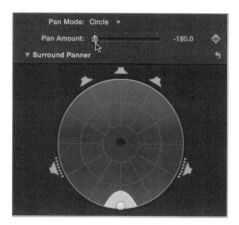

5   Click the Keyframe button for the Pan Amount slider.

6   Move the Timeline playhead forward by five seconds (to approximately 35:00).

7   Drag the Pan Amount slider to the right.

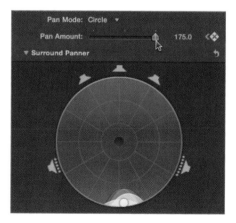

A keyframe is automatically added, and the sound is animated to move around the room in a circle.

8   Play across Shot_04 to hear the results.

Alternatively, rather than creating a circle effect, you could select one of the other pan modes.

9   Set Pan Mode to Back to Front.

   NOTE ▶ Changing the pan mode automatically erases any keyframes assigned to the Pan Amount slider.

10 Move the Timeline playhead to the beginning of **Shot_04** and repeat steps 5 through 9 as you observe the difference in the movement of the sound.

Managing Audio Channels

Most clips include multiple audio channels. This could be two discrete mono tracks recorded in the camera, a stereo track in which the left and right channels are intended to pan in a specific way, or a multitrack clip with many audio channels that actively need to be managed. One common example of this is footage in which audio was recorded on a device separate from the video and the two signals were joined inside Final Cut Pro using the Synchronize Clips function as described in Appendix A.

Regardless of the number of tracks, you can manage which audio channels are *active* and which are ignored when you play a particular clip.

   NOTE ▶ You can change the active channels at any point in the editing process—either in the Event Browser before the clip is used, or after an instance of a clip has been added to a project.

Furthermore, active channels can be displayed in the Timeline collapsed into a single bar combined with the video, expanded into a separate audio-only bar, or broken apart so that each individual channel can be seen and modified independently.

Enabling and Disabling Channels

You manage audio channels in the Audio Inspector for the selected clip. There, you can skim the individual channels to identify the contents of each channel. You can also enable or disable individual channels, and select the audio format (stereo, surround, and so on). This latter setting instructs Final Cut Pro how to pan the individual channels by default.

1   In the Timeline, select **Shot_05**.

2   In the Audio Inspector, scroll down to view the Channel Configuration section. This clip contains two audio channels, marked as stereo. Because they are a stereo pair, they are represented by a single bar.

3   From the Channels pop-up menu, choose Dual Mono. The two individual items are broken out into two individual channels.

NOTE ▸ The contents of the Channels pop-up menu changes dynamically based on the number and type of channels in the currently selected clip. Clips with an even number of channels can display as stereo pairs or individual mono channels. Clips with six channels can also be marked as 5.1 surround channels. Always check the pop-up menu to see the options available for the current clip.

4   Skim the two individual tracks to hear the difference between them.

The first channel contains clear, sharp audio; the second sounds inferior. That's because channel 1 was recorded with a boom mic pointed directly at the subject's mouth, and channel 2 was recorded using the built-in camera mic, which was much farther away.

5   Deselect the checkbox to the left of the second channel to disable it. Now, the clip in the Timeline will play only the higher-quality channel 1 audio.

Breaking Apart Audio Clips

When you have more than one audio channel, you can expose each of the components as separate bars in the Timeline. This allows you to independently keyframe the volume, pan, and effects settings for each channel.

1   In the Timeline, select **Shot_06**, and in the Audio Inspector, scroll to see the Channel Configuration section.

This clip contains four audio channels: two mono channels and a stereo pair. Yet, in the Timeline, the audio is represented by a single bar connected to the video.

TIP ▶ You can reconfigure these four tracks as four mono channels, two stereo pairs, L, R, C, S, or other configurations by choosing from the Channels pop-up menu.

This bar can be *expanded*, as described earlier in the lesson, or it can be detached to be treated as a separate entity from the video.

2   With audio selected, choose Clip > Detach Audio, or press Control-Shift-S. The audio is detached from the video and appears as a connected clip, synchronized to the first frame of the video.

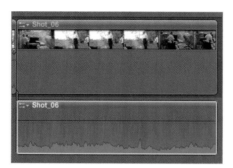

However, the four individual audio channels are still combined and treated as a single entity in the Timeline. This is helpful when adjusting the audio as a single unit, but if you want to change individual channels you need to go one step further.

3   Choose Clip > Break Apart Clip Items, or press Command-Shift-G. Each channel is broken into its own bar and can be adjusted individually.

Lesson Review

1. What three things do Audio meters show?
2. Should dialogue levels be set to: A) 0 db, B) –12 db, C) –31 db, or D) none of these options?
3. Should you change audio levels in the Timeline or the Inspector?
4. What is the finest resolution that audio can be adjusted to?
5. Which kinds of clips can have an audio fade effect applied?
6. How many fade shapes are there and what are they called?
7. Can you crossfade between two connected clips?
8. How many speakers can you use for audio panning?
9. True or false: Panning can be animated in stereo but not in surround.
10. How do you display individual audio channels of a multichannel clip in the Timeline?

Answers

1. Average audio levels, peak audio levels, and overmodulation
2. B or C are both acceptable answers. Never set audio to 0 db.
3. You can set audio levels in either the Timeline or the Inspector.
4. Audio can be adjusted to the individual sample level.
5. All clips that contain audio can be faded.
6. There are four audio fade shapes: Linear, S-curve, +3 dB, and –3 dB.
7. Yes, although they will automatically be converted into a storyline.
8. Two speakers in stereo and five speakers in surround. (Surround mixes also include a low-frequency channel that is not affected during panning.)
9. False. You can animate panning settings in both stereo and surround mixes.
10. Select the clip, and choose Clip > Break Apart Clip Items.

Keyboard Shortcuts

Control-A	Open Audio Animation Editor
Command-J	Open Project Properties
S	Toggle skimming on and off
Control-S	Expand/collapse Audio/Video
Control-Shift-S	Detach audio from video and display as a connected clip
Control-Z	Zoom to Samples
Shift-Z	Zoom to fit
Option-Down Arrow	Reduce level of the selected keyframe
Option-Up Arrow	Increase level of the selected keyframe
Option-' (apostrophe)	Navigate to next keyframe
Option-; (semicolon)	Navigate to previous keyframe
Command-= (equal sign)	Zoom in on Timeline
Control-= (equal sign)	Increase volume level by 1 dB
Control-− (minus sign)	Decrease volume level by 1 dB
Command-4	Open Inspector
Command-Shift-8	Display large Audio meters

5

Time

This lesson takes approximately 60 minutes to complete.

Goals

Use equalization to improve your clips' sound quality

Understand EQ effects

Manage audio effects in the Inspector

Copy audio effects between clips

Utilize reverb and echo

Apply distortion presets to create distressed sound

Perform pitch shifting and other voice alterations

Animate audio effects over time in the Timeline and Inspector

Using Audio Effects

Lesson 4 focused on audio basics: levels, fades, and panning. But Final Cut Pro offers far more audio manipulation tools and techniques.

Every clip has a built-in equalizer that allows you to independently adjust the level of specific frequencies. You can apply over 100 built-in audio effects ranging from versatile limiters, compressors, and noise-gates to echo, reverberation, and pitch-shifting effects. You also have access to modulation and distortion effects typically used for musical instruments.

Each effect has a custom interface designed to visually represent the audio manipulation. Plus, many effects are actually compound presets that combine other filters and preassigned parameters to create fun and practical one-click effects such as Cartoon Animals, Telephone, Underwater, Car Radio, Spaceship, Robot, and so on.

Finally, you can also animate the parameters for any of these effects so, for instance, your character's transformation from human to monster can develop gradually and organically.

> **MORE INFO** ▶ Final Cut Pro X also offers a variety of automatic audio enhancements such as background noise and hum removal, loudness adjustments, and matching of audio EQ. To learn more about those features, visit help.apple.com.

Understanding Equalization

The most basic type of audio effect is equalization, or EQ, which is a way to adjust the volume of particular frequencies (or *bands*) of your clip's audio. You can use EQ to turn down the low-pitched rumbling of nearby traffic or the high-pitched whirr of a vacuum cleaner while leaving your actor's voice relatively unaffected.

Unfortunately, most sounds are not neatly divided. They spread across many different frequencies, so turning down the lower (bass) bands may make your actor's voice sound tinny and small, and turning down the high (treble) bands can make his voice sound muddy or muffled. No perfect EQ setting exists, and knowing when your settings are closest to "correct" is difficult. You just have to listen and trust your ears.

To further complicate things, different loudspeakers have different characteristics that affect audio reproduction. Some speakers are much louder in the higher frequencies than the lower frequencies, and some don't play certain frequencies at all.

Thus, it's very important to adjust EQ (and any audio adjustments, really) while listening to a speaker system that closely matches your intended playback environment. If your program is an airline safety video that will be viewed on a noisy airplane, you should simulate that environment when finalizing your audio or risk your audience hearing a very different soundtrack mix than the one you delivered.

> **NOTE** ▶ Some of the changes you make in this lesson will be subtle and may be nearly undetectable in some listening environments.

The built-in equalizer applied to every clip in Final Cut Pro X divides your sound into 10 or 31 bands, each of which can be independently *boosted* (made louder) or *attenuated* (made quieter).

> **TIP** ▶ As a general rule, attenuate the sounds you don't want rather than boost the sounds you do want, lest you risk the danger of hitting 0 dB and causing unwanted distortion.

You also have eight EQ presets to choose from if don't want to get your fingers dirty or are intimidated by the EQ interface.

1   In the Project Library, open the Lesson 05 folder, and double-click the *Sound Effects* project to open it into the Timeline.

2 In the Timeline, select Shot_01, and in the Audio Inspector, double-click the Audio
Enhancements section to expand the controls, if necessary.

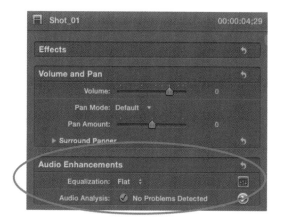

3 Press / (slash) to play the clip and hear its tonal balance, and then from the
Equalization pop-up menu, choose Bass Boost and play it again.

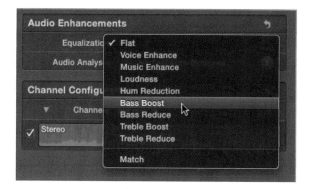

The Bass Boost preset increases the level of the lower-frequency bands to create a
richer, warmer tone. However, taken to an extreme, this boost could make the sound
muddy or thick.

4 From the Equalization pop-up menu, choose Treble Boost, and play the clip again.

Treble Boost increases the level of the higher-frequency bands, which can make
your clip sound brighter or sharper, though if you go too far it can sound thin,
tinny, or piercing.

NOTE ▶ Sound designers have developed a whole language to describe the feeling that different sound tones impart. There is no science to it; they're just trying to articulate one sense to describe another. Feel free to use your own adjectives to spice things up and impress your clients. I've heard all of the following said with a straight face: chewy, spicy, round, fuzzy, tight, and bodacious.

Any of these presets can quickly adjust (and hopefully improve) the sound of your clips. But you can also control the equalizer manually.

5　Click the Controls button (the EQ icon) to the right of the Equalization pop-up menu.

The Graphic Equalizer window opens.

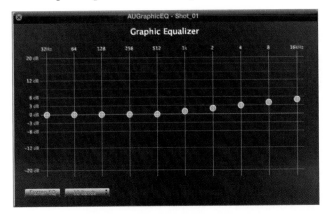

The Graphic Equalizer contains 10 sliders to manipulate the level of 10 bands of frequencies. The sliders on the left control the lower frequencies, and the sliders on the right control the higher frequencies. When a slider is set above the central baseline, that frequency is boosted; when the slider is set below the baseline, that frequency is attenuated.

Currently this clip is set to the Treble Boost preset, and you can see that the sliders on the right are elevated above the baseline.

6   Click the Flatten EQ button.

The sliders are all reset to their "flat" positions.

7   Drag the leftmost slider down to about –6 dB to attenuate the lowest frequencies by 6 dB, then play the clip to hear the result.

You can also modify more than one band at a time.

8   Drag across the three sliders on the left to select them as a group.

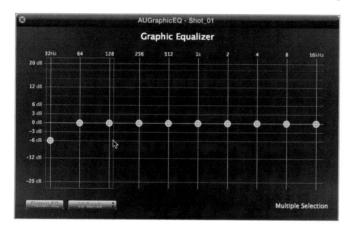

NOTE ▸ To select multiple sliders, begin dragging one of the sliders.

9   Drag any one of the sliders down by about 3 dB.

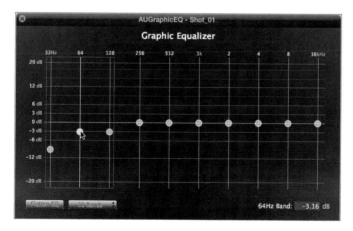

The leftmost slider is lowered to –9 dB, and the next two sliders are set to –3 dB. This creates a common effect called a *bass roll-off* that tapers off the volumes of the lowest frequencies (which frequently contain more noise than useful content).

If you need more adjustment precision than 10 bands, you can set the graphic equalizer to 31 bands.

NOTE ▸ Switching between 10 and 31 bands automatically flattens the equalizer.

10 Click the 10 Bands button, and from the pop-up menu, choose 31 Bands.

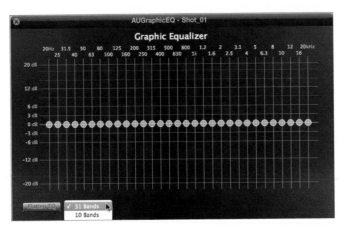

The equalizer changes to contain 31 frequency sliders. You operate the 31-band equalizer the same way you operate the 10-band one. However, the increased number of bands allows you to make more narrow and precise EQ adjustments.

11 Click the close button to close the Graphic Equalizer.

Applying Equalization Effects

In addition to the Graphic Equalizer, Final Cut Pro includes a variety of filters that provide similar or overlapping functionality. The filters have some advantages in that they have customized (and in some cases, more elaborate) user interfaces. Additionally, some filters are effectively presets created using the built-in filters.

Ultimately, there is no overall advantage or disadvantage to using EQ filters over the Graphic Equalizer. Effectively they are just different ways to achieve the same results. The filters do offer more extensive presets than the eight built into the Graphic Equalizer.

Some filters incorporate EQ presets in combination with other audio filters. This is how complex effects like Telephone, Vintage Radios, or Underwater are created.

NOTE ▶ Filters are applied to clips on top of any adjustments made in the Graphic Equalizer.

1   In the Timeline, select Shot_01, if necessary.

2   In the toolbar, click the Effects button, or press Command-5. The Effects Browser opens to the right of the Timeline.

3   Scroll down in the Effects Browser to the Audio section, and select the EQ category.

4   Double-click the Less Bass effect to apply it to the selected clip.

5   Locate the effect in the Audio Inspector.

The Less Bass effect has two controls: an Amount slider and a parameter called Fat EQ, which is actually the name of the plug-in used to create the Less Bass effect.

NOTE ▶ Many of the plug-ins used to create the audio effects are the same as you'll find in Logic, the Apple professional audio mixing and editing application.

6   Click the Controls button to the right of the Fat EQ parameter. The Fat EQ window opens, revealing its custom interface.

Fat EQ is a five-band equalizer plug-in. You may recognize that the preset is another example of a bass roll-off.

You have many manual controls in the Fat EQ window to further modify the equalization; but because this effect was applied as a preset, you can also just modify it using the slider in the Audio Inspector.

TIP ▶ You can also apply a generic Fat EQ effect by double-clicking the icon in the Logic section of the EQ category of the Effects Browser.

7   In the Audio Inspector, drag the Amount slider to the right and observe the result in the Fat EQ interface.

The farther right the slider is set, the more frequencies are rolled off. The farther left you drag the slider, the fewer frequencies.

8   Press / (slash) to play the clip as you drag the slider and listen to the difference of various settings.

9   Drag the slider to 25, and close the Fat EQ window.

10 In the Effects Browser, double-click the Remove High Frequencies effect to apply it to the clip. This second effect is added to the clip, and the controls appear beneath the Less Bass effect.

Remove High Frequencies is similar to the Less Bass preset; but instead of attenuating the lower frequencies, it affects the higher ones. The effect has a Preset pop-up menu in which you can choose the type of filter; an Amount slider; and instead of using the Fat EQ, this preset uses the Channel EQ.

NOTE ▸ Depending on the chosen preset, this effect uses either the Channel EQ or the Fat EQ plug-in. For the purposes of this lesson, keep the Preset pop-up menu set to High Cut or Strong Cut.

11 Click the Controls button to the right of the Channel EQ parameter name to open the Channel EQ interface.

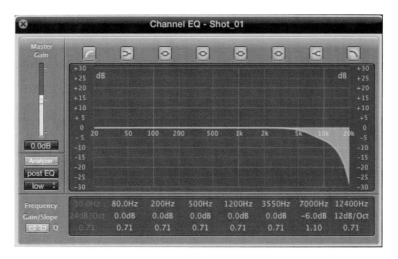

Channel EQ is an eight-band equalizer, but you can see that this preset affects only the two rightmost bands.

12 In the Audio Inspector, drag the Amount slider to the right and observe the change in the Channel EQ window.

The Channel EQ window has another very useful feature called the Analyzer. It provides a visual representation of the frequencies present in the clip and can help you choose how to equalize the clip.

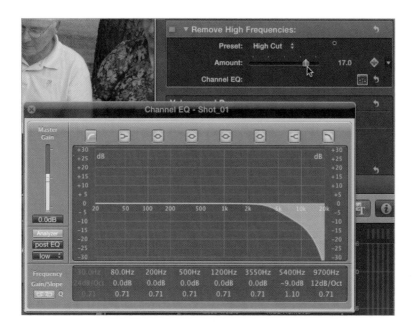

13 In the Channel EQ window, click the Analyzer button.

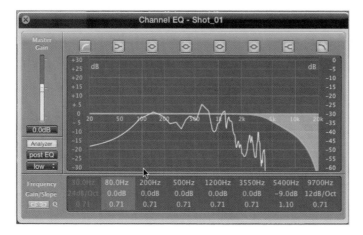

14 Play the clip.

You can see a line representing the active frequencies in the audio as it plays. You can see that there are no frequencies in the high end because the filter is rolling them off.

15 Click the Post EQ button (below the Analyzer button) to change it to Pre EQ.

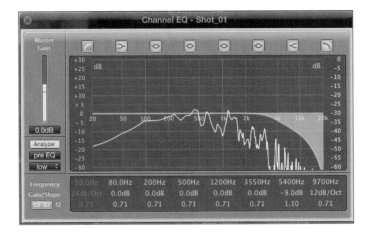

Now the analyzer shows the frequencies in the source clip *before* the results of the EQ. You can see that level indicators are now present in the high frequencies.

NOTE ▶ Regardless of the setting, the audio you hear is the post-EQ result. To hear the clip without the filter applied, you must disable the filter in the Audio Inspector as described in the following section.

16 Close the Channel EQ window.

Controlling Audio Effects

Once you begin adding and manipulating audio effects, learning how to manage those effects is important—choosing the order in which they are applied, enabling and disabling specific effects, and moving effects from one clip to another.

Toggling Clip Effects

Each effect appears in the Audio Inspector and can be enabled or disabled without permanently removing the effect. Toggling clip effects allows you to sample or audition the clip with and without a particular effect applied.

1 Select Shot_01 in the Timeline, if necessary.

2 In the Audio Inspector, deselect the blue checkbox to the left of the Remove High Frequencies effect name to disable the effect.

3   Press / (slash) to play the clip. The clip plays without the Remove High Frequencies effect.

4   Select the blue checkbox to enable the effect again.

> **TIP** ▶ You can toggle the effect checkbox dynamically while the clip is playing.

Removing Clip Effects

When you decide that a particular effect is not working the way you want, you can remove it completely.

1   In the Audio Inspector, click the name of the Less Bass effect to select it.

2   Press Delete to permanently remove the effect from the clip.

> **NOTE** ▶ Be sure that the effect name is selected in the Inspector (the title bar will turn blue). If it is not selected, you will delete the entire clip from the project.

Transferring Clip Effects Between Clips

When you have an effect that you're happy with, you can copy it to one or more clips in the project.

1   In the Timeline, select **Shot_02**.

2   In the Effects Browser, select the Distortion category, and then double-click the Car Radio effect to apply the effect to the clip.

> **NOTE** ▶ Be sure to select the Audio > Distortion category, not the Video > Distortion category.

3   Select **Shot_02**, and then choose Edit > Copy, or press Command-C, to copy the clip
to the clipboard.

4   In the Timeline, select **Shot_01**, and choose Edit > Paste Effects, or press Command-
Option-V, to copy the effect from **Shot_02** to **Shot_01**.

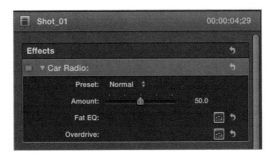

Paste Effects always pastes all effects (video and audio) from the clip on the clipboard
to the selected clips.

Notice that the Remove High Frequencies effect was removed from **Shot_01**. Pasting
effects *replaces* any existing effects with the pasted ones.

TIP ▶ You can paste effects to multiple clips by selecting multiple clips in the
Timeline and choosing the Paste Effects command.

5   Select **Shot_02** again, and delete the Car Radio effect.

Using Other Types of Effects

Final Cut Pro offers scores of other audio effects and presets, and don't forget that you can
also use third-party Logic effects if you have access to them. These additional effects are
grouped into categories that suggest when and how you may want to employ them.

Levels Effects

Aside from equalization, levels effects—which alter the basic volume of a clip—are the
next most common type. Final Cut Pro has a Loudness setting in the Audio Enhancements
Inspector that attempts to automatically set the volume of your clips to a "good" level. But
professionals will inevitably want more precise control than that setting can provide, and
they will find it in the various levels effects.

Typical Levels (or *dynamics*) effects include limiters, compressors, and gates. A description of all available filters is beyond the scope of this book, but the following descriptions may aid you in selecting from the many levels effects. In practice, each filter is unique, and many filters incorporate more than one of the following categories:

▶   *Limiters* turn down the volume of the loudest parts of a shot (determined by identifying a *threshold* level) without affecting the rest of the audio. You can use them when a few brief loud noises are much louder than the rest of the shot.

▶   *Compressors* are similar to limiters in that a compressor identifies the loudest portions of a clip and turns down those bits, but then it increases the overall volume of the clip without the risk of overmodulating. This effect is often used to raise the perceived volume of TV commercials and give dialogue more "presence" in the mix. Because compressors reduce *dynamic range*, overuse can create an unnaturally flat sound.

▶   *Expanders* are the opposite of compressors. An expander increases the dynamic range, effectively stretching the volume of the signal so the quieter parts get quieter and the louder parts get louder.

▶   *Gates* are somewhat like the inverse of limiters. A gate can identify the quietest parts of a clip and turn them down. Gates are often used to reduce noise or to highlight the desired sound in a shot with limited background noise.

Using Reverb, Spaces, and Echo Effects

These three types of effects produce similar results, but are typically employed in different situations.

Reverb effects (called *spaces* in the Final Cut Pro X Effects Browser) can produce natural effects that simulate real environments. They are especially useful for matching audio recorded in dissimilar settings, and are commonly used in animated or green screen productions where the scene appears to take place in a very different type of space than the soundstage in which it was recorded.

Echo effects (also called *delay* effects) simulate natural phenomena, too, but they're also great fun when used to represent a disturbed or confused character's mental state. Each echo can be assigned a different volume, pitch, and pan setting, permitting a wide range of complex effects.

Final Cut Pro has a variety of customizable preset effects in both categories to speed your work, or you can choose from one of the core effects and manually adjust all the parameters for total control.

1 In the Timeline, select Shot_02.

2 In the Effects Browser, select the Spaces category, scroll to the Logic effects section, and double-click the Space Designer effect.

The effect is added to the clip and its controls appear in the Audio Inspector.

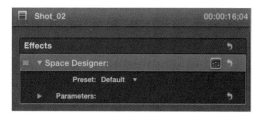

At first glance, this effect appears to have no parameters (they're hidden in the collapsed Parameters section), but the Space Designer is one of the most powerful reverb effects, and has more than 50 built-in presets.

3 From the Preset pop-up menu, choose 02 Medium Spaces > 06 Indoor Spaces > 1.6s Narrow Staircase.

4 Press / (slash) to play the clip and hear the results.

5 From the Preset pop-up menu, choose 01 Large Spaces > 06 Outdoor Spaces > 05.2s Deep Canyon, and press / (slash) to hear the difference.

6 Experiment with some of the other presets.

NOTE ► Some presets are labeled based on the type of space being simulated (such as cathedral, cave, garage, and so on). Others are labeled for a type of mechanical reverberation originated in traditional analog reverb devices (such as plate or spring). Still others are labeled to indicate the musical instrument that might best benefit from that preset (piano reflection, horn chamber, small guitar hall). Every situation is different, and you'll likely want to experiment with a variety of settings before settling on one. You can also click the Controls button and further customize any of the presets using the custom graphical interface.

7   In the Audio Inspector, click the Space Designer title bar, and press Delete to remove the effect from the clip.

8   In the Effects Browser, select the Echo category, scroll to the Mac OS X group, and double-click the AUDelay preset.

9   In the Inspector, click the Controls button to the right of the effect name to open the Apple Delay window.

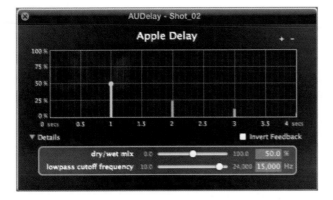

The vertical bars indicate the echo. By default, the echoes occur once every second, and the volume (represented by the height of the line) is reduced on each repetition.

10   Press / (slash) to play the clip.

11   Drag the first echo handle to the left until it lines up with the 0.5 seconds indicator, and raise the top of the bar until it reaches 75%.

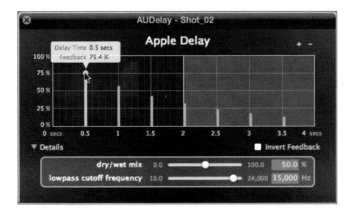

12 Press / (slash) to play the clip again.

Now the echoes occur more frequently and are louder. The farther you drag the bar to the left, the faster the echoes will occur.

This Apple Delay effect provides very precise control over the speed and volume of the echo, but other echo effects provide even more control and include presets that let you choose from predetermined settings rather than manually assigning them.

For example, the Delay Designer effect lets you modify pitch, panning, and many other parameters, as well as the duration and volume of each echo. You can also enable a recording mode and tap out the echoes manually.

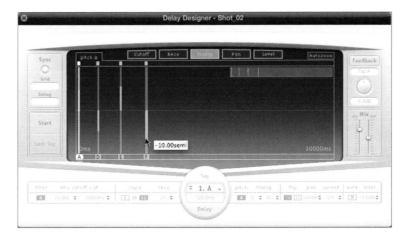

For extra credit, experiment with the Delay Designer effect (or any of the others) to learn more about the power these effects provide.

Employing Distortion Presets

Another category of audio filters is distortion effects. Some of these are the kind of distortion that rockers apply to their guitars to make them sound grungy; another collection of preset filters are used to make your audio sound like it's coming out of a poor-quality speaker.

Distortion presets include Car Radio, Television, Telephone, Underwater, Walkie Talkie, and more. And, as expected, each of those presets has additional settings. For example, the Vintage Radios preset allows you to choose from one of four radio types identified by date and style.

1   In the Timeline, select Shot_03.

2   In the Effects Browser, select the Audio > Distortion category.

3   Click the Low Tech effect once to select it (don't double-click), and press the Spacebar to hear a preview of the effect.

> **TIP** When audio skimming is enabled (Shift-S), you can skim the mouse over the effect to hear a choppier version of the effect preview.

4   While the preview is playing, click some of the other effects to preview those effects.

5   Press the Spacebar again to stop the preview.

6   Double-click the Vintage Radios effect to apply it to the clip.

7   Play the clip to hear the effect.

Distortion presets such as this combine multiple core plug-in effects to create a particular result. For example, the 1931 Radio preset uses three separate plug-ins to create its unique sound.

You can click the Controls button for any of the plug-ins to further customize the effect and make it perfect for your situation.

8   Click the name of the Vintage Radios effect in the Audio Inspector and press Delete to remove the effect.

Using Pitch Shifting and Voice Effects

Voice effects are similar to the distortion effects, but as the name implies, specifically designed to modify/distort human voices. Presets make it easy to quickly turn your boss into a Robot, Alien, Cartoon Animal, or Monster. Less extreme effects such as Brightness, Voice Over Enhancement, and De-esser can improve human voices in subtle ways, as can as a variety of more multipurpose pitch- and voice-related plug-ins, each with its own presets and custom user interface.

1   In the Timeline, select Shot_03, if necessary.

2   In the Effects Browser, select the Voice category.

3   Click the Alien effect to select it (don't double-click), and press the Spacebar to preview the effect.

4   While the preview is playing, click some of the other effects to preview them, too.

5   Press the Spacebar again to stop the preview.

Just as with the distortion effects, the voice effects are based on a group of plug-ins you can further modify to customize the results.

▶ **Preserving Pitch When Retiming**

Speeding up or slowing down a clip by using the retiming effects can impact the pitch of your audio clip. Speeding up a clip typically raises its pitch and slowing down a clip lowers it. When you want to retime a clip, but leave the audio pitch unaffected, you can try using one of the pitch-altering effects described in this section and experiment with the settings to get it just right. But there's a much easier way:

1   In the Timeline, select **Shot_03**, if necessary.

2   In the toolbar, from the Retime pop-up menu, choose Slow > 50%.

    The clip is slowed to half-speed.

3   Click the Retime pop-up menu again, and ensure that the Preserve Pitch setting is enabled.

4   Play the clip.

    When Preserve Pitch is enabled, the clip audio will play at the normal pitch, even when the clip speed is faster or slower than normal.

5   From the Retime pop-up menu, choose Preserve Pitch to disable it.

6   Play the clip again.

    Now the pitch is lowered in accordance with the 50% speed setting. Using this control you can choose whether or not retiming effects affect the pitch of the audio.

Animating Audio Effects

As if experimenting with all these powerful audio filters wasn't enough, Final Cut Pro also allows you to animate any of these effects to change the results over time.

So, you can have your hero's voice *gradually* turn into that of a cartoon moose. Or more practically speaking, you can change the amount and type of reverb dynamically as your character walks through the hallway and out into the courtyard.

1   In the Timeline, select Shot_02.

2   In the Audio Inspector, delete any filters currently applied to the clip.

3   In the Effects Browser, select the Audio > All category, and then in the search field at the bottom of the window, type *cathedral*.

Searching for specific text will filter the Effects Browser to show only effects containing the search term.

4   Double-click the Cathedral effect to apply it to the selected clip.

5   In the search field, click the Reset button to show all the effects.

6   In the Timeline, position the playhead over the first frame of the clip.

7　In the Inspector, drag the Amount slider of the Cathedral effect all the way to the left to 1.0.

8　Click the Keyframe button to the right of the slider.

9　In the Timeline, position the playhead five seconds into the clip at 10:00.

10　In the Inspector, drag the Amount slider to 50.

11 Press / (slash) to play the clip. The reverb effect appears gradually over five seconds.

Many audio filters don't have an Amount slider. In that case, you may need to click the disclosure triangle next to the Parameters section of the Inspector and keyframe the specific parameters you want to change over time.

NOTE ▶ Some audio effects have no keyframeable parameters.

Modifying Audio Effect Animations

You can also animate audio effects directly in the Timeline. Doing so enables you to see a graphical representation of the changing parameters displayed over time.

1 Ensure that **Shot_02** is still selected, and choose Clip > Show Audio Animation, or press Control-A. The keyframe graphs for the audio effects appear and display the two keyframes you added to the Cathedral Amount slider.

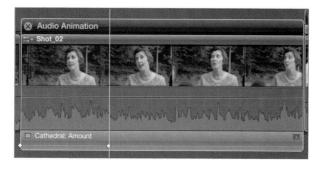

By default keyframe graphs are collapsed, so you can see where the keyframes appear in time, but the actual keyframe values are not apparent.

NOTE ▶ If the Solo Animation command in the Clip menu is selected, only one effect graph will appear at a time. If Solo Animation is disabled, you will see graphs for each effect.

2   Double-click the keyframe graph. The graph expands to show the positions of the keyframes and their relative values.

3   Drag the first keyframe up to about 20.

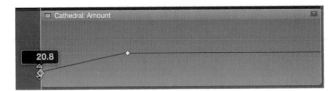

NOTE ▸ You can drag a keyframe either horizontally (to change its place in time), or vertically (to change its value), but not in both directions at once.

The clip now begins with a small amount of reverb, which increases from that point until the second keyframe.

If you wanted the reverb to decrease towards the end of the clip, you could add a new keyframe.

4   Near the end of the clip, Option-click the keyframe line twice to add two new keyframes.

5   Drag the last keyframe to the lower-right corner of the graph.

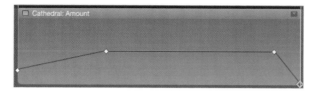

6   Play the clip. The reverb effect now fades out as the clip comes to an end.

When you are satisfied with the settings you have made, you can collapse the graph or hide it completely.

7   Double-click the keyframe graph to collapse it.

8   On the Audio Animation bar above the clip, click the close button, or press Control-A. The audio animation graph disappears, but the animated settings you made remain applied.

Lesson Review

1. What is equalization?
2. What is an EQ band?
3. Is it better to boost the desired frequencies of an audio clip or attenuate the undesired parts?
4. Which EQ effect has the Analyzer function?
5. Can you copy one of two applied audio effects from one clip to another?
6. What does a Compressor effect do?
7. In which category of effects does a delay effect belong?
8. Where would you find a preset to simulate the sound of a telephone speaker?
9. True or false: When speeding up a clip using the Retime pop-up menu, the pitch of the audio will always go up.
10. How many keyframe graphs can you view in the Timeline at once?

Answers

1. Independently modifying the volume of different frequencies
2. A range of frequencies
3. It's generally preferable to attenuate the less desirable frequencies.
4. Channel EQ
5. No, you can only copy all clip effects at once.
6. It reduces the dynamic range of a clip, enabling you to make it louder.
7. Echo effects
8. Distortion category
9. False, you can enable the Preserve Pitch setting, which will compensate for the pitch shift that would otherwise occur.
10. You can view as many graphs as you have effects (just be sure the Solo Animation setting is disabled).

Keyboard Shortcuts

Control-A	Open/close the Audio Animation graph.
Command-5	Open the Effects Browser
Command-Option-V	Paste effects

6

Time

Goals

This lesson takes approximately 60 minutes to complete.

Create multicam clips from multiple-camera footage

Control the multicam clip view using the Angle Viewer

Edit multicam clips on the fly

Control audio and video of multicam clips separately

Rearrange, add, and delete angles from a multicam clip

Adjust the sync of angles within a multicam clip

Apply effects to multicam angles

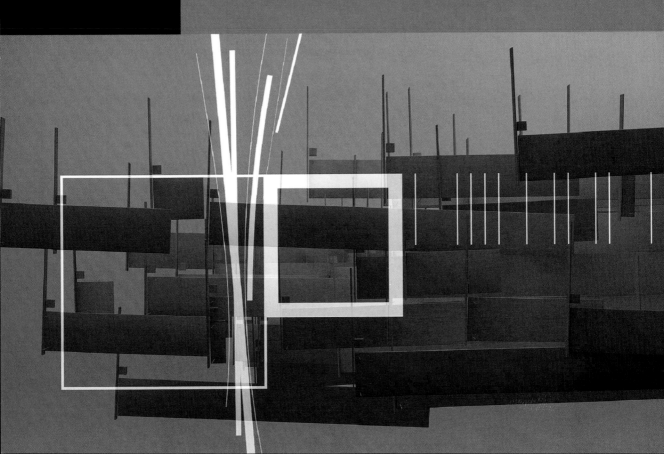

Lesson 6
Editing Multicam Clips

Although traditional films are shot using a single camera, many types of productions use several cameras operating at the same time. Most often this *multicamera* technique is used when documenting a live event, such as a concert, theatrical performance, or sporting event. Multiple cameras are also frequently used for complicated stunts or for action that is difficult to stage or repeat, such as improvisational performances.

Some compromises are necessary when shooting with more than one camera. Framing options are severely limited if you want to avoid showing other cameras in the shots, and lighting must be unnaturally even to ensure that all angles get an acceptable image. This explains the very formulaic and artificial look employed by many television sitcoms and soap operas in which three cameras are operated simultaneously and the show is edited on the fly using a broadcast switcher.

Still, given the plummeting price of cameras and recording media, more and more productions are choosing to use multiple cameras for all sorts of events, even those traditionally shot with a single camera. As an editor, you'd best be able to manage multicamera footage because you're almost certain to work with it eventually. Fortunately, editing multicamera footage is fun, exhilarating, and often easier than editing single-camera footage.

Using Multicamera Footage

When multiple cameras capture the same action at the same time, you can effortlessly cut from one angle to another without worrying about matching the timing. Not only will audio be in sync from angle to angle, but so will any action that occurs simultaneously in all the shots. In many ways, multicamera shoots are an editor's dream, even though the limited camera angles sometimes mean that you may not have the exact close-up or insert that most clearly tells the story.

Final Cut Pro X has a special feature designed to take advantage of multicam footage: You can group multiple clips into a *multicam clip*. A multicam clip can hold up to 64 *angles*, and each of those angles can contain multiple clips. When the multicam clip is used in a project, you can move between the angles to choose which one is currently visible.

Although you can create and use multicam clips in a variety of ways, this lesson focuses on a recommended workflow that takes advantage of special features in Final Cut Pro X and also serves the creative needs of multicam editing.

Creating a Multicam Clip

Although you can combine any group of clips into a multicam clip, the feature is primarily designed for synchronous clips—especially clips photographed simultaneously by more than one camera.

Final Cut Pro X is designed to automatically ensure that all the clips are properly aligned. The software compares the timecode of the selected clips, their creation times and dates, and even optionally compares the audio waveforms, which will nearly always result in perfect sync.

1   In the Event Library, select the *Fairytales* Smart Collection in Lesson_06.

2   Skim through the clips to become familiar with the footage.

3   Select all the clips, and choose File > New Multicam Clip. The Multicam Clip sheet appears.

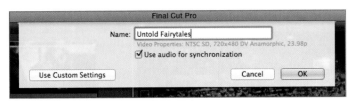

4 Name the clip *Untold Fairytales*, and click OK.

Multicam clip icon

A new multicam clip is created and added to the project. (It does not inherit the keywords from its constituent clips, so it will not appear in the *Fairytales* Keyword Collection.) The multicam clip has a unique icon that appears both in the list view and in the thumbnail.

TIP ▸ You can create a Smart Collection for the multicam clip type so you can easily group your multicam clips. For more on creating Smart Collections, see Lesson 1.

NOTE ▸ Final Cut Pro uses a variety of information to synchronize and arrange the clips. The options for customizing or overriding its automatic settings are discussed later in this lesson.

Viewing a Multicam Clip

Before getting too deep into the options for creating multicam clips, let's look at one.

1 From the Viewer Options pop-up menu, choose Show Angle Viewer, or press Command-Shift-7. The Angle Viewer appears to the left of the Viewer.

TIP ▸ You may want to hide the Inspector if it is showing, and increase the size of the Viewer area to better see the details in the Angle Viewer.

2 Skim or play the clip in the Event Browser.

You'll see four of the clips skimming along in the Angle Viewer. The active angle (highlighted in yellow) also plays along in the main Viewer.

NOTE ▶ Some black frames are visible at the beginning of some of the angles. These frames are applied to shorter clips to maintain proper sync with the other angles.

3 In the Angle Viewer, click the different angles to change the active angle.

As you select each angle, it becomes active and appears in the Viewer.

Changing the Angle Viewer

This multicam clip contains seven angles, but only four are currently visible. There are several options to view the remaining angles. At the bottom of the Angle Viewer, two icons represent different *banks* of clips. The active angle is highlighted in yellow.

1 Click the right bank icon to display the remaining three clips in the Angle Viewer.

By limiting the Angle Viewer to showing no more than four angles at a time, each of the angles displays larger, and you have fewer separate angles to pay attention to. You can switch between banks while the video is playing.

TIP If you drag the divider bar between the Viewer and the Angle Viewer left, you can force the Angle Viewer to display the clips vertically.

2   Play the multicam clip in the Event Browser to see that all the angles play at the same time.

▶ Playback Performance

Final Cut Pro X allows you to play up to 64 angles simultaneously. That's a lot for you to track all at once! It's also a lot of data that must be streamed from your hard drive. Furthermore, the drive is reading from 64 separate places on the drive—at the same time!

Working with just the seven angles in this exercise may be too much for some hard drives (such as the bus-powered USB drives that are so popular with laptop users).

If you experience dropped frames or stuttering playback, you can monitor your hard disk performance by choosing Final Cut Pro > Preferences and selecting "Warn when frames are dropped due to hard disk performance."

continues

▶ **Playback Performance** *(continued)*

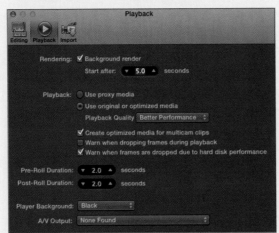

You can find out if something other than the hard disk is causing the problem by selecting "Warn when dropping frames during playback."

If you're dropping frames, enabling "Create optimized media for multicam clips" can help. This option transcodes video recorded in a long-GOP format (such as H.264) to the Apple ProRes 422 codec format, which provides improved performance during multicam editing. Although this option is turned on by default, if the original camera format can be edited with acceptable performance, you can deselect this checkbox.

3   While the clip plays, click the left bank icon, or press Shift-Option-; (semicolon).

The bank changes and you can see the alternative angles.

4   Press Shift-Option-' (apostrophe) to select the next bank.

If you prefer to see all seven angles at once, you can change the Angle Viewer view settings.

5   Click the Angle Viewer Settings button, and from the pop-up menu, choose 9 Angles.

Now all seven angles are visible at once.

TIP You can also change the number of angles displayed while the clip plays.

If you're having trouble remembering which angle is which, you can turn on text overlays that display the angle name or the clip name as well as the timecode for each angle.

6   Click the Angle Viewer Settings button, and from the pop-up menu, choose Display Name > Angle.

The angle name is displayed in the lower-left corner of each clip in the Angle Viewer. By default, the angle name is taken from the Camera Angle field in the Info Inspector for each clip at the time the multicam clip is created.

7   Click the Angle Viewer Settings button again, and from the pop-up menu, choose Timecode. The clip timecode is displayed in the lower–right corner of each clip.

If the angle names are not very helpful, you can alternatively use the clip names.

8   Click the Angle Viewer Settings button and from the pop-up menu, choose Display Name > Clip.

NOTE ▶ Changing the Camera Angle field in the Inspector for a source angle in the Event Browser after the multicam clip has been created will not have any effect.

Editing with Multicam Clips

Viewing a multicam clip is fun, but the Angle Viewer really becomes useful when you edit a multicam clip into a project. You can cut between angles as the clip plays, allowing you to build an edit out of the various angles in a single pass.

Adding Multicam Clips to a Project

Multicam clips are edited into a project just like any other clip using an insert, overwrite, append, connect, or replace edit. You can backtime and set project edit points, and you begin—as with any other clip—by setting start and end points to identify the section of the multicam clip you want to add.

But remember: You will be able to switch back and forth between any of the angles after adding the multicam clip to the project, so generally you'll want to add a large section into your project in one step, and later add interim edits within the clip.

1   In the Event Browser, play or skim until just before the song begins (at 14:02), and press I to set a start point.

   The clip is automatically selected through the end of the shot, which is fine for this exercise.

2   Open the Project Library, and in the Lesson 06 folder, open *Untold Fairytales*. This project is currently empty, waiting for you to add the multicam clip.

3   Press E to add the selected portion of the multicam clip to the project.

Cutting Between Angles

Once the clip is in the project, the fun begins.

1   Play the project from the beginning.

As the clip plays, the Angle Viewer displays all seven angles. If you hover the mouse pointer over the Angle Viewer, the pointer changes to the Blade tool icon to indicate that clicking will perform a cut.

2   While the clip is playing, click a different angle when you want to cut to a new shot. Each time you cut to a new angle, a dotted line appears in the Timeline to indicate the edit.

3   Stop playback.

4   Return the playhead to the beginning of the project and play the entire project to see the results of your work.

You'll probably notice a pretty glaring problem: The sound quality is different in each of the different takes, so each time you cut, you create a jarring audio edit. You could fix the problem after the fact, but starting over and doing it right the first time would be easier

5   Position the playhead at the very beginning of the project, and press D to overwrite
another copy of the original multicam clip and erase the edits you made.

Performing Video-Only Cuts

In this example, as in many real-world cases, only one of the clips has the correct audio,
and the others all have scratch tracks that shouldn't be heard in the edited version. Final
Cut Pro X allows you to edit the audio and video elements separately, so you can edit the
audio from one angle and the video from a different angle at the same time.

1   In the Angle Viewer, Option-click 01 Concert Footage.

This switches the clip to display Angle 1, which has the correct audio. You still want
to edit between cameras on the fly, but you want to keep playing the clean music. In
this case, you want to perform *video-only* cuts.

2   At the top of the Angle Viewer, click the filmstrip icon, or press Shift-Option-2.

This sets the Angle Viewer to edit only video. You could also click the waveform icon (or press Shift-Option-3) to perform audio-only edits (although that is far less common).

TIP Pressing Shift-Option-1 resets to performing audio plus video edits.

3 Play the project again from the beginning, and as it plays, click the various angles to cut between them.

TIP You can also press the number keys 1 through 9 to cut to angles one through nine, respectively. No modifier key is necessary. This is best attempted on an extended keyboard with a numerical entry pad.

The bank switcher indicates which angle is active for video and audio.

Now, only the video is cut. The audio remains consistent, playing the audio from Angle 1. The active angle in the Angle Viewer is highlighted in blue for the video and green for the audio.

NOTE ▶ The bank switcher also displays the active angles using the same color coding, which is helpful when one of the active angles is currently in a hidden bank.

4 Stop playback, return to the beginning of the project (press Home), and play the project to see the result of your work.

Displaying Angle Names

You may want to change the display of clip names in the Timeline to show the currently selected angle instead of the name of the multicam clip.

1   Click the Clip Appearance button.

2   In the window that appears, set the Show pop-up menu to "Clip Names or Angles."

Non-multicam clips will still show the clip names, but multicam clips will show the name of the active angle.

Switching Angles

After your multicam clip is edited into separate clips, you may want to choose a different angle for a particular segment. This is called *switching* angles, and it can be done in many ways.

1   Play or skim to the third clip in the project.

NOTE ▶ Your project might not look exactly like the one pictured. Also, you may have to zoom in on the Timeline if your shots are very short.

2   In the Angle Viewer, Option-click an angle other than the currently selected angle.

The third clip is switched to the new angle, but no new edit is added.

You can just as easily change angles in the Timeline.

3   Control-click, or right-click, the fourth clip, and from the shortcut menu, choose Active Video Angle. Then choose one of the other angles to switch to that angle.

TIP ▶ By selecting multiple clips, you can use the Active Angle setting in the Inspector to change the selected clips to a single angle all at once.

4   Press Command-4 to open the Inspector, if necessary.

5   Select a clip in the Timeline, and in the Info Inspector, from the Active Video Angle pop-up menu, choose a new angle. (The currently selected angle has a checkmark beside its name.)

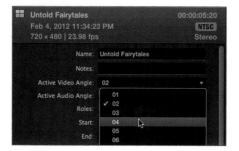

TIP ▶ You can also press Option-1 through Option-9 to switch the currently selected clip to angles one through nine.

You can also use keyboard shortcuts to step through the angles one at a time, switching from one to the next.

6   Press Control-Shift-Right Arrow to switch the currently selected clip to the next angle in the list.

7   Press Control-Shift-Left Arrow to switch to the previous angle.

Trimming Multicam Clips

When you make cuts in a multicam clip, Final Cut Pro X treats those edits as *through edits*. A through edit is what you get immediately after blading any normal clip: A line is drawn in the Timeline to indicate the edit, but the clip plays smoothly across that point.

With a multicam clip, the edit is likely a cut between different angles, but they're all part of the same clip.

One advantage to through edits is that you can delete them, making the two adjacent clips into one longer clip.

1 In the Timeline, click the edit between the first and second clips to select it.

2 Press Delete.

The edit is removed, and the angle from the first clip now extends all the way to the subsequent edit.

Rolling Edits

With the Select tool, when you move the pointer over a multicam through edit, the pointer changes to the Roll icon (because any other type of edit could ruin the angle synchronization in your multicam clip). Rolling allows you to change the position of the edit—making one clip shorter and another longer simultaneously. This way you could move the edits to align on music beats or to correspond with important action within the scene without ever knocking a clip out of sync.

1 With the Select tool, position the pointer over any edit in the Timeline.

The pointer shows the Roll icon. (If this were not a multicam clip, the pointer would change to the Ripple icon.)

2 Drag the edit to the left to roll it earlier in time, or drag to the right to roll the edit later in time.

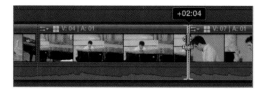

Rolling an edit on a multicam clip will never change the sync. It just changes the specific frame where the cut occurs.

▶ Using Other Trim Types

Although rolling is the default, nothing prevents you from rippling or performing another trim command on a multicam clip. It doesn't make sense in this music video example used here, but you might want to trim pauses or dead sections from a multicam interview or use trimming to fix the timing on a stunt or dramatic sequence shot with multiple cameras.

Many modifications (such as split edits, markers, connected clips, and retiming) remain in place on a multicam clip in the Timeline even after you switch the angle. But certain editing operations are associated directly with the specific (active) angle and are not retained when you switch angles.

The following modifications are specific to the active angle and are *not* retained when you switch angles:

- ▶   Video and audio effects
- ▶   Keyframing (including audio volume and panning)
- ▶   Roles

Customizing Multicam Clip Settings

Now that you've seen the basic multicam clip workflow, let's explore some additional options you can use when creating a multicam clip. In most cases, the Automatic settings will yield desirable results, but in other cases you may need to override or customize them. You can instruct Final Cut Pro X to use specific fields and specific data to control how the multicam clip is constructed.

1   In the Event Library, select the *Lesson 06* Event.

2 In the Event Browser, select `Shot_01` and `Shot_02`.

3 Choose File > New Multicam Clip to open the Multicam sheet.

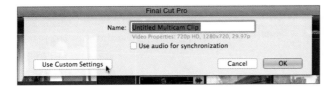

4 Click Use Custom Settings. The sheet expands to show a variety of additional options.

The various pop-up menus and other settings allow you to specify precisely what data you want Final Cut Pro X to use in order to construct the multicam clip.

Angle Assembly

The Angle Assembly setting determines how many angles are available and which clips belong in which angle. This setting is primarily used when you started and stopped one or more of the cameras during the production, but still want them linked into one tidy multicam clip.

The Angle Assembly pop-up menu allows you to specify the metadata used to determine which clips are from which cameras. You can choose among Automatic, Camera Angle, Camera Name, or Clips (which looks at the clip name and the creation time and date).

The Automatic setting scans all the metadata fields—including the Camera ID field, which is stamped onto each clip by your camera and can't be modified after the fact—to determine the proper arrangement of clips into angles. If it guesses wrong, you can use one of the other options.

To ensure that your multicam clip is created correctly, name your camera and provide an angle name or number in the Info Inspector.

The following steps must be done prior to creating the multicam clip.

1   Click Cancel or press Esc (Escape) to exit the Multicam sheet without creating a new clip.

2   In the Event Browser, select **Shot_01**.

3   In the Info Inspector, in the Camera Angle field, type *Side Angle*.

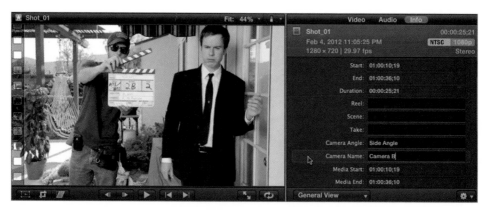

4   In the Camera Name field, type *Camera B*.

NOTE ▶ You may need to switch to the general view or extended view in the Info Inspector to see the Camera Angle field.

5   Select Shot_02.

6   In the Camera Angle field, type *Front Angle*; and in the Camera Name field, type *Camera A*.

Although entering this information isn't required, doing so helps to ensure that the multicam clip is created in the most logical and useful way.

TIP ▶ Remember, you can select multiple clips in the Event Browser and change their settings in the Inspector simultaneously. If you had more than one clip from the same camera, this would be quicker than entering the data one clip at a time.

Angle Clip Ordering

The Angle Assembly setting determines how many angles are available and which clips belong in which angle. The Angle Clip Ordering setting controls the chronological order of each of those clips within each angle.

In most real-world scenarios, you can use the Automatic setting, which checks the starting timecode and the creation date for each clip and determines the most logical arrangement. But when you combine shots with no metadata or combine clips that were not originally shot as a multicamera scene, you may want to override the defaults.

TIP ▶ Take care to set the clock of each camera prior to shooting the scene so you'll have that matching data in each clip, thereby making multicam clip creation much easier. This is especially recommended for non-timecode devices such as DSLRs, iOS devices, GoPro or Flip cameras, and so on.

You can modify a clip's Content Created Date and Time field by selecting the clip and choosing Modify > Adjust Content Created Date and Time. Changes you make in that window will override whatever metadata was originally in the clip.

Angle Synchronization

The Angle Synchronization setting determines which sync point should be used to align the multiple angles. The Automatic setting does a great job of syncing your clips without much fuss; but, once again, at times you may want to override the setting.

When the cameras are *jam-synced* to give all clips an identical timecode, you can use that timecode to determine the sync point by choosing Timecode from the Angle Synchronization pop-up menu.

If the cameras all have accurate Content Created Date and Time settings, you can choose Content Created.

If neither of those metadata fields are available, but you have a visual slate (as in Shot_01 and Shot_02), you can manually set a sync point using a marker.

1   Select Shot_01.

2   Skim or play until you find the frame where the slate clapper closes (at about 01:00:10:26).

3   With the playhead or skimmer on exactly that frame, press M to add a marker to the clip.

4   Select **Shot_02**.

5   Find the frame where the clapper closes the second time (at 01:00:10:19).

NOTE ▶ Be aware that this shot includes two slate claps. Use the second one!

In this case, you'll have to refer to the sound of the clapper because you can't easily see the slate in the frame.

6   Press M to add a marker on that frame.

7   Select **Shot_01** and **Shot_02**, and choose File > New Multicam Clip to open the Multicam sheet.

8   Click the Use Custom Settings button to expand the sheet.

9   From the Angle Synchronization pop-up menu, choose "First marker on the Angle" to instruct Final Cut Pro to use the markers you just added as the sync point.

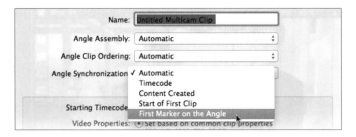

TIP ▶ Notice that the option is "*First* Marker." If you're using this method, be sure you don't have any stray or extraneous markers prior to the intended sync point.

Using Audio for Synchronization

You can use one more tool to ensure accurate alignment of multiple angles, and it works like magic! Final Cut Pro can compare the audio waveforms in the clips to determine where they overlap, and then use this information to align the angles.

This option is reliable, powerful, and makes short work of what used to take many hours of manual syncing—although in some situations you may want to disable the setting.

For example, you may have non-identical audio on the shots or you are deliberately grouping non-synchronous clips into a multicam clip. The audio analysis in this case can be time consuming. As a result, you might want to deselect the "Use audio for synchronization" checkbox.

TIP ▶ If "Use audio for synchronization" is selected and you are syncing using a slate marker, the audio is analyzed only in the area surrounding the marker. This means, if common audio exists around the marker, waveform analysis will be faster, and the markers need not be frame accurate.

Setting Multicam Clip Properties and Timecode

You can optionally change a few additional settings when using the custom settings for multicam clip creation. For example, you could assign a specific timecode for the first frame of the multicam clip. You could also choose exactly which video and audio settings you want your multicam clip to use.

If all your source clips are in identical audio and video formats, it makes sense for the multicam clip to inherit exactly those properties. But Final Cut Pro allows you to combine clips of different formats into a single multicam clip. You can even use still images and audio-only clips.

When clips are in several formats, you can choose a setting manually.

1 In the Video Properties section, click the Custom radio button.

Three pop-up menus appear, in which you can choose a new format. Choosing a setting in the Format pop-up menu automatically enters values in the other two menus.

When choosing an ideal format, ask the following questions:

▶ What is the format of the target project receiving this clip?

If your multicam clip contains a range of formats from NTSC SD to 1080p HD, but your existing project is 720p HD, there is little advantage to making the clip resolution higher than the project resolution.

▶ What are the settings for the clips being joined together?

A rule of thumb is to choose the settings of the highest-quality clip in your group. So if you have four 1080p clips and two 720p clips, set the multicam clip to 1080p. The 720p shots will be scaled up (and, thereby, be of potentially lower quality), but you will have access to the full quality of the higher-resolution shots.

▶ In what format are the majority of the shots?

If you've got six 720p shots and one 1080p shot, setting the multicam clip to 720p may be preferable. That way, the one 1080 shot is scaled down, but the majority of shots remain at their native (and, therefore, at the highest-quality) resolution.

TIP You can similarly override the audio settings (although this is less likely to be necessary in real-world situations).

2 For the purpose of this exercise, change the video properties back to "Set based on common clip properties."

Gray text beneath the control indicates the format of the majority of selected clips.

3 Set Angle Synchronization to Timecode. (Yes, you did add those markers previously, but these clips also have identical timecode.)

4 Make sure "Use audio for synchronization" is deselected.

5 Name the new multicam clip *Ukulele Girl* and click OK.

The new multicam clip is created and appears in the Event Browser.

6 Select the **Ukulele Girl** clip to view it in the Angle Viewer.

7 Click the Angle Viewer Settings button, and from the pop-up menu, choose 2 Angles.

The Angle Viewer switches to a two-up display, which makes sense because this multicam clip contains only two angles.

Modifying a Multicam Clip

You may want to make a variety of modifications to your multicam clip that aren't possible in the Angle Viewer—for example, to rearrange the order in which the angles appear in the Angle Viewer, or to adjust one of the angles for sync. Or, you might want to delete an angle, or add a new one. All of these tasks are performed in the Angle Editor.

The Angle Editor looks quite a bit like the Timeline, and it replaces the Timeline onscreen when it is open. In many ways the Angle Editor works just like a Timeline, but it is different and has the sole purpose of allowing you to edit the contents of multicam clips.

1   Double-click the **Ukulele Girl** multicam clip. The Angle Editor opens, and each of the clips is shown on its own row.

The Angle Editor displays a gray highlight around one of the angles. This indicates the monitoring angle, which is not the same as the active angle. The monitoring angle determines which angle displays in the Viewer when the Angle Editor is open. It is also used for syncing and aligning clips within the Angle Editor, as you'll learn in the next few exercises.

The monitoring angle is relevant only when the Angle Editor is open. It does not have any impact on the angle shown when a clip is used in a project.

The upper-left corner of each row displays icons for the video and the audio to further indicate which angles are currently being monitored.

Only one video angle can be set as the monitoring angle, but you can monitor multiple audio angles simultaneously. This can be very helpful for identifying sync problems—when a clip is out of sync, you'll hear an echo.

2   On Front Angle, click the Video Monitor icon to make it the monitoring angle.

Monitoring icons

This sets that angle to display in the Viewer while the Angle Editor is open.

Fixing Sync Errors

Although Final Cut Pro X generally does a great job of ensuring that clips are properly lined up, sometimes it makes mistakes. When that happens, you can realign the clips in the Angle Editor.

1   Press Spacebar to play the multicam clip. Watch carefully all the way to the end. Although it looks like the two shots are in sync, they are slightly misaligned. This is most evident when you see the woman swing the ukulele near the end of the shot.

In the side angle (on top), the woman has yet to start swinging the ukulele, while in the front angle (bottom), she's already completed her swing. This error happened because the timecodes for the two clips were slightly off—the cameras were not started at exactly the same time—and you were instructed to use timecode as the alignment method in the previous exercise.

NOTE ▶ If you had chosen the First Markers option, or selected the "Use audio for synchronization" checkbox, the clips would have been perfectly aligned (but you'd have no sync mistake to fix now).

2   Press Command-= (equal sign) to zoom in on the area where the ukulele is being swung.

3   Place the playhead in the frame in the monitoring angle where the ukulele is directly in front of the man's face (at 33:05).

4   Click the arrow to the right of the Side Angle name, and from the pop-up menu, choose Sync to Monitoring Angle.

The Viewer is temporarily replaced by the Sync Angle window.

5   In the Angle Editor, skim **Shot_01** until you find the corresponding frame where the ukulele is directly in front of the man's face. Click that frame.

6   Click Done to close the Sync Angle window. **Shot_01** is moved to better align with the monitoring angle.

> **NOTE** ▶ In a case as simple as this, you could also have used the Position tool to drag the side angle to the left until the two markers at the beginning of the clips line up, but then you wouldn't have learned about this nifty feature.

7   Play the end of the multicam clip (or step through it with the arrow keys) watching the two angles in the Angle Viewer. You'll see that now the clips are properly synced.

> **NOTE** ▶ Be aware that this change (like all changes performed in the Angle Editor) affects all instances of the multicam clip.

There is no close button to exit the Angle Editor when you finish using it. To exit the window, click the Timeline History Back button.

8   Click the Timeline History Back button.

The *Untold Fairytales* project reopens, replacing the Angle Editor.

TIP You can also close the Angle Editor by opening the Project Library.

Modifying the Angle Structure

You can also use the Angle Editor to change the order in which angles appear in the Angle Viewer. Additionally, you can delete or remove angles from the multicam clip.

Remember, changes made in the Angle Editor affect all instances of the multicam clip in use. So, for example, in the *Untold Fairytales* project, you have many instances of the Fairytales clip. Modifying any one instance in the Angle Editor will update all of them.

1   Control-click any of the clips in the Timeline.

2   From the shortcut menu, choose Open in Angle Editor.

The Timeline is replaced with the Angle Editor, and the seven angles in the Untold Fairytales clip are all visible.

To see all the angles, you may want to decrease the height of the clips.

3   Click the Clip Appearance button, and click the right-most icon size (no thumbnails). Then click anywhere outside the Clip Appearance control to dismiss it.

Let's say you want to rearrange the angle order so the close-ups (Angles 2, 5, and 7) appear in one bank along with the concert footage, and the remaining three angles go into a second bank.

4   Click the Angle Viewer Settings button, and from the pop-up menu, choose 4 Angles. Make sure the first bank is selected.

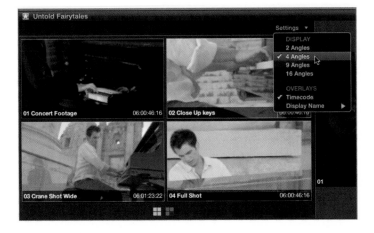

5   In the Angle Editor, drag up the handle in the upper-right corner of the angle for Angle 5 until it is between Angles 2 and 3. The angles are rearranged, changing their display order in the Angle Viewer.

6   Drag the same handle to move Angle 7 until it is the fourth angle from the top.

Arrange the angles until bank one contains Angles 1, 2, 5, and 7; and bank two contains Angles 3, 4, and 6.

Now let's say that you want to delete Angle 7 entirely.

7   Click the arrow to the right of the Angle 7 name, and from the pop-up menu, choose Delete Angle to remove Angle 7 from the multicam clip.

8   Click the Timeline History Back button to return to the *Untold Fairytales* project.

Any clips that previously used that angle now read "Missing" and display black frames when played or skimmed.

9   Click the Timeline History Forward button to open the Angle Editor showing the the **Untold Fairytales** multicam clip.

10   Click the arrow next to the Angle 5 name, and from the pop-up menu, choose Add Angle.

A new, empty angle is added to the clip below Angle 5.

11 Double-click the Untitled Angle name, and when the field becomes editable, type *07*.

12 Click the Video Monitor icon to make the new Angle 7 the monitoring angle.

13 In the Event Browser, select the **07 CU Profile** clip.

14 Position your pointer over the empty fourth angle, and press E to add the angle back into the multicam clip.

Syncing the Added Clip

Although you added the clip, you have no way of knowing if it's properly synced with the rest of the multiclip. Let's make sure it's synced.

1 Click the Video Monitor icon for Angle 1.

2 Click the arrow next to the Angle 7 name, and choose "Sync Angle to Monitoring Angle Using Audio." The clip's audio is analyzed, and the clip is automatically adjusted to sync it to the monitoring angle. Beware that this will not automatically reassign those clips pointing to the angle you deleted in the project.

Although in this instance you have added a previously deleted angle, the software doesn't know it's the same angle. As a result, you'll have to manually switch those angles that previously pointed to Angle 7 to point to the new Angle 7.

3   Click the Timeline History Back button, or press Command-[(left bracket), to reopen the *Untold Fairytales* project.

4   Select an angle that is currently labeled as missing, and in the Angle Viewer, Option-click the Angle 7 image to switch the clip to Angle 4, the added angle.

TIP▶ Be sure to hold down Option when clicking, otherwise you'll perform a cut and add a new (unwanted) edit to the clip.

5   Repeat step 4 for any other clips marked missing.

Adding Effects or Other Trimming

The Angle Editor is a lot like a Timeline, and there's no reason you can't utilize the powerful editing tools available in a regular Timeline in the Angle Editor.

You can add effects, transitions (if you have more than one clip on an angle), color correction, retiming, keyframing, and other effects to any of the clips within the multicam clip.

All of these changes will propagate and appear in every instance of that angle when used in a project.

1   Click the Timeline History Forward button to reopen the Angle Editor.

2   Press Command-5 to open the Effects Browser, if necessary.

3   In the Angle Editor, select the clip in Angle 5 (**05 Close Up 1**), and in the Effects Browser, double-click the 50s TV effect to apply it to Angle 5.

4   Press Command-[(left bracket) to return to the *Untold Fairytales* project.

5   Play or skim any clips that are set to Angle 5 to verify that the 50s TV effect is applied to those clips.

Adding Effects in the Timeline

When you apply an effect to an angle on a multicam clip in a project, the effect is applied only to that angle.

1   Select one of the clips in the Timeline, and in the Effects Browser, double-click the Aged Paper effect to apply it to the current angle.

2   With the clip still selected, in the Angle Viewer, Option-click another angle to switch to it. Note that the Aged Paper effect is not applied to this new angle.

3   Option-click the previously chosen angle and note that it retains the Aged Paper effect.

Similar results would occur if you applied any color correction, retiming, or transformations effects. The effect would be applied only to the angle active when the effect was applied.

NOTE ▶ Applying an effect to a clip in the Timeline will *not* cause that effect to appear on other instances of that angle in other clips. If you want an effect to apply to every instance of a particular angle, apply that effect in the Angle Editor.

Lesson Review

1.   What is a multicam clip?

2.   How do you create a multicam clip?

3.   How are the angles in a multicam clip ordered?

4.   How are the angles in a multicam clip synced?

5.   Can audio and video be edited separately?

6.   What's the difference between cutting and switching?

7.   Is the monitoring angle the same as the active angle?

8.   How do you rearrange the order of angles appearing in the Angle Viewer?

9.   What happens if you delete an angle that is currently in use?

10. Can filters and effects be applied to multicam clips?

Answers

1. A multicam clip is a special type of clip that contains from 2 to 64 angles, any one of which can be used at one time.

2. Select the clips in the Event Browser, and choose File > New Multicam Clip.

3. Angles are ordered automatically based on the metadata in the Camera Angle, Camera Name, and other fields; or manually ordered by choosing which field should be used for that purpose.

4. Angles are synced automatically by using the timecode or the content created date and time, by matching audio waveforms, or by manually specifying one of those options. Angles can also be synced using the first marker in the clips or the beginning of the clips.

5. Yes. Use the controls at the top of the Angle Viewer to determine which components are edited.

6. Cutting adds an edit in the Timeline and the clip after the cut points to the new angle. Switching changes the existing clip to a new angle.

7. No. The monitoring angle is used strictly in the Angle Editor for manually syncing angles and certain other tasks.

8. Control angle order by dragging the drag handles in the Angle Editor.

9. Clips pointing to a deleted angle display black frames, and the angle name is listed as missing.

10. Effects can be applied to individual angles within a multicam clip.

Keyboard Shortcuts

1 through 9	Switch to angles 1 through 9
Option-1 through Option-9	Switch the current-selected clip to angles 1 through 9
Shift-Option-2	Set Angle Viewer to edit only video
Shift-Command-7	Show Angle Viewer
Shift-Option-' (apostrophe)	Select the next bank
Shift-Control-Left Arrow	Switch to the previous angle
Shift-Control-Right Arrow	Switch to the next angle

Advanced Compositing
and Effects

7

Time

Goals

This lesson takes approximately 60 minutes to complete.

Retime video to audio cues

Key and mask video clips with keying effects

Create a garbage mask

Use advanced keying features

Browse, composite, and modify generators

Composite with blend modes

Understand layered graphics files

Keying and Compositing

While you are familiar with the feature-rich editing capabilities of Final Cut Pro X, you may not know that you can also create complex, multi-layered, and animated composite images directly in the Final Cut Pro Timeline.

In this section of the book, you'll explore compositing, effects, titling, and animation in Final Cut Pro while building a show open. You can combine the extensive library of titles, transitions, effects, and generators built into Final Cut Pro to add professional title sequences, lower thirds, animated graphics, and other composited elements to your projects, even if you have little or no original content.

This lesson focuses on laying the foundation: editing video clips, timing clips to music, and then combining layers of video and graphics to form a composite image. You'll explore keying green screen footage, using generators for content, working with a luma keyer, and compositing with blend modes.

Laying the Groundwork

Assume you were asked to create an opening title sequence for a new web show called iJustine: a fun, campy, weekly video podcast featuring Internet personality Justine E. The producers provided you with a few clips of Justine shot in front of a green screen, a simple graphic, and a music clip. It's up to you to create a fast-paced, light, and fun introduction to the show.

To get started, you'll edit the video clips together and time them to the music clip to create the basic project structure. Then you'll replace the green background behind Justine with some background graphics.

Using a Compound Clip in the Event Browser

The show open you create is intended for a project that hasn't yet been made, and will be used in multiple projects for each show that is produced. Therefore, you'll start by creating a compound clip directly in the Event Browser, and then build the show open in this compound clip. This method makes the open available for editing into any project right from the Event Browser. To start, you'll need to mount the disk image for the Advanced Compositing and Effects section.

1   In the Finder, locate and double-click the APTS FCP X ADV Part 2.sparseimage disk image to mount it.

2   In Final Cut Pro X, click the disclosure triangle for the Disk APTS FCP X ADV Part 2 image mounted drive in the Event Library, if necessary, and then select the *iJustine* Event.

> **TIP** To ensure that the clips in your Event Browser match the following images, from the Action pop-up menu, choose Name, or choose Arrange Clips By > Name and choose Group Clips By > None. Then drag the Duration slider all the way to the right (the word *All* will appear next to it). Click the Clip Appearance button and set the slider so that you can see all six clips in the Event Browser and still read the complete clip names.

This Event contains four video clips, a graphic, and an audio clip. The video clips and audio clip each have a range rated as a Favorite. You'll use these ratings when creating a compound clip.

3   From the Filter pop-up menu, choose Favorites, or press Control-F.

Now only the range marked as a Favorite for each clip is available.

4   Select each video clip and press the / (slash) key to preview them in turn.

> **TIP**   If you enable looping (choose View > Playback > Loop Playback, or press Command-L), you can press / (slash) once and then press the Up and Down Arrow keys to navigate to each clip and view each of them in playback.

Each clip shows Justine performing a short action. Together, they will serve as the foundation for your show open. You'll edit them into a compound clip and then time them to the audio clip.

5   Select the **Justine_funny_spin** clip. Then Command-click **Justine_flip_roar**, **Justine_ selects**, and **Justine_turn_look** to select all four clips

6   Choose File > New Compound Clip, or press Option-G.

7   In the window that appears, name the clip *Show Open*, and click OK.

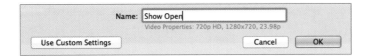

TIP ▶ When you are working with clips in different formats, resolutions, and frame rates, or when you want to render to a different codec, you can click the Use Custom Settings button and choose custom video properties, audio properties, and render properties.

A new compound clip named **Show Open** appears in the **iJustine** Event.

NOTE ▶ The Filter pop-up menu has automatically returned to Hide Rejected so that you can see the compound clip.

8 Double-click the **Show Open** compound clip to open it in the Timeline.

The compound clip contains just the range of each clip that was rated as a Favorite, and the clips have been edited into the clip in the same order you selected them.

NOTE ▶ Because you'll change these clips frequently in these three lessons, you should consider turning off background rendering by choosing Final Cut Pro > Preferences, clicking the Playback icon, and deselecting the "Background render" checkbox.

9 In the Event Browser, scroll down, if necessary, and click the green bar at the top of the **Two Seater Short** audio clip to select the Favorite range.

10 With the playhead at the beginning of the Timeline, press Q to connect this clip to the primary storyline at the playhead.

11 Press Command-2 to make the Timeline active, and then press Shift-Z to fit the audio clip to the window.

The compound clip now contains the primary elements you'll use to create the show open.

12 Press the Home key and play the Timeline.

The sequence obviously needs work, but the key elements—the shots of Justine combined with the music clip—are in place. The next step is to time the video clips to the music.

Timing Edits with Markers and Hold Segments

To introduce the character of iJustine, you'll freeze the video of Justine after each move she makes, and onscreen text will describe aspects of her show persona. To determine how long she should freeze, you can use beats in the music track that you'll identify with markers.

1 In the Timeline, select the **Two Seater Short** audio clip, and play it from the beginning. As it plays, count the beats in (four beats per measure), and press M to set a marker on the first beat of each measure.

When you've gone through the entire clip, you'll have a total of four markers, each positioned at or near these timecode values: 2:05, 4:07, 6:14, and 8:17.

TIP ▶ Press Control-' (apostrophe) to jump to the next marker, or press Control-; (semicolon) to return to the previous marker. When the playhead is parked on a marker, you can nudge it forward or backward in time by pressing Control-. (period) or Control-, (comma), respectively. You can also choose these commands from the Mark menu.

Now you can use Hold segments to extend the duration of each clip to a marker.

2 Select the first clip, **Justine_funny_spin**.

3   Press the Down Arrow to move the playhead to the first frame of the next clip, and then press the Left Arrow to move the playhead to the last frame of that clip.

4   In the toolbar, click the Retime pop-up menu and choose Hold or press Shift-H to create a 2-second Hold segment starting at the playhead.

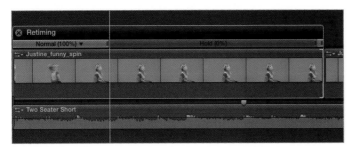

Retiming bars automatically appear over the clip, including the new Hold segment. The hold duration extends well past the first marker.

5   Drag the end point of the first clip to the left to trim it back to the first marker.

TIP ▶ You can turn on snapping (choose View > Snapping, or press N) to snap the edit point to the marker. Press Command-= (equal sign) to zoom into the Timeline to make it easier to trim the clip to the marker.

You'll repeat this process for the second clip.

6   Select the second video clip, Justine_flip_roar, and press the Down Arrow followed by the Left Arrow to place the playhead at the end of the that clip. Press Shift-H to create a Hold segment on the last frame of the clip, and trim the end point of the clip back to the second marker.

The third video clip extends well past the next *two* markers, so instead of extending it with a Hold segment, you'll shorten it by speeding it up to fit to the last marker. The action in this clip is a little slow for a fast-paced opening title anyway, so speeding up the clip will also improve the pacing.

7 Select the third video clip, **Justine_selects**, click the Retime pop-up menu, and choose Show Retime Editor (or press Command-R).

8 Drag the retiming handle located at the right edge of the green speed segment to the left until it aligns with the last marker.

> **NOTE ▶** This time you aren't trimming the end point of the clip, but rather changing the speed of the clip by dragging the retiming handle.

The speed segment turns blue to indicate that it will now play faster. It shows a speed of about 115%.

For the last clip, you'll hold the final frame until the end of the music clip.

9 Select the last video clip, **Justine_turn_look**, and move the playhead to the last frame (press Down Arrow followed by Left Arrow). Press Shift-H to create a Hold segment, and then drag the retiming handle of the red speed segment to line up with the end point of the audio clip.

> **NOTE ▶** Be sure to drag the retiming handle of the red speed segment, and not the retiming handle of the very small green speed segment next to it.

The clips are retimed so that the edit points land on key beats of the music.

10 If necessary, press Shift-Z to fit the Timeline to the window, move the playhead to the start of the sequence, and play the Timeline.

The timing looks good. Even though there is no edit point on the third marker, Justine's action of spreading her arms nicely matches that beat.

11 Select all the video clips in the Timeline, and press Command-R to hide the Retime Editor for every clip. Then press Command-Shift-A to deselect everything. You no longer need to see the timing properties and you now have more screen real estate for editing additional content.

With the basic project timing of the project in place, you can now start compositing layers together by removing Justine from the green background using a process known as *keying*.

Using Keying and Masking Effects

Keying is the process of removing part of a video or graphic based on color or luminance (brightness) information. The video clips of Justine were shot in front of a bright green wall so that the editor could remove this background and replace it with something else—anything else! Final Cut Pro X contains a category of keying effects for this purpose. In this exercise, you'll combine a keying effect and a masking effect to remove that green background.

Keying Automatic and Manual Sampling

We'll begin by using automatic and manual color sampling to create a key.

1 In the toolbar, click the Effects button, or press Command-5, to open the Effects Browser.

The Effects Browser contains over 200 video and audio effects you can use in your projects, all organized into categories.

2   Select the Keying category.

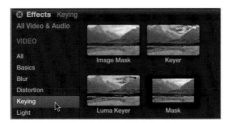

NOTE ▸ You'll work with several other effects categories in a later lesson.

The Keying category contains four effects, each designed to remove elements of a video clip. The Keyer effect can remove, or *key*, a colored background out of a shot.

NOTE ▸ The Keyer effect does a remarkable job of pulling a good key on most footage, but you'll get the best results with a shot in which the colored background is evenly lit and adequate separation exists between the background and the subject.

3   Select the first video clip in the Timeline, `Justine_funny_spin`, and then move the pointer over the Keyer effect (without clicking the mouse).

The selected clip appears in the effect's thumbnail and also in the Viewer against a black background. Using these views, you can preview the effect before applying it.

4   Double-click the Keyer thumbnail image to apply the effect to the selected clip. Then, reselect the first Justine clip.

In the Viewer, Justine appears in front of a black background. This new background is actually transparent, which will become obvious later when you composite a new background beneath it. But first, let's examine and adjust the Keyer effect.

5   In the toolbar, click the Inspector button, or press Command-4 to open the Inspector.

In the Video tab of the Inspector, you have access to all the parameters of applied effects, as well as controls to adjust the color and other properties of the video clip.

The keyer seems to have done a great job of removing the green background without the need to adjust anything at all, but let's check it out a little more thoroughly to make sure. By doing so, you'll also learn how to key a shot by manually sampling colors. After all, not every green screen shot is lit as well as this.

6   In the Timeline, skim through the clip, stopping on a frame where Justine's hair is flying in the air—such as at 0:13.

Strands of hair can be challenging to separate from the background, so it's a good idea to select a frame that includes fine detail.

You are currently looking at the final results of the Keyer effect, the *composite*. But another way to examine the key is to look at the *matte* that creates the key.

7   In the Video Inspector, to view the matte, select Matte (the center button) in the View area.

The Matte view uses grayscale values to indicate areas of the image that are visible or transparent. Anything that is white is fully opaque; anything that is black is completely transparent; and shades of gray indicate partial transparency.

By default, the Keyer effect works in an automatic color sampling mode: It samples the background color and determines how the matte should appear on the inside (the *core matte*) and on the edges (the *edge matte*).

A good matte (and, therefore, a good key) will appear as solid white on a solid black background, while the edges of the subject may have areas of gray, particularly around soft areas such as hair.

Any areas within the subject that are not completely white will be partially transparent in the composite. If any areas of the background are not completely black, some of the green screen will still be visible in the composite. When keying footage, you may need to deal with either or both of these situations.

When the automatic sampling results aren't quite good enough, you can also key a shot by sampling colors manually. Although the automatic results are very good in this example, sampling the colors manually will help you to understand how to address less than ideal situations.

8   Select Composite in the View area (the black silhouette on the checked background) to return to the Composite view.

9   Drag the Strength slider to 0%.

The Strength parameter determines how much of the automatic color sampling is being used by the Keyer effect. At 0%, no automatic color sampling is used, allowing you to manually select the color you want to key out of the video. If the automatic key doesn't provide satisfactory results, setting the slider to 0% is a good first step toward sampling manually.

10   In the Refine Key controls, click the Sample Color thumbnail, and then in the Viewer, drag a selection rectangle over a representative section of the green background.

Sample an area of the background color close to the subject being keyed because the key color can change near the frame's edges when the lighting is not even. Note the slight halo around the edges of the shot. The green color is slightly darker at the edges and hasn't been completely removed by the keyer.

NOTE ▸ You can draw more selection rectangles to take additional color samples in multiple regions of the screen. Multiple samples can be helpful when your subject moves around in the shot or the lighting is uneven. You can even take color samples in different frames of your video clip, and the Keyer effect will adjust the key over time to compensate for any changing lighting conditions.

Sampling the background color creates the core matte, separating the primary subject from the green screen. To refine the edges of the matte, you can use the Edges tool.

11   Click the Edges thumbnail and then draw a line across Justine's hair so that one end of the line is in a transparent area and the other is in an opaque area.

12 In the View controls, select Matte to switch to the Matte view, and drag the line between the two end points of the edge sample to adjust the transparency of the fine hair detail. If you move the line too close to the core matte, the inside of the white matte will start to turn to shades of gray, indicating areas of transparency, which is not what you want. Drag the line back toward the end point in the transparent area until the core matte returns to a solid white.

NOTE ▸ You can also reposition the end points of the Edges sample, and add multiple samples to the image. If you still cannot get the fine edge detail without introducing areas of transparency to the core matte, drag the Fill Holes slider to "clean up" the core matte. The Edge Distance parameter determines how close to the edge of the matte the Fill Holes parameter will work.

13 Select Composite in the View controls to return to the composite image.

When a subject is shot in front of a colored background, that color often bounces or *spills* back on the subject, introducing a green cast along subject edges and hair. The Keyer effect's Spill Level parameter automatically attempts to correct for this spill. Let's see what it's doing in our example.

14 Drag the Spill Level slider to 0%.

The green spill is now obvious in Justine's hair and along the edges of her arms.

15 Increase the Spill Level to 100%.

To correct for the green spill, the Keyer effect adds the complementary color, magenta. When complementary colors are added in the additive RGB color space of Final Cut Pro X, the result is shades of gray. In other words, all hue and saturation is removed. However, if too much magenta is added, the result is the pink/purple tint we see here on the subject.

16 Adjust the Spill Level until any green or magenta color cast disappears. Skim the clip.

> **NOTE ▸** As you skim or play the clip, you'll notice that the color and edge samples disappear. This occurs because the samples were applied to just one specific frame of the clip. To see them, click the appropriate Jump to Sample arrow in the Keyer controls in the Inspector.

Your key is looking pretty good. However, the outer edges of the matte are still not completely transparent. Rather than create another color sample, you can generate a mask to hide the edges of the shot.

Using a Garbage Mask

Frequently a green screen shot will contain extraneous elements you don't want to see. For example, a light stand or a boom mike may appear in the shot, or perhaps the edges of a small portable green screen. To eliminate these items—or just to reduce the overall keying area to the most evenly lit part of the background—you can use a mask. Often called a *garbage mask* or *garbage matte*, you use the mask to quickly matte out the "garbage" that can litter the edge of a green screen shot. After applying and adjusting the mask, you'll refine the key and then quickly key all the rest of the shots in the Timeline using a copy-and-paste operation.

1 Make sure the first clip in the Timeline is still selected. (It should have a gray outline.) Then in the Effects Browser, double-click the Mask effect to apply it to the selected clip.

In the Viewer, onscreen controls appear at the four corners of the mask. You may notice that the background of the video inside the mask is not as black as the areas outside of the mask. The key isn't quite as good as we thought!

2   Drag the onscreen controls to adjust the shape of the mask. Skim the clip to make sure Justine's hair and arms never move outside the mask.

TIP ▶ If you don't see the onscreen controls, select the Mask effect in the Video Inspector.

NOTE ▶ Depending on your screen resolution, you may need to adjust the Viewer zoom level to be able to adjust the position of the matte corners using the onscreen controls.

3   In the Inspector, in the Keyer effect, select Original (the silhouette on the blue background) in the View controls to switch to the original view of the Keyer effect. This view lets you see the mask more clearly.

4   Click the disclosure triangle to reveal the Mask effect parameters, if necessary. Increase the Feather and Roundness values to create a softer edge.

A softer mask edge is likely to key more easily. Now you're ready to finalize the key.

5   In the Inspector, click the word *Keyer* to select the Keyer effect, and then return to the Composite view.

6   Click the Jump to Sample arrows to locate the frame containing the color and edge samples, and create another color sample within the masked area to eliminate any remaining traces of the background.

You now have a nicely keyed shot. Only three more shots to go! Instead of repeating this entire process three more times, you can copy and paste these effects to the other clips, and then set the other clips to be keyed with automatic sampling.

NOTE ▶ The stacking order of effects can impact your key. Specifically, if you first apply the Mask effect, and then apply the Keyer effect, you may see the edges of the mask. To eliminate the edges, in the Inspector, drag the Keyer effect above the Mask effect.

7   Select the first clip in the Timeline, and press Command-C to copy it.

8   Drag a selection rectangle around the last three clips in the Timeline, and choose Edit > Paste Effects (or press Command-Option-V).

The Video Inspector now shows the effects applied to all three selected clips as indicated by the "Inspecting items" text at the top. You can adjust the effect on all three clips at once.

9   In the Inspector, drag the Strength slider to 100% to enable automatic sampling.

10 Select just the second clip, select the mask in the Inspector, and adjust the onscreen controls as necessary. Skim the entire clip to make sure that Justine's arms and hair are not cut off by the mask. (Feel free to switch to the Original view if you find it helpful.)

11 Adjust the mask on the remaining two clips and adjust the key, if necessary.

All the shots are now nicely keyed.

Using Advanced Keying Features

While these shots were not too difficult to key, the Keyer effect includes several advanced controls for more challenging situations. Let's see how they work.

1   In the Timeline, select the second clip, **Justine_flip_roar**, and move the playhead to a frame where she is flipping her hair up into the frame, at about 2:13.

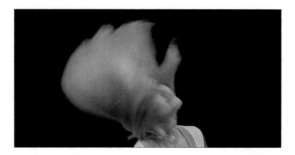

Because of the motion blur created by the rapid movement, her hair looks unnaturally thick with very little detail. While you could probably make it look better with the Edge tool, let's look at how much more control you have with the advanced features.

2   In the Inspector, select the Keyer effect. Make sure the Strength parameter is set to 100%, and then click the disclosure triangle for the Color Selection controls.

When using the Color Selection tools, you can start with an automatically sampled key such as we have here, or with a key in which you manually sampled the color and edges of the matte. However, the Strength parameter must always be greater than zero to access all of the Color Selection controls.

The heart of the Color Selection controls is the Chroma color wheel. It lets you set the range of hue and saturation included in the key.

You interact with this wheel in two modes based on your Graph selection. Scrub Boxes, the default, allows you to affect only the edge transparency, while leaving the core transparency untouched. The edge transparency is represented by the high-lighted "pie slice" on the wheel.

The impact of changing the Chroma color wheel can often be more clearly seen in the Matte view.

3   In the View controls, switch to the Matte view.

4   Move the pointer over the right edge of the "pie slice" in the Chroma wheel. This is the outer graph. Drag right to expand the range of hues that are being keyed out.

The edges of the matte thin out, revealing more hair detail and transparency.

To adjust the range of hue and saturation that is keyed further, you use the Chroma Rolloff parameter.

5   Drag the Chroma Rolloff slider to zero to reveal more detail in the matte.

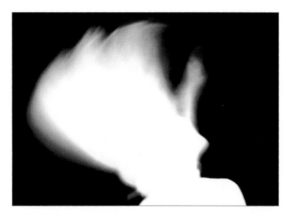

This Chroma Rolloff allows you smooth the transition between colors that are keyed and those that are not, thereby creating a softer edge.

TIP ▶ To best evaluate the matte, set the Viewer zoom level to 100%.

The Luma curve under the Chroma wheel represents the brightness, or luminance, of the pixels that are being keyed, and allows you to adjust the range of pixels included in the key. You can feel free to drag the curve, but you'll likely find that it won't improve this particular key. The Luma Rolloff parameter is analogous to the Chroma Rolloff parameter: It adjusts the smoothness of the transition between keyed and non-keyed pixel, but based on brightness rather than color.

To reveal a little more detail in Justine's blurred hair, you will want to adjust the core transparency. It is represented by the small box inside the "pie slice" on the Chroma wheel, called the *inner graph*. It can only be adjusted with the Graph set to Manual.

6   In the Graph controls, click the Manual button.

NOTE ▶ Once you have selected Manual, if you want to return to Scrub Boxes, you should reset the Color Selection by clicking the Reset button (hooked arrow) to avoid unexpected combinations of color samples.

The core transparency box is very small. Let's get a closer look.

7 Hold down the Z key and click several times on the green box in the top left of the Chroma color wheel to zoom in. Then hold down H and drag to center the box in the frame.

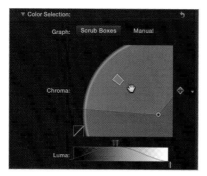

8 Drag the left and right sides of the inner graph to expand the range of hues included in the key for the core matte (and thus being removed from the matte).

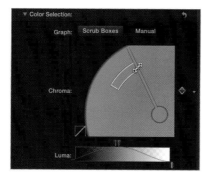

9 Drag the top and bottom sides of the inner graph to expand the range of saturation included in the key (which are being removed from the matte). Don't go too far, or you'll start removing edge detail.

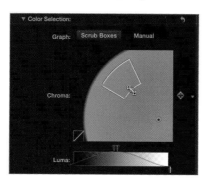

You should now see more detail in the matte.

You can refine the matte further using the Matte Tools.

10 Click the disclosure triangle to reveal the Matte Tools parameters.

Here, you can adjust the contrast, shrink or expand, soften, and erode the matte. You want to use these tools sparingly, if at all, to avoid damaging the work you've already done. Feel free to experiment, but then reset these tools by clicking the Reset button because you don't need them for this key.

11 In the View controls, select the Composite view to see the result of your adjustments.

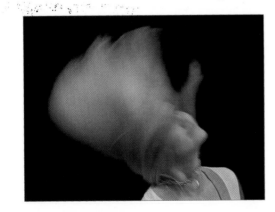

The next advanced feature, Spill Suppression, is best used when viewing the composite image.

12 Open the Spill Suppression controls.

This section gives you more control over the Spill Level you set above. In particular, the Spill Contrast gradient can eliminate gray fringing you may see around the edges of your keyed subject by making it darker or lighter. It can also help recover some motion-blurred detail.

13 Drag the White point handle (under the right edge of the Spill Contrast gradient) to the left to about 0.82. This will reduce the fringing and reveal more detail in Justine's hair.

The Tint and Saturation parameters can help restore the natural color to the video that was affected by the spill suppressor.

14 Set Tint to 0% and Saturation to about 85%.

The last advanced feature, Light Wrap, matches a keyed element to a background element more naturally by blending the background colors into the keyed image. You can try it out once you have a background in place.

Just because this frame looks good, doesn't mean you are finished.

15   Press the Arrow keys to step through all the other frames of the clip. If you find any hairs that are separated from Justine because you got too aggressive with the key, adjust the inner graph on the Chroma wheel to make a smaller hue selection (a skinnier box). Then set the Viewer zoom level back to Fit.

The advanced features of the Keyer give you the power to make a poorly-lit green screen shot workable—and a well-lit shot beautiful.

Compositing Generators

In the next exercises, you'll be transforming, animating, and adding effects to these shots of Justine; but first let's give her a background so that she's not just hanging around in empty space.

Although you could add any video or graphic as a background element, Final Cut Pro X includes a large amount of content you can use in your projects. This content takes the form of Motion projects called generators. In this exercise, you'll browse, apply, and modify generators for use as background and foreground elements. To get started, you'll choose a background for your show open.

1   In the Timeline, click above the primary storyline to deselect everything, and then move the playhead back home.

2   In the toolbar, click the Generators button.

The Generators Browser contains 26 generators, including several that have multiple design options. You can preview the default state of each generator by skimming its thumbnail.

3   Move the pointer over several of the generator thumbnails to preview them.

The preview appears in both the thumbnail and in the Viewer. Some generators are animated; others contain still graphics.

As opposed to effects, which are applied to a clip in the Timeline, generators are clips in and of themselves that you can use much as you would a video clip.

4   Select the Grunge thumbnail, and press Q to connect the generator to the primary storyline. Then, drag its end point to trim it to match the duration of the primary storyline. (If snapping isn't enabled, press N.)

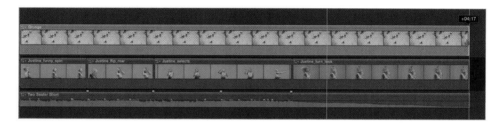

By default, generators are connected above the primary storyline, but that's not what you want to do here.

5   Select the Grunge clip in the Timeline, and then Shift-drag it below the primary storyline. Justine now appears properly composited on top of the generator.

TIP ▶ Holding down the Shift key while dragging prevents the connected clip from moving left or right.

Let's look at the options for this generator.

6 In the Inspector, select the Generator tab, if necessary, and then try out the Published Parameters, including Type options, Tint Color, and Tint Amount.

As you can see, you can make this generator look much different than the default settings.

NOTE ▶ All generators—as well as almost all the effects, titles, and transitions—are Motion projects that were published to Final Cut Pro. The Published Parameters in the Generator Inspector are Motion parameters that were published by the generator designer to appear in Final Cut Pro. You can modify any of these effects in Motion, or you can create your own. For more information, see *Apple Pro Training Series: Motion 5* by Mark Spencer (Peachpit Press).

The grungy textures are interesting, but none are appropriate for this show open. Rather than deleting the generator, you can replace it, as you would replace a video clip.

7   In the Generators Browser, scroll down to locate the Retro thumbnail. Drag it to the Grunge generator in the Timeline, and choose Replace from Start.

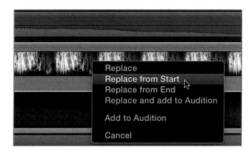

8   Select the new generator in the Timeline and look at the Inspector.

The producer loves this graphic but wants it to have more of a purple-pink color. Unfortunately, this particular generator has no published parameters! No problem. Just as you can apply effects to video clips, you can also apply them to generators.

9 Return to the Effects Browser, and select the Basics category. Here you'll find 11 handy effects.

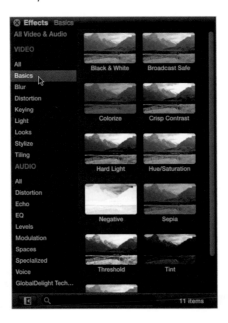

10 Drag the Tint effect onto the Retro generator in the Timeline. Select the generator, and in the Inspector, click the Video tab to locate the Tint effect. To change the color to a bright purple, you can click the triangle next to the color swatch and use the eye-dropper to sample a color. Or, you can click the color swatch directly to open the Mac OS X color picker and enter specific values for the color you want.

With the background in place and tinted, you'll now add a foreground element.

NOTE ▶ Now that you have a background placed and tinted, feel free to select the second Justine clip, and in the Keyer effect, try out the Light Wrap controls.

11 Select the third video clip, **Justine_selects**, press / (slash) to play it, and press X to select a range for the clip.

In this clip, Justine sees something above her, drags it down, stretches it out, and finally tosses it to the side. You can use a generator to serve as this object. By selecting a clip range, you can edit the generator to match the clip duration.

12 Open the Generators Browser, and then select the Elements category.

This category includes a Counting generator that can display animated numbers, a Placeholder generator for adding storyboard images, a Timecode generator, and the Shapes generator you'll use here.

13 Select the Shapes generator, and press Q to connect it to the primary storyline based on the range you selected in the Timeline.

14 In the Timeline, select the Shapes generator. In the Generator tab of the Inspector, change the Shape to a Square. Deselect Fill, change the Outline color to a dark purple, and increase the Outline width to 40.

TIP ▶ Rather than dragging the slider to adjust the Outline Width parameter, you can click the number to the right and type in an exact value.

You'll animate this shape's scale, position, and other properties to follow Justine's hand movements in a later lesson. For now, let's add a transition to animate the shape onto the screen.

15 Click the left edge of the Shapes generator to select the start point, and then in the toolbar, click the Transitions button.

The Transitions Browser contains 89 transitions you can preview by skimming their thumbnails. You can apply transitions to the edit points between clips or to the start or end of any clip. You can even apply transitions directly to connected clips and automatically create a storyline.

16 Skim the thumbnails of several transitions to see how they animate. Then select the Dissolves category and double-click the Cross Dissolve transition to apply it to the selected edit point of the Shapes generator in the Timeline.

 You can also press Command-T to add a Cross Dissolve transition to a selected edit point.

A new storyline is created for the generator, and the transition is added to the beginning of the clip. However, the transition is much too long for this fast-paced show open.

17 Control-click (or right-click) the transition and choose Change Duration from the shortcut menu. Type *10* (to set the transition duration to 10 frames), and press Return.

You've added two generators, an effect, and a transition to your composite. Next, you'll turn your attention to a few more compositing techniques, including compositing graphics based on luminance values and compositing using blend modes.

Compositing Graphics

In addition to compositing generators with your footage, you can composite graphics or video you imported into the Event Library. If the graphics don't contain any transparency, you can remove the brighter or darker areas using a *luma key* effect. You can even composite copies of video clips on top of themselves and make the layers interact using *blend modes*. Before adding any more layers to your composite, make some room in the Timeline by adjusting the clip appearance.

1 Press Shift-Z to fit the Timeline to the window, then at the lower-right side of the Timeline, click the Clip Appearance button, and select the smallest display option at the far right. Now you have plenty of room for compositing more elements. Click the button again to hide the window.

Let's start by spicing up the background with a graphic.

2   Move the playhead to the start of the Timeline, and in the Event Browser, select the
     Stars graphic. Press Q to connect this graphic to the primary storyline at the playhead
     position. Then, trim the clip to match the end of the last video clip. (The Shapes clip
     will move up to make room as you drag.)

3   Select the **Stars** clip, and then Shift-drag it between the **Justine** clips and the Retro
     generator. (It doesn't matter whether it is above or below the audio clip.)

Because this graphic doesn't have any transparency, it completely obscures the Retro generator underneath it. You'll want to remove the white background from this graphic to reveal the generator. You can do this using a blend mode.

4   In the Video Inspector, scroll down to the Compositing section and click the Blend Mode pop-up menu.

Blend modes combine the selected clip with one or more clips beneath it by performing mathematical operations on the RGB values of each overlapping pixel. These modes are available in many applications that allow for compositing of layers, such as Adobe Photoshop and Motion.

The modes are separated into logical groups from top to bottom. The default mode, Normal, just displays the selected clip. The first grouping contains five blend modes that usually darken the combined image. Because these blend modes eliminate brighter pixels, they are good candidates for separating the stars in your graphic from the white background.

5   Try each of the five blend modes in the first grouping. Then try the Overlay mode in the third grouping.

While all the blend modes in the first group knock out the white background, some reveal the Retro generator pattern inside the stars. Subtract turns the Retro generator completely black. Color Burn reveals the generator and also blends a color into some of the stars, but a few are turned black.

Notice how Overlay doesn't remove the white background intact, but it does blend a nice color into all the stars. It would be great if you could keep the Overlay blend mode *and* knock out the white background.

Fortunately, there is a technique that will allow you to remove the white areas, and apply a blend mode independently. You'll do this using a luma key.

6   Return the Blend mode to Normal. In the Effects Browser, in the Keying category, drag the Luma Keyer effect onto the **Stars** clip in the Timeline.

7   Select the **Stars** clip and go to the Luma Keyer section of the Video Inspector.

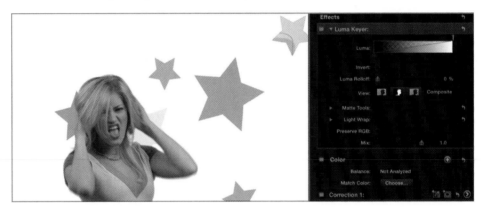

The Luma Keyer's controls look similar to the Keyer effect controls because they work much the same way. But instead of keying out a specific color range, the Luma Keyer keys out a specific brightness, or *luminance*, range you can adjust. By default, it keys out the darker pixels in the image.

8   In the Luma Keyer, select the Invert checkbox.

Inverting the keyer knocks out the white pixels, but now some of the stars are partially transparent. The brightest pixels are completely removed, but some of the darker pixels are also removed, as indicated by the slope in the Luma graph.

9 Drag the Luma Rolloff slider to 100%, while you watch the Luma graph and the opacity of the stars in the Viewer.

The stars become more opaque, as reflected by the steeply sloping Luma graph.

TIP The Luma Keyer effect has a set of advanced controls that work almost exactly like the Keyer effect: Matte Tools and Light Wrap.

Now that the background is "out of the picture," you can choose a blend mode that works best for the stars.

10 Scroll down in the Video Inspector and change the blend mode to Overlay. Experiment with the other blend modes as well, and then return to Overlay.

The Overlay blend mode creates a nice look. By keying out the white background with the Luma Keyer, you have many more creative options when using blend modes.

Another interesting use of blend modes is compositing a clip on top of itself.

11 Select the last clip, **Justine_turn_look**, and press the Up Arrow to move the playhead to the start of the clip.

12 Press Command-C to copy the clip, and choose Edit > Paste as Connected Clip (or press Option-V).

This command connects a copy of the entire clip starting at the playhead location. Because the playhead was placed at the start of the clip, the copy is perfectly registered above the original clip. Blend modes applied to the copy will combine the two clips.

13 Select the top clip. Scroll down to the bottom of the Inspector and experiment with different blend modes, finally selecting Hard Light.

The blend modes in the third group increase contrast and add some "punch" to the clip. However, that punch is a little too intense. Fortunately, it's easy to modify the impact of a blend mode by lowering the opacity of the clip.

14 Decrease the Opacity parameter to about 60%.

▶ Layered Graphics Files

When you want to add layered graphics files to you project, such as Adobe Photoshop® files saved in the .psd format, Final Cut Pro X provides access to the individual layers in the file.

When you import a layered graphics file into an Event, it appears in the Event Browser with a layered badge in the upper-left corner to indicate that it is a layered file.

If you select Clip > Open in Timeline, the file will appear in its own Timeline with each layer represented by a connected clip.

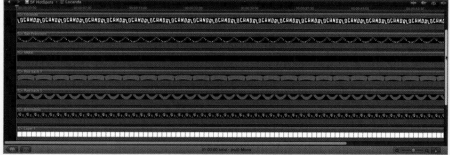

You can now transform, animate, and add effects to these clips just as with any other clips. You can also copy and paste them into a project.

Note that any vector-based effects applied to layers in Photoshop® files, such as layer styles, must be rasterized to appear on the layer in Final Cut Pro X.

You've made good progress on your show open by editing clips into a compound clip timed to a music clip, keying footage, and compositing a few elements. In the next chapter, you'll take things further with transformations, effects, and titles.

Lesson Review

1. What is the advantage to creating a compound clip in an Event rather than in a project?
2. How can you freeze a video clip at a specific frame?
3. Describe the difference between the Keyer effect and the Luma Keyer effect.
4. How do you turn off automatic sampling in the Keyer effect?
5. What value must the Strength parameter of the Keyer effect be set to in order to use the Manual graph mode for the Color Selection?
6. How can you preview an effect, generator, or transition without adding or applying it to the Timeline?
7. True or false: Transitions can be added only to connected clips that are part of a storyline.
8. Can effects and transitions be applied to generators?
9. Name two blend modes that will remove the white areas of a clip if placed over a clip that has no white pixels.
10. How can you alter the impact of a blend mode?

Answers

1. Compound clips in an Event can be edited into a project just like any other clip.
2. Select the clip, move the playhead to the desired frame, and then click the Retime pop-up menu in the toolbar and choose Hold (or press Shift-H). Then, trim the duration of the Hold segment in the Timeline.
3. The Keyer effect creates transparency in a video clip or graphic by removing a specific color range. The Luma Keyer creates transparency by removing a specific range of brightness values.
4. Change the value of the Strength parameter to 0.
5. The Strength parameter can be set to any value other than 0 to set the Color Selection graph mode to Manual.
6. Skim the thumbnail of any effect, generator, or transition to see a preview in both the thumbnail and in the Viewer.
7. True. However, adding a transition to a connected clip automatically creates a storyline if one doesn't already exist.
8. Yes

9. Any of the blend modes in the first grouping—Subtract, Darken, Multiply, Color Burn, and Linear Burn—will replace white pixels with something darker as long as no white pixels are underneath.

10. Reduce the opacity of the clip to which it's applied.

Keyboard Shortcuts

Control-M	Delete a marker
Control-; (semicolon)	Move the playhead to the previous marker
Control-' (apostrophe)	Move the playhead to the next marker
Control-, (comma)	Nudge a marker to the left
Control-. (period)	Nudge a marker to the right
Shift-H	Create a two-second Hold segment on the selected clip at the playhead location
Option-V	Paste as a connected clip

8

Lesson Files	Lesson 8 > Lesson 8 Start
Time	This lesson takes approximately 75 minutes to complete.
Goals	Transform clips
	Browse and apply effects
	Combine and modify effects
	Edit and stylize titles
	Save title presets
	Animate titles
	Assign subroles to titles

Transformations, Effects, and Titles

In addition to compositing video clips with graphics and generators using transparency, keying, and blend modes, Final Cut Pro X includes tools for transforming clips. You can change the position, scale, rotation, and other attributes of any clip interactively in the Viewer, or by entering specific values in the Inspector. These tools let you choose only a portion of a video or graphic, and place it exactly where you want it.

You can also control the appearance of your video by choosing from a large variety of effects that can distort, blur, stylize, tile, or colorize video in many ways.

Finally, you can use titles to communicate key messages to your audience by leveraging the vast number of text animations provided with Final Cut Pro X. You can use them "as is" or modify them to create highly customized and animated titles. And you can use roles metadata to easily work with multiple language versions of your project.

In this lesson, you'll use transform tools, effects, and titles to give your show open a unique look and polish.

Transforming Clips

In the previous lesson, you keyed the clips of Justine onto background graphics, but the layout could still use some work. Each shot of Justine is dead center on the screen with too much empty headroom. To achieve a more dynamic feel and create room to add titles, you can transform the clips by changing their scales and positions, either directly in the Viewer or in the Inspector. You'll use the **Show Open** compound clip you started building in the last lesson.

> **NOTE** ▸ If you didn't complete the previous lesson, you'll find a completed project on the APTS FCP X ADV Part 2 mounted disk image. Open the Lesson 8 folder and double-click the *Lesson 8 Start* project to open it into the Timeline.

1   Select the first video clip in the Timeline, **Justine_funny_spin**.

At the lower left of the Viewer are three buttons that allow you to apply effects and change the clip directly in the Viewer. You can transform, crop, or distort a clip.

2   Click the Transform button to apply the Transform effect.

The button turns blue when it is selected. In the Viewer, a bounding box appears around the clip with blue control handles at the corners and midpoints of each side. At the upper left of the Viewer are controls for setting and navigating keyframes. (You'll work with these in the next lesson.) And at the top right is a Done button for exiting the Transform effect.

Let's increase the scale of the clip so that Justine fills more of the frame, and then move the clip to the right to make room for text you'll add later. First, you may need to zoom out so that you can see, select, and move the control handles.

3 Click the Viewer zoom level and choose a value that allows you to see all the control handles.

NOTE ▶ Depending on your screen resolution, you may require a different zoom level than the one shown in the screenshot.

4 Drag out any corner control handle to increase the size of the clip. Then drag inside the clip to reposition it up and toward the right side of the frame.

NOTE ▶ Dragging a corner control handle scales the clip proportionally, but dragging an edge control handle scales the clip only horizontally or vertically. Shift-dragging a handle reverses this default behavior for both types of control handles.

5   Click Done to turn off the Transform effect.

> **TIP** ▶ You can also click the Transform button again to turn off the effect, or press A to return to the Select tool.

That looks better, but what exactly did you just do? How much did you scale the image and how far did you move it? The Inspector provides the answers.

6   If the Inspector is not already open, click the Info button in the toolbar, or press Command-4. Click the Video tab, if necessary, and scroll down to the Transform section. If it's closed, click the word *Show* that appears when you move your pointer over the title bar.

Here, you can view, change, and even reset all the Transform parameters.

7   Click the Reset button (the curved arrow) to return all the Transform parameters to their default values. Then press Command-Z to undo.

The Reset button is a convenient way to restore your video clip to its original position, scale, rotation, and anchor point settings.

For consistency, you'll make Justine the same size in each clip. To make this value easier to remember, let's change the current Scale value to a round number.

8   Click the Scale field, type *115*, and press Return.

To change the Transform parameters in the Viewer, you clicked the Transform button to enable the Transform effect. But in the Inspector, you can make these changes without enabling the Transform effect.

Applying transformation changes in the Viewer is more direct and intuitive, but you can make more precise changes in the Inspector.

9   Set the Viewer zoom level to Fit, and in the Timeline, select the second clip, **Justine_flip_roar**.

> **TIP** ▶ When the Viewer is the active window, press Shift-Z to fit the Viewer to the window.

Since you'll be transforming the clip in the Inspector, you no longer need to make it smaller in the Viewer to access the control handles.

10   In the Inspector, scroll down to the Transform section and change Scale to 115%. Then, drag left in the Position X field to move the clip to the left. Drag right in the Position Y field to move the clip up a little. However, make sure you don't reveal the lower edge of the clip.

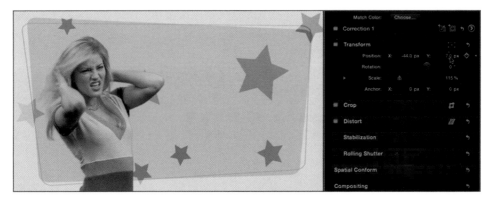

> **TIP** ▶ Option-drag in a parameter's value field in the Inspector to change the value more slowly, allowing for finer adjustments. Command-drag to change the value more quickly, allowing for very large adjustments.

11   In the Viewer, enable the Transform effect once again, and experiment by changing the Anchor Point and Rotation properties in the Inspector. Then press Command-Z to undo the changes.

The anchor point is in the middle of the bounding box, represented by a control handle that extends to the right. It is the point around which a clip scales and rotates. You can drag the handle to rotate the clip.

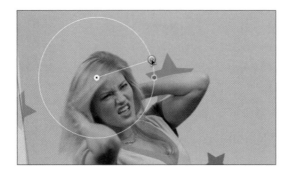

TIP ▶ When rotating a clip, Shift-drag to snap the rotation values to 45-degree increments.

The next clip must remain centered to suit the animation you'll create later, but you can change its scale to match the first two clips.

12 Select the third clip in the Timeline, **Justine_selects**, and change its Scale to 115%.

13 Select the upper copy of the last video clip in the Timeline, **Justine_turn_look**.

This clip was shot with the camera zoomed in, so it needn't be scaled. You'll move it to the left to make room for the final title.

14 In the Inspector, change Position X to –50.

> **NOTE** ▶ These Position X and Y values in the Inspector represent the percentage of the height of the clip. So a value of -50 moves the clip to the left 50 percent of its height.

The duplicate clip no longer aligns with the original. You could individually enter the same value for the lower clip, but the Inspector allows you to transform multiple clips at the same time.

15 Press Command-Z to undo the previous position change. Then in the Timeline, drag a selection rectangle to select both of the **Justine_turn_look** clips, and in the Inspector, change Position X to −50.

The value change is applied to both clips at the same time, and they stay perfectly aligned.

You can also crop and distort clips in both the Viewer and the Inspector. Although you don't need to apply these effects here, understanding how they work is useful.

16 In the Viewer, click the Crop button to enable the Crop effect and experiment with the onscreen controls, as well as changing the parameters in the Inspector. In the Inspector, click the Reset button to reset all the parameter values when you are done. Also enable the Distort effect and experiment by changing its parameters.

Each Justine clip now has a more visually dynamic and pleasing composition, plus you now have room to add titles to three of them. Before adding those titles, however, let's stylize each of the clips with some effects.

Working with Effects

You applied several keying effects in the previous lesson, but Final Cut Pro includes many other effects that allow you to create interesting looks for your footage. Once applied, many effects have parameters you can use to customize their results. You can even combine effects, and change the end result by switching their stacking order. In this exercise, you'll apply a variety of effects to give your show open a more stylized look.

Browsing, Previewing, and Applying Effects

Let's take a deeper look at the variety of effects available in Final Cut Pro X.

1 In the Timeline, select the first video clip.

2 In the toolbar, click the Effects button (or press Command-5), and select the Looks category.

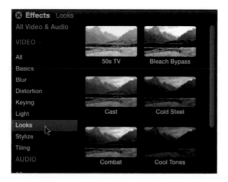

This category includes 25 effects to give your footage a specific visual character. To see more effects onscreen at once, you can hide the category names.

3 At the lower left of the Effects Browser, click the Show/Hide button.

4 Skim a few of the Looks effects to see how they appear on the first shot of Justine.

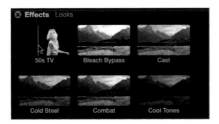

As with the Keying effects, the preview thumbnail is replaced with the shot of Justine with the effect applied, and the shot also appears in the Viewer with the effect preview applied.

NOTE ▶ The effect preview in the thumbnail and the Viewer shows just the selected clip, separate from any other composited clips.

5   Scroll down to the last row of the Looks effects, and locate the Teal & Orange effect. Double-click it to apply it to the selected clip.

TIP ▶ You can also drag an effect onto a clip. When dragging, you don't need to select the clip first. If you select multiple clips before double-clicking an effect, that effect will be applied to all the selected clips.

The Teal & Orange effect creates an interesting look. Let's leave it in place for now.

6   In the Timeline, select the second video clip.

7   In the Effects Browser, click the Show/Hide button to show the category names. Select the Stylize category.

While most of the effects in the Looks category change only the colors of a video clip, these 22 effects add textures, graphics, and even animation.

8   Preview a few of the effects. Then, locate the Graphic effect and apply it to the second Justine clip.

This effect's default parameters create an extreme black-and-white version of the image, which looks interesting but may be too different compared to the other clips. You'll readjust these effects shortly; but first, you'll apply an effect to each of the last two clips.

9 In the Timeline, select the third video clip, and in the Effects Browser, select the Basics category.

The Basics category contains some of the most useful and versatile effects.

10 Preview several of the effects, and then apply the first Basic effect, Black & White, to the selected clip.

Later, you'll isolate this effect so that Justine will appear in color inside the shape she draws in front of her, and black and white outside the shape.

11 In the Timeline, select the top copy of the last video clip, and from the Basics category, apply the Hue/Saturation effect.

The default settings of the Hue/Saturation filter make the shot of Justine pop with color.

Now that you have applied an effect to each clip, let's see how to modify them.

Modifying and Combining Effects

Some effects are pretty much "what you see is what you get," while others include adjustable parameters that can create many different looks. Let's see how you can alter the effects you've applied.

1   Select the first video clip. Open the Inspector, if necessary, and locate the Teal & Orange effect controls.

The Amount parameter is set to 50 by default.

2   Drag the Amount slider to increase its value to 100, and then experiment with the other parameters.

Notice that when you adjust the Protect Skin parameter, it removes the Teal & Orange effect from Justine's skin. In this case, it just barely affects her gray clothing, so you can return its value to 0.

Having played with the other parameters, you may have noticed that the overall impact of the effect is a little too intense with an Amount value of 100.

3   Set Protect Highlights back to 0. Set Amount to about 70, and Shadows to about 0.8, and then toggle the effect visibility off and on by clicking the blue checkbox next to the effect name. Because your eyes quickly adjust to an effect, it's easy to forget how much it impacts a clip until you turn it off.

You can also apply multiple effects to a single clip. While the order of the effects can change their impact, it's easy to reorganize them.

4   In the Effects Browser, select the Light category, and add the Glow effect to the first
video clip.

The Glow effect appears in the Inspector below the Teal & Orange effect. Effects are
applied in the Inspector from the top down. In this case, the stacking order blows out
the highlights in Justine's face and hair to a complete white.

5   In the Inspector, drag the Glow effect above the Teal & Orange effect.

The hair highlights now have more detail, but they have turned too yellow, and this
combination of the two effects causes the overall image to be overly bright.

6   In the Teal & Orange effect parameters, drag the Protect Highlights slider all the way
to the right and the Shadows slider all the way to the left. Toggle each effect on and
off to see its impact.

That looks better. Let's move on to the next clip.

7 Select the second video clip, and in the Inspector, locate the controls for the Graphic effect.

> **TIP** You can click the disclosure triangles to hide added effects in the Video Inspector and reduce the need for scrolling. You can hide the parameter controls for the default Color, Transform, and other properties by placing the pointer over the top edge of each effect's title bar and clicking the word *Hide* when it appears.

8 Set the Amount to about 50.

Decreasing the Amount value reintroduces some color into the clip and makes its appearance more consistent with the first clips. Still, it's different enough to indicate a new "look."

> **NOTE** ▶ In the next lesson, you will animate parameters of this effect so that it changes over time.

You don't need to adjust the Black & White effect on the third clip, but the last clip could use some tweaking.

9 Select the top copy of the last video clip.

10 Try adjusting the Hue/Saturation effect parameters, turning the effect off completely, changing the blend mode or the opacity of the clip, or using a combination of these adjustments to get a look that you like.

> **TIP** Press V to temporarily disable the top clip and see just the bottom clip.

By combining effects with blend modes and opacity levels, you have a great deal of control over the look of your footage.

11 Experiment with different effects and combinations of effects on each of the video clips. There is no right answer here. Just make sure to leave the third clip with only the Black & White effect applied because you'll continue to work with it in the next lesson.

Creating Titles

The written word can support, clarify, and amplify the communication of your video and graphics. And by animating that text, you increase your viewer's attention.

To be effective, all text and its animation should support the look and feel of the video. The Final Cut Pro Titles Browser contains myriad animated text options, all of which can be customized in the Viewer and the Inspector.

In this exercise, you'll browse, apply, edit, and stylize an animated title. Then you'll build your own text animation using another title as a starting point. You'll finish by creating Spanish versions of your English titles, and you'll use roles and subroles to organize, view, and export those titles.

Modifying Titles

Your show open will have four titles, one for each video clip. The first three will be "teaser" titles, describing different aspects of iJustine's character: Bold, Brash, and Colorful. The last title will display the name of the show (iJustine) and its time slot (Tuesdays 8pm).

1   In the Timeline, move the playhead to the frame in the last video clip where Justine freezes, at about 10:05. This is the frame where the title should begin animating onto the screen. (Note that no clips need to be selected.)

   TIP ▶ To locate this frame precisely, you could select one of the copies of the final video clip, press Command-R to show the Retime Editor, and place the playhead at the start of the Hold segment.

2   In the toolbar, open the Titles Browser.

The Titles Browser contains over 160 title styles, organized into five categories. Most of the titles animate, and you can preview and modify all of them to suit your needs.

3   Select a few categories and skim the thumbnails slowly to preview several titles.

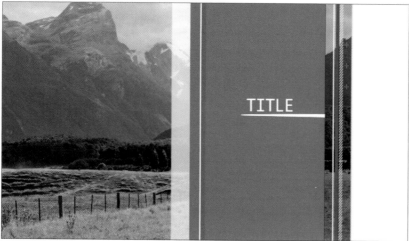

Some titles include animated graphics. Some are part of a theme, as indicated by the theme name below a divider bar.

TIP ▶ Titles and transitions that are part of a theme are also available in the Themes Browser, which you can open by clicking the Themes button in the toolbar.

For this show open, you don't need any additional graphics, just an animated title.

4   Select the Build In/Out category, and skim the Drifting thumbnail to preview the title animation. This title could work well as a starting point.

5   Click the Drifting thumbnail to select the title, and press Q to connect it to the primary storyline at the playhead position. Instead of pressing Q, you can also drag a title to the Timeline.

NOTE ▶ If you don't select the title before pressing Q, the last selected clip in the Event Browser is edited into the Timeline.

TIP ▶ Two titles—Basic Title and Basic Lower Third—can be added to the Timeline by choosing Edit > Connect Title, or pressing Control-T for the Basic Title or Shift-Control-T for the Basic Lower Third.

The title appears in the Timeline as a purple bar with its name, Drifting, and a line connecting it to the primary storyline.

6   Click the purple bar to select the title, and press / (slash) to play the title.

The title animates onto the screen, drifts, and then animates off. If you enabled looping (choose View > Playback > Loop Playback, or press Command-L), it will continue to play. However, the repeating music track can be distracting.

7   Select the green **Two Seater Short** audio clip. Choose Clip > Disable, or press V, to disable the clip. Then reselect and play the title clip.

You can now concentrate on the title design in silence. As a first step, the title might look more integrated into the scene if it animated onto the screen from behind Justine.

8 Shift-drag the Drifting title below the two **Justine_turn_look** clips.

The title now animates behind Justine. The white borders around each line of text indicate that you can change the text directly in the Viewer. You can even independently change the position of each line of text.

9 With the playhead near the middle of the title clip (so that you can see most of the text in the Viewer), double-click the word *Title* and type *iJustine*.

Notice that while you are in text-entry mode the box around the text is replaced by a white underline, and a control handle appears at the midpoint of that line.

10 Drag the control handle to move the top line of text up and to the right.

11 Double-click the *Subtitle* text, and type *Tuesdays 8pm*. Drag this title below and slightly to the left of the iJustine title, and then press Esc (Escape) to exit text-entry mode.

Clearly, the font is too large for this second line of text. You can change its size and other attributes of the text in the Inspector.

12 Open the Inspector by pressing Command-4, if necessary, and click the Title button.

Remember, like the effects, transitions, and generators you've been working with, all of these titles are Motion projects. The Title Inspector contains only those parameters that the Motion title designer published to Final Cut Pro X. Sometimes they are duplicates of parameters in the Text Inspector.

For this title, you can quickly change its font, size, and color in the Title Inspector. You can also turn off the incoming and outgoing animations.

13 In the Title Inspector, from the Line 1 Font pop-up menu, choose the Coolvetica font.

TIP ▶ Fonts are listed alphabetically.

Each font listed in the pop-up menu appears in the correct style, and as you scroll through the list, the text in the Viewer updates so you preview each font in context.

NOTE ▶ The menu includes all the fonts installed on your system, so your menu may differ from the previous screenshot.

14 Change the Line 2 Font to Helvetica and the Line 2 Size to 100. Then, double-click the second line in the Viewer and drag the control handle to move this line closer to the first line. Press Esc to exit text-entry mode.

15 In the Title Inspector, click the arrow next to the Line 1 color well and change the color of the iJustine text to a deep purple. Then, play the title.

The font, size, position, and color of the text all look good, as does the incoming animation. However, because this is the last shot and the text is the key information you want the viewers to read, it shouldn't animate offscreen.

16 At the top of the Title Inspector, deselect the Build Out checkbox.

Now the text continues to drift right to the end of the title. However, the title is a little shorter than the video clip.

17 Stop playback, and in the Timeline, trim the end point of the title clip to match the end points of the video clips above it.

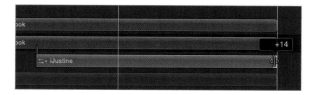

The text could use a more prominent drop shadow to separate it from the background. Text attributes not available in the Title Inspector are found in the Text Inspector.

18 In the Inspector, click the Text button.

While the parameters available in the Title Inspector will differ from title to title (depending on which parameters the title designer published in Motion), the parameters in the Text Inspector are always the same. Here, you can change the basic formatting of the text (including the Font and Size parameters that you already adjusted in the Title Inspector), as well as the style of the text, including its Face, Outline, Glow, and Drop Shadow parameters.

19 Move the pointer over the Drop Shadow title bar, and click the word *Show* when it appears. Then increase Blur to 6 and Distance to 20.

A soft drop shadow sets the text off from the background.

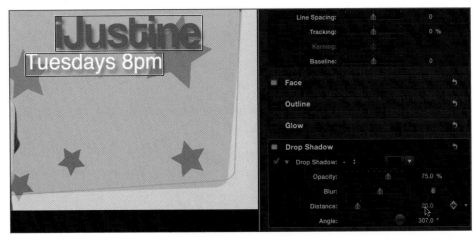

TIP ▶ When nothing is selected in the Viewer, parameter changes made in the Text Inspector affect all lines of text. To change a specific line of text, select it in the Viewer before changing parameters in the Text Inspector. You can also change individual characters or a range of characters by first selecting them in the Viewer.

20 Press / (slash) to play the title.

The titles are looking good! Now let's take advantage of all the work you've done to make it easier to create the remaining three titles.

Using Text Styles and the Custom Title

Final Cut Pro includes a variety of text styles to apply to your text. You can also save your own text styles and apply them to text in any generator or to the title of any project. In the next exercise, you'll save the iJustine text style to use as you build the three remaining titles for this project. And instead of using a title that is already animated, you'll use a custom title that lets you design your own animation.

1 In the Viewer, double-click the iJustine text to select it. Then, in the Text Inspector, click the Style pop-up menu (the bar at the top that reads *Normal*).

From this menu, you can choose a preset text style or you can save your own.

2 Choose Save All Basic+Style Attributes, name the preset *iJustine*, and click Save.

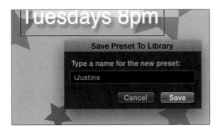

Choosing Save All saves the preset with both the basic font information (font, size, and alignment) and the Style attributes (face color, drop shadow, and so on). Let's apply this preset to a new title template.

3   In the Timeline, move the playhead over the first video clip and place it on the frame where Justine freezes, at about 0:23.

4   In the Titles Browser, in the Build In/Build Out category, select the Custom title. Press Q to connect it to the primary storyline at the playhead position. Then, trim the end point of the title to match the end point of the first video clip.

The title now matches the duration of the Hold segment. Let's apply the new text style to it.

5   In the Timeline, select the Custom title. In the Text Inspector, from the Style pop-up menu, choose the iJustine style that now appears in the list.

The font, size, color, and drop-shadow settings all change to match the saved text style. That's quite a timesaver! However, the title still needs a few tweaks to work in the context of this video clip.

6   In the Viewer, double-click the text and type *Bold*. Then move it to the left, press the Esc key, and increase the Size to about 350. Press / (slash) to play the title.

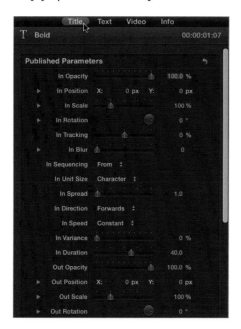

By default, the Custom title isn't animated. Rather, you choose the parameters you want to animate.

7   Stop playback. In the Inspector, click the Title button.

The Title Inspector contains a long list of Published Parameters. The first 13 parameters start with the word *In* and control the title's animation onto the screen. The next 13 parameters are exactly the same except that they start with the word *Out* and control the title's animation off the screen. You'll just animate the title onto the screen by first animating its Opacity value.

8   Drag the In Opacity parameter slider to 0, and then press / (slash) to play the title clip.

Each letter of the word *Bold* now starts with an opacity of 0% and animates to an opacity of 100%, one after the other.

9   Stop playback and increase the In Scale parameter to 400%. Play the title.

Now each letter starts at 0% opacity and 400% scale and animates to 100% opacity and 100% scale, thereby creating the appearance of floating down onto the screen. Because text scales from its baseline, each letter starts high on the screen. You can use the Position parameter to center them.

10   Stop playback and drag left in the In Position Y field to about –25 as you watch the animating character in the Viewer move down until it's centered horizontally with the characters that have finished animating. Play the title.

11   Stop playback. To add a little more spice to the animation, change the In Rotation value to –90 degrees. Play the title.

Now each character starts rotated 90 degrees clockwise and spins into place as it scales down, fades up, and moves up.

Currently, each letter completes its animation before the next one begins, which can feel a little "clunky." The In Spread parameter determines how many characters are animating at once.

12 Stop playback, change the In Spread value to 3, and play the title.

The animation lasts for the same total duration (determined by the length of the bar in the Timeline); but at any point in time, three letters are animating at once. In other words, the animation spreads across more characters, resulting in a smoother animation sequence.

However, it still takes too long for the animation to complete. The clip ends before the animation is finished!

13 Stop playback and reduce In Duration from the default value of 40 to 12 frames.

The title now animates on in just 12 frames. The snappier animation matches the feel that you want and gives the viewer enough time to read the word.

From this point, it's quick and easy to apply copies of this title to the next two video clips.

14 Press Command-C to copy the selected Bold clip, move the playhead to the first Hold segment of the second video clip (at about 3:11), and press Command-V to paste a copy of the clip, which will connect to the primary storyline at the playhead.

15 Trim the copied title to match the end of the second video clip. Then select the title, and edit the text to read *Brash*. Reposition the title next to Justine and adjust the font size as necessary. Feel free to play with the animation settings to create a different animation.

16 Move the playhead over the third clip on the frame where Justine finishes expanding the imaginary square and looks at the camera, at about 7:00. Paste a copy of the title here, trim it to match the end of the video clip, and change the text to read *Colorful*.

Drag it directly above Justine. Adjust the font size to fit the box. Select each letter, and in the Face section of the Text Inspector, assign a new color to every other letter. Again, feel free to adjust the animation.

NOTE ▶ You'll make Justine herself appear "colorful" in the next lesson.

17 Select the audio clip, press V to enable it, and play the full project.

NOTE ▶ Depending on your hardware, you may need to render the project to play it at the full frame rate. To do so, choose Modify > Render All, or press Control-Shift-R to render the project.

You've integrated titles into your show open that match the look and pacing of the video and background graphics. As a final step, you'll use the powerful roles feature to create an alternate version of the titles in another language.

Using Roles with Titles

Roles allow you to tag audio clips based on the contents, such as dialogue, music, or effects. But roles can also be used on clips and titles. For example, many shows are produced in multiple languages for international viewing. You can create and assign subroles to different versions of a Titles role, and then enable just the language you want to view or export.

For your show open, you'll first create copies of each title and translate them into Spanish. Then you'll create new English and Spanish subroles for the Titles role, and assign these subroles to the appropriate titles. Finally, you'll learn how you can export different language versions of your show open.

1   In the Timeline, select the first title, Bold. Press the Up Arrow to move the playhead to the start point of the title. Press Command-C to copy it and then press Command-V to paste a copy directly above it.

> **NOTE ▶** If the copied upper clip is positioned one frame before the lower clip, press Command-Z to undo, press the Right Arrow key to move forward one frame, and press Command-V to paste.

2   Select the lower Bold clip, and press V to disable it. Then select the upper Bold clip, and in the Viewer, change the text to *Audaz*, which is the Spanish word for "bold." Adjust the font size and title position as necessary, and press Esc to exit text-entry mode.

> **TIP ▶** In addition to working in the Viewer, you can also change text in the Text Inspector's Text box.

By disabling the lower copy of the title, you have an unobstructed view of the top copy. Because the Spanish translation contains more characters, you need to reduce the font size.

3   Repeat the previous two steps with the next title. Duplicate the *Brash* title, disable it, change the duplicate to read *Pintoresca*, and adjust the font size and position as necessary.

TIP ▶ You may find it easier to change the font size before typing the new characters because the Spanish word is so much longer than the English word.

4   Repeat the steps with the next title, replacing the copied title *Colorful* with *Atrevida*.

TIP ▶ If you select and replace one letter at a time, you can maintain the unique face color of each letter. Fortunately, in this case, the translated word has the same number of characters.

5   For the final title, once again copy and paste it with the playhead on the first frame, and change only the *Tuesdays 8pm* line to read *Martes 20:00*. Press the Esc key.

TIP ▶ Instead of copying and pasting each title individually, you could select all the titles, and with the playhead located at the start point of the first title, press Command-C and then press Command-V to create a copy of every title on top of itself.

6   Select one of the lower English titles, then Command-click the others to select them all. Press V to enable them all. Then click in an empty area to deselect everything.

Rather than selecting every title in a language to disable or enable them, you can use the power of roles. To do so, you will start with every title enabled.

7   Press Shift-Z to fit the Timeline to the window. At the lower left of the Timeline, click the Show/Hide Timeline Index button, or press Command-Shift-2.

8   In the Timeline Index, click the Roles button, if necessary, and then select the Titles role.

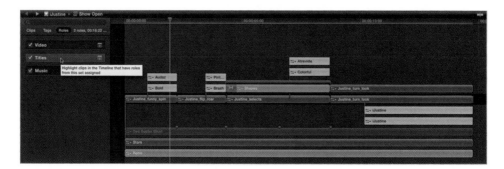

All the titles in the timeline are highlighted because they all are assigned to the Titles role. To distinguish between English and Spanish titles, you'll create subroles.

9   Choose Modify > Edit Roles to open the Role Editor.

10 In the Role column, select the Titles role. Then, in the Subrole column, click the Add (+) button twice to create two new subroles. Name the first subrole *English* and the second *Spanish*.

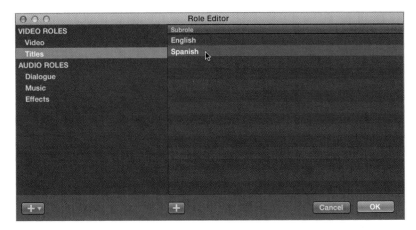

With the subroles defined, you can assign them to the appropriate titles.

11 Click OK to close the Role Editor. In the Timeline Index, click below all the roles to deselect the Titles role.

12 In the Timeline, select the first lower title (English), and then Command-click the other three English titles.

13 In the Inspector, click the Info button. From the Roles pop-up menu, choose the English subrole.

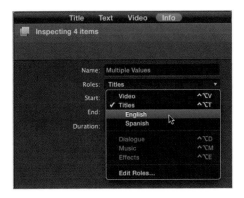

TIP ▶ Alternatively, you could choose Modify > Assign Roles > English.

The new subrole is assigned to the selected titles, and appears in the Timeline Index.

14 Select all the upper titles (Spanish), and in the Info Inspector, assign the Spanish subrole. Now both subroles appear under the Titles role in the Timeline Index.

15 In the Timeline Index, deselect the English subrole.

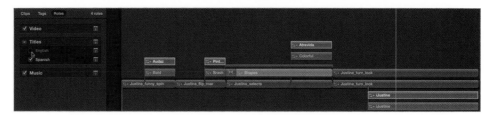

Now only the Spanish titles are visible in the project because all the English titles are disabled. As you can see, by using roles you can quickly turn the titles for a specific language on or off, and then export a movie for a particular language.

You can also export the titles as separate tracks of a QuickTime movie.

16 Choose Share > Export Media.

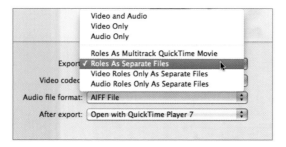

In the Export options, you can choose to export roles as tracks in a multitrack QuickTime movie or as separate files. You can also choose to include an alpha channel to export your titles with a transparent background.

17 Choose "Roles as Separate Files," and from the Video Codec pop-up menu, choose ProRes 4444. Then, click the Roles button.

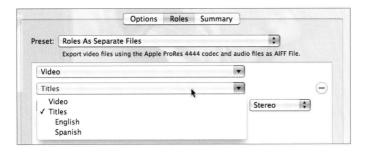

Here, you can choose which title subroles to export. By default, all titles will be exported, but for this project, you want to export English titles separate from the Spanish titles.

18 From the Titles pop-up menu, choose English. Click the Add Video File button, and from the pop-up menu, choose Spanish.

Now you will export each title language as a separate movie, so that it can be composited back into the show in another application.

19 Click Next, choose a location, and click Save to render the movies. Then, play the movie files.

Good work. You've applied the edited and keyed clips you created in the last lesson, and given your show open a better layout by transforming clips. You've also achieved a stylized look by adding effects, and added punch and meaning with animated titles. In the next lesson, you'll complete your iJustine open by animating many of its other components.

Lesson Review

1. True or false: When dragging a corner control handle to scale a video clip with the Transform effect enabled, you need to hold down the Shift key to scale the clip proportionally.

2. How can you change the position or scale of a video clip without enabling the Transform effect?

3. Describe two ways to apply an effect to a selected clip.

4. When applying multiple effects to a clip, what determines the order in which the effects are applied?

5. In what two ways can you change the content of a title?

6. You've modified a line of text in a title by changing the font to Impact and the face color to red. You then saved a text style by choosing "Save Style Attributes." When you apply this new text style to a title that is in the Helvetica font, will the font change to Impact? Will the color change to red?

7. What role is automatically assigned to titles by default and how can you tell?

8. Describe one way to create a new subrole.

Answers

1. False. You need to Shift-drag only when moving one of the control handles at the midpoint of a bounding box edge.

2. Change the Transform parameters in the Video Inspector.

3. Double-click the effect, or drag it onto the clip.

4. The stacking order of the effects in the Inspector. The effects are applied from the top down.

5. With the title in the Timeline selected, double-click the text in the Viewer to enter text-entry mode and type the new text; or, in the Text Inspector, type in the Text box.

6. The color will change to red but the font will not change. To change both, you need to choose Save All Basic+Style Attributes from the Text Styles pop-up menu in the Text Inspector.

7. Titles are assigned the Titles role, which you can see by opening the Timeline Index and selecting the Titles role. This action will highlight all the titles in the Timeline. Or, you can select a title, and in the Info Inspector, the Roles pop-up menu will identify the assigned role.

8. Choose Modify > Edit Roles; or in the Info Inspector, from the Roles pop-up menu, choose Edit Roles. Then, select the role, click the Add (+) button in the Subrole column, and name the new role.

Keyboard Shortcuts

Command-Shift-2	Show/Hide Timeline Index
Command-E	Export media
Command-L	Loop playback
Control-R	Render selection
Control-Shift-R	Render all
Control-Option-T	Assign the Titles role to a clip
Control-Option-V	Assign the Video role to a clip

9

Time

Goals

This lesson takes approximately 90 minutes to complete.

Create animation using keyframes

Keyframe in the Inspector

Keyframe in the Video Animation Editor

Animate a generator

Create a travel matte

Animate with transitions

Lesson **9**

Creating Animation

Video is all about movement: engaging the eye with moving light and shadow that the viewer interprets as a sun rising, a man and woman dancing, or smoke drifting lazily from a chimney.

You can support and enhance movement in your videos by creating motion of your own, as you did in the previous lesson with animated titles. In this lesson, you'll learn how to enhance any clip by animating its properties.

In Final Cut Pro X, you can create animation with keyframes. You set keyframes with different values for a single parameter at two points in the Timeline, and Final Cut Pro will animate, or *interpolate*, the parameter values between the keyframes.

You can also create animation using transitions, and certain effects can be animated to turn on and off with a simple slider.

In this lesson, you'll complete your show open by animating the position of the video clips, animating an effect, and animating the rectangle shape to match Justine's hand movements. You'll build on your compositing skills as you make her appear in color inside the rectangle. Finally, you'll apply transitions to create animation from one clip to the next.

Animating Clip Position

Justine makes a dramatic move at the beginning of the first two video clips: spinning around in the first clip, and flipping back her hair in the second. But in each shot, she starts onscreen with her back to the camera. You can use keyframes to slide her onto the screen as she makes her move.

A keyframe locks the value of a specific parameter value—such as position, scale, or blur amount—at a specific point in time. By creating two or more keyframes at different points in time, each with different values, Final Cut Pro will change, or *interpolate,* the parameter value between the keyframes, thereby animating the parameter.

You can create and manipulate keyframes in the Viewer, the Inspector, and the Timeline.

To start working with keyframes, you'll continue to use the **Show Open** compound clip you've been building in the preceding two lessons.

> **NOTE ▶** If you didn't complete the last lesson, you'll find a completed project for you to use on the APTS FCP X ADV Part 2 mounted disk image. In the Project Library, open the Lesson 9 folder, and duplicate the **Lesson 9 Start** project (don't include the render files.) Double-click the duplicate to open it into the Timeline.

Keyframing in the Viewer

You can set keyframes to animate clip transformations directly in the Viewer. In this exercise, you'll animate the position of the starting video clip so that Justine flies in from the left as she spins around to face the camera.

1   In the Timeline index, make sure that only the English titles are enabled, and then close the Timeline Index and any Effects Browsers. Press Shift-Z to fit the project to the window.

2   In the Timeline, select the `Justine_funny_spin` clip, and then move the playhead to the start of the project. This is the first frame of the first video clip, and Justine's back is to the camera. You'll move her offscreen at this frame.

3   In the Viewer, click the Transform button to enable the Transform effect.

As you've already seen, a bounding box appears around the clip.

4   In the Viewer, drag the clip to the left until Justine disappears completely offscreen. Watch the bottom of the bounding box to keep the clip aligned to the bottom of the frame.

You've now changed the position of the clip for every frame—so Justine will never appear. You want to set this new position value for the starting frame only; you do so by setting a keyframe.

5   At the top left of the Viewer, click the Add Keyframe button.

The white diamond turns orange to indicate that a keyframe now exists at the current playhead location for all the Transform properties: Position, Rotation, Scale, and

Anchor. The values for each of these parameters are now "fixed" for this frame. The only parameter you want to change is Position.

However, adding a keyframe for a parameter at one point in time does not create animation. You need at least two keyframes, at different points in time, with different values.

6   Tap the Right Arrow key six times to move the playhead forward six frames, to 0:06.

This is the frame where you want Justine to arrive at her "landing" position.

7   In the Viewer, drag the clip right to the middle of the frame. Make sure to keep the bottom bounding box line just outside the frame so that Justine isn't cut off.

Because you already set one keyframe for the position of this clip at a different point in time, Final Cut Pro automatically sets a keyframe when you change the position of the clip directly in the Viewer. The red line, called the motion path, indicates the clip's line of movement.

8   Press the / (slash) key to play the clip. Observe the animation, and then stop playback if looping is enabled.

Justine now animates onto the screen from the left as she spins around. However, since she stops in the center of the frame, the word *Bold* appears on top of her.

To fix this, you must adjust the value of this second keyframe; but to do so, you need to park the playhead on the frame that contains it. You can navigate to keyframes directly in the Viewer.

9   Stop the playhead when you can see the *Bold* title over Justine so that it is past the second keyframe. In the Viewer, click the left arrow near the Add Keyframe button to move the playhead to the last keyframe.

The Add Keyframe button turns orange to indicate that the playhead is parked on a keyframe.

10 In the Viewer, drag the clip to position Justine a bit farther to the right. Then, play the clip.

11 If you've moved her so far that her left hand is cut off, stop playback, move the playhead back to the second keyframe, and readjust her position.

NOTE ► If you adjust the position of the clip when the playhead is not parked on a keyframe, you'll set a new, third keyframe at this frame.

TIP ► To move the entire motion path without setting a new keyframe, Command-Option-drag one of the keyframes on the red motion path line.

Using two keyframes, Final Cut Pro creates a straight motion path. But you can also create a curved path.

12 Control-click (or right-click) the endpoint of the motion path, and from the shortcut menu, choose Smooth.

With Smooth chosen, you can create a curved motion path by dragging the Bezier handles that extend from the endpoint of the motion path.

13 Drag an end of the Bezier handles to create a curve in the motion path, and then play the clip to see the result.

TIP ▶ To see exactly how the animation unfolds, tap the Right and Left Arrow keys to step through the animation frame-by-frame.

Justine now dips down as she comes into the frame and then pops up again. For this clip, however, a straight horizontal animation is all you need.

14 Adjust the Bezier handles so that they are horizontal with the motion path.

Setting keyframes in the Viewer is tactile and intuitive, but it does have limitations. For example, when you dragged the clip of Justine left and right, you might also have accidentally dragged her up or down, changing the end points of her motion path. You also can't set specific values for keyframes in the Viewer, and you can't change the location of keyframes in time to speed up or slow down the animation.

To perform those actions, you use the Inspector and the Video Animation Editor.

Keyframing in the Inspector

In the Inspector, you can set keyframes for just those parameters you want to animate, and you can change their values precisely. Let's use the Inspector to animate the position of the second video clip.

1   In the Timeline, select the **Justine_flip_roar** clip, and then tap the Up Arrow until the playhead moves to the start of the clip.

In this first frame, Justine is bending forward before she rises up and flips back her hair. Let's position her below the screen, and then animate her up into view. You'll work backwards this time: first, you'll set the keyframe for her final position, and then you'll set the keyframe for her offscreen starting position.

2   Tap the Right Arrow key six times to move the playhead forward six frames, to about 2:12. Make sure the Transform effect is still active in the Viewer (the button should be blue, and you should see a bounding box around the clip).

This six-frame animation will match the duration of the first clip's animation.

3   Open the Inspector, if necessary (press Command-4), and scroll down to the Transform section.

For the previous clip, you clicked the Add Keyframe button in the Viewer to set a keyframe. Let's now see exactly what that does.

4   In the Viewer, click the Add Keyframe button while keeping an eye on the Inspector.

In the Inspector, orange diamonds appear next to all four Transform parameters, indicating that a keyframe is set for each parameter at the current playhead location. It doesn't hurt to have them all keyframed (because you need two keyframes at different points in time with different values to create animation), but by creating keyframes in the Inspector instead of in the Viewer, you can set keyframes for just those parameters you want to animate.

5   Press Command-Z to undo the keyframes. Then in the Inspector, move the pointer over the Position parameter, click the triangle that appears to the right, and from the pop-up menu, choose Add Keyframe.

Now an orange diamond appears only next to the Position parameter, indicating a keyframe at the playhead.

TIP ▶ You can also create a keyframe by clicking the gray diamond that highlights yellow with the + (plus sign) when you move the pointer over a parameter.

With the clip's ending position locked in place, you can now set its starting position.

6   Press the Up Arrow to move the playhead to the start of the clip.

7   In the Inspector, drag left on the Position Y value until Justine moves down out of the shot. A red line in the Viewer indicates the motion path, and a small gray arrow indicates the starting and ending keyframes.

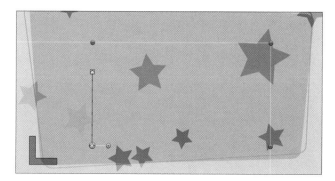

8   Press / (slash) to play the clip.

Justine now animates up from offscreen. And because you changed just the Y-position value in the Inspector, you know her motion path doesn't shift right or left.

NOTE ▶ You don't need to enable the Transform effect to set keyframes in the Inspector. However, you can't see the resulting motion path or switch between Linear and Smooth without enabling the effect.

Keyframing in the Video Animation Editor

You've keyframed the position of the first two video clips using both the Viewer and the Inspector. But you can also work with keyframes in the Timeline using the Video

Animation Editor. You can set keyframes, move keyframes in time, change the value of certain parameters, and fade certain effects.

1   Select the first video clip, **Justine_funny_spin**, and choose Clip > Show Video Animation (or press Control-V). Then press Command-= (equal sign) to zoom in. You may need to scroll vertically and/or horizontally to frame the clip.

The Video Animation Editor opens above the selected clip with blue bars for opacity, transformations, color corrections, and applied effects stacked up from the bottom. As in the Inspector, each bar contains a blue checkbox you can click to toggle the effect on or off.

2   Click the blue checkbox for the Transform effect, and then play the clip.

The bar turns gray to indicate that the effect is disabled, and the clip position no longer animates.

The diamonds along the line in the Transform effect bar indicate the keyframes for this effect. Notice that two diamonds are stacked on top of each other at the start point of the clip. These indicate that keyframes are set for at least two parameters on this frame. You can choose which keyframes to display.

3   Enable the Transform effect again, and then click the triangle next to "Transform: All", and choose Position.

Now only the single Position keyframe appears at the start point of the clip.

You can change the timing of a keyframed animation by moving the keyframes in the Video Animation Editor.

4   Drag the second keyframe to the right and play the clip.

Justine now takes much longer to slide across the screen.

You can also use the Video Animation Editor to animate other effects.

5   Undo the keyframe move, click the close button (X) at the upper left to close the Video Animation Editor for this clip, and then select the next video clip. Press Control-V to open the Video Animation Editor for that clip.

TIP   Pressing Control-V will also close the Animation Editor if it is open.

Effects that include a small disclosure triangle in the upper right of the bar can be animated to fade in and out by dragging handles.

6   Click the disclosure triangle for the Graphic effect to expand it. If necessary, click the triangle next to the name of the Graphic effect and select the Amount parameter.

TIP   You can also double-click any effect that has a disclosure triangle to expand or collapse it.

The horizontal line in the middle of the bar represents the value of the selected parameter—in this case, the Amount for the Graphic effect. You can drag up or down on the line to change the value.

7 In the Video Inspector, locate the Graphic effect, and note that the Amount value is around 50. In the Video Animation Editor, drag up and down on the horizontal control to change the value, noting the change in the pop-up window, the Inspector, and the Viewer.

Rather than setting a constant value, we'd like this effect to "turn on" over time. In other words, we'd like the Amount value to change from 0 to 50. You can accomplish this task in the Video Animation Editor by dragging the fade handles or by creating keyframes.

8 Drag the left fade handle to the right about 15 frames to fade in the Amount parameter, and play the clip.

The effect now animates on during the first 15 frames. But it would look better if the effect didn't start fading on until the point that Justine freezes. For this task, you need to use keyframes.

9 Undo the fade adjustment, or drag the fade handle back to 0.

10 Move the playhead to the frame where Justine freezes, at about 3:11 (where the titles start). Then, Option-click the horizontal control at the playhead to set a keyframe.

Option-clicking anywhere on the horizontal control sets a keyframe for the selected parameter.

11 Set a second keyframe about six frames later.

TIP ► You don't have to move the playhead to the frame where you want the keyframe, but doing so can help guide you to a specific frame.

12 Drag the first keyframe all the way down to 0, and then play the clip.

The clip starts out with no effect applied, and then the Graphic effect ramps up quickly when Justine freezes.

You can even change how an effect changes between the two keyframes.

13 Control-click the sloped line between the two keyframes.

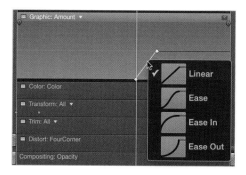

The pop-up menu includes four options. The default option, Linear, creates a constant rate of change between the parameter values. The other options create a smoother start or ending to the animation, or both. In this case, the animation is so short that these changes won't be perceptible.

You can also adjust all the keyframes on a curve at once.

14 Click to close the pop-up menu, then drag the sloped curve up between the keyframes. The entire curve moves up so that the Amount parameter starts with a nonzero value.

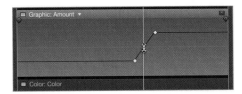

TIP ▶ When more than two keyframes are applied, dragging a segment between two keyframes moves only part of the curve. To move the entire curve in those cases, Command-Option-drag any part of the curve.

Now that you've covered the basics of creating animation in the Viewer, Inspector, and Video Animation Editor, let's tackle an animation that requires animating more than one parameter and more than two keyframes.

NOTE ▶ The Audio Animation Editor, also available from the Clip menu, works in a similar fashion when animating audio effects.

Animating a Generator

In the third video clip, Justine reaches up to grab something, pulls it down, expands it, gives an approving look, and finally swipes it away. In an earlier lesson, you composited a rectangle on top of her using a generator. Now, you'll use keyframes to animate the rectangle to follow her hand movements. As you work, you'll use the Viewer, Inspector, and Video Animation Editor.

1 With the second video clip selected, press Control-V to close its Video Animation Editor. Now select the storyline containing the Shapes generator, and scroll over in the Timeline to frame it.

NOTE ▶ Make sure you've selected the Storyline containing the Shapes generator and not the clip itself.

Animating the generator will be easier if it isn't in a storyline.

2   From the Clip menu, choose Break Apart Clip Items, or press Shift-Command-G. In the warning dialog that appears, click Break Apart.

The storyline and the transition are removed, and you have direct access to the connected Shapes clip.

3   Press Control-V to reveal the Video Animation Editor for the Shapes clip, and zoom in and scroll down, if necessary, to frame it in the Timeline.

You'll animate both the Position and Scale parameters of this generator to have it follow Justine's fingers. You'll start in the middle of the clip, at the point Justine has expanded the rectangle to its full size, and then work backward and forward from this frame.

4   Move the playhead to the frame where Justine has finished moving her fingers outward to expand the square, at about 6:16.

This is the frame where the rectangle will stop scaling up. You'll use the Transform effect to line up the rectangle corners with her fingers, and then set keyframes for Scale and Position parameters.

5   In the Viewer, click the Transform effect button if necessary, and then scale and reposition the square so that the upper-left and lower-right corners align with Justine's

fingertips. Drag the control handles along the sides of the bounding box to scale it non-proportionally, as needed.

TIP You may want to change the zoom level in the Viewer to make it easier to select the bounding box handles, and you may also want to turn off snapping by pressing N.

6   In the Video Inspector, set keyframes for Position and Scale.

With the rectangle now locked in place at this frame, you'll move to the frame where Justine starts to drag out the edges, add keyframes for Position at that frame, and then move the rectangle to once more align with her fingers.

7   Press the Left Arrow key to move back frame by frame until just before Justine's fingers start to move apart, at about 6:04.

8   In the Viewer, drag the center of the bounding box to position it on Justine's fingertips.

TIP You could make the rectangle small enough to place her fingers behind the corners, but the overall animation will work better if you leave it large enough to frame her eyes and center it on her fingers.

A red motion path appears in the Viewer, yellow diamonds appear for all the Transform parameters in the Inspector, and blue double diamonds appear in the Video Animation Editor in the Timeline.

9   Press / (slash) to play the clip.

The rectangle moves into position, but it doesn't grow at all. We didn't change its scale because of what Justine does before this animation.

10   Move the playhead to the frame where Justine stops pulling her finger down, at about 5:08.

At this frame, her finger is quite far from the center of the rectangle. To deal with this, we can scale down the rectangle so that its edge covers her finger here.

11 With the playhead positioned at 5:08, in the Viewer, drag a corner bounding-box handle to decrease the scale until it covers her finger.

This action set new Scale keyframes at 5:08.

12 Play through the animation.

It's getting there, but you don't want the scale of the rectangle to change between 5:08 and 6:04. So, you need to place a Scale keyframe at 6:04 with the exact same values as at 5:08.

13 In the Inspector, click the disclosure triangle for Scale to reveal the individual X and Y parameters. Change their values to the nearest whole number to make them easier to remember.

14 Click the arrow to the right of the yellow Scale keyframe icon in the Inspector to move to the next keyframe at 6:04. At that frame, enter the same Scale X and Scale Y values.

TIP ▸ If you don't remember a value, click the arrow to the left of the keyframe icon to jump back to the earlier keyframe.

15 Skim, scrub, or step through the animation.

The rectangle seems to move just a small amount between the first two keyframes, before she moves her fingers apart.

When you create a motion path with more than two keyframes, Final Cut Pro assumes you want a smooth interpolation between the frames, which can result in movement between them, even if the keyframes have the same values.

16 In the Viewer, Control-click the gray arrow at the bottom of the animation path, and from the shortcut menu, choose Linear. Step through the animation.

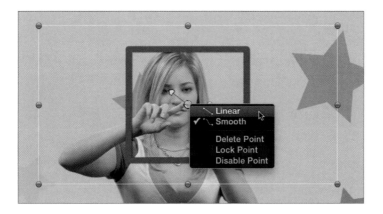

The rectangle now stays rock solid and motionless between the first two keyframes. With the middle part of the animation completed, you can move to its beginning and the end.

17 Move the playhead to the frame just before Justine begins to drag her finger down, at about 4:21.

18 In the Viewer, drag the rectangle up and over so that Justine is touching the left edge near the bottom corner. The new motion path appears in the Viewer.

19 Tap the Right Arrow key to step through the animation.

The shape moves down with her finger; but once again, it continues to move after the keyframe at 5:08—even though the next keyframe at 6:04 has the same position values. (You can verify this by clicking the arrows on either side of the keyframe icon in the Inspector.)

Even though you set the keyframe to Linear, another keyframe is actually beneath it that isn't selectable.

NOTE ▶ If the keyframe is already set to Linear, you'll still need to perform the following steps.

20 In the Viewer, drag the white diamond to the right to reveal the keyframe underneath it.

You can see that one segment of the motion path is curved and the other is straight.

21 Change the exposed keyframe's interpolation to Linear, and then drag the moved keyframe back on top of it. In the Inspector, click the arrows on either side of the keyframe icon to move between these two keyframes. Type values for X and Y so that they match exactly. Then play the clip.

Now you just need to animate the shape off the screen.

22 In the Inspector or the Video Animation Editor, set a keyframe for the position of the shape at about 8:09, just before Justine swipes her finger off to the right. Change the interpolation of this keyframe to Linear, if necessary, so the shape will remain still between 6:04 and 8:09.

23 Press the Down Arrow and then the Left Arrow to move the playhead to the last frame of the clip, and in the Viewer, drag the shape straight off the right edge of the screen. If necessary, change the keyframe in the Viewer to Linear.

24 In the Viewer, click Done to disable the Transform effect, and play the clip. Adjust the position and font size of the English and Spanish titles to align with the new shape position.

By setting and adjusting keyframes in the Viewer, Inspector, and the Video Animation Editor, you've created a fun, engaging animation. In the next exercise, you'll complete the effect by making Justine more colorful.

Creating a Travel Matte

A travel matte, a mask also known as a *travelling matte*, creates transparency that changes over time. The Keyer effect you used in an earlier lesson is a type of travel matte.

Another type of travel matte applies transparency to a clip based on the transparency of another clip. For example, you could mask a video clip so that it appears only inside a shape from a generator clip.

Your goal is to keep Justine black and white outside the rectangle shape, but appear in full color inside the shape—no matter how the rectangle moves and scales.

To accomplish this task, you'll build on the compositing skills you developed earlier by duplicating clips, employing a compound clip, and using a blend mode to create the travel matte.

1   In the Timeline, with the **Shapes** clip selected, click to close the Video Animation Editor (or press Control-V).

2   Trim the Start point of the **Shapes** clip to match the start of the video clip. Select the **Shapes** clip, move the playhead to its start point, press Command-C to copy it, and then press Option-V to paste the copy as a connected clip at the playhead. Select the copy and Shift-drag it below the titles.

    NOTE ▶ If the copy is pasted a frame early, undo the paste operation, move the play-head forward one frame, and paste again.

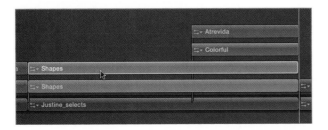

    You will use this copy to matte a full-color copy of the Justine clip below. First, you need to make a copy of that video clip and put both copies into a compound clip.

3   Select the **Justine_selects** clip. Move the playhead to the start point, press Command-C to copy it, and then press Option-V to paste it as a connected clip at the playhead. Select the copy and then Shift-drag it below both **Shapes** clips.

Now you'll combine the two middle clips into a compound clip.

4   Select the lower **Shapes** clip, and Shift-click the upper **Justine_selects** clip. Choose File > New Compound Clip, or press Option-G.

You have created a connected clip "sandwich." You will leave the top Shapes clip and the bottom video clip unaltered. In fact, if you play the clips now, you'll see that nothing has changed. You'll use the copies inside the compound clip to create the travel matte. To do so, you need to open the compound clip.

5   Double-click the compound clip to open it in the Timeline. Move the playhead to the point where Justine has expanded the shape, at about 2:08.

You are now looking at just the copied clips outside the context of the full project. Because the clip copies contain all the applied effects, Justine appears in black and white, keyed over a black (transparent) background.

In this compound clip, you want Justine to appear in color, and only inside the shape.

6   Select the **Justine_selects** clip, and in the Video Inspector, deselect the Black & White effect.

For Justine to be visible only inside the rectangle, you'll need to fill it with a solid color so that you can apply a blend mode to reveal her.

7   Select the Shapes layer, and in the Generator Inspector, select the Fill checkbox.

NOTE ▸ The fill color does not matter. The key is that no transparency exists inside the shape.

8   Select the Video Inspector, and set the Blend Mode to Stencil Alpha. Play the clip.

Justine appears only inside the animating shape. Let's see how this compound clip looks in the context of the project.

9   At the upper left of the Timeline, click the left arrow to go back in the Timeline history, and then play the clip.

Sure enough, Justine is in color inside the shape, and black and white on the outside. However, the difference is a little too subtle. Let's see if we can make her even more colorful.

10   At the upper left of the Timeline, click the right arrow to return to the compound clip (or double-click the clip.)

11 Select the **Justine_selects** clip, move the playhead to its start point, press Command-C to make a copy, and then press Option-V to paste the copy as a connected clip at the playhead. Select the copy and Shift-drag it below the **Shapes** clip.

12 With the upper video clip selected, go to the Video Inspector, scroll down, and from the Blend Mode pop-up menu, choose Hard Light. The blend mode increases the intensity of the color.

13 Click the left arrow at the top left of the Timeline to return to the full project. Play the compound clip.

Justine now appears much more colorful inside the shape.

Your project is almost complete. To give it a final polish, you'll use transitions to create animation between video clips.

Animating with Transitions

Transitions offer fast and easy ways to create animation without setting keyframes. The Transitions Browser includes myriad ways to animate from one clip to the next. For this project, the Slide transition can animate Justine on and off the screen.

1   Press Shift-Z to fit the Timeline to the window, and then move the playhead to the edit point between the first and second clips. Press Shift-/ (slash) to play around the playhead.

TIP ▶ You may want to disable the audio clip by selecting it and pressing V. You may also want to enable looping by pressing Command-L.

Currently the edit point is a straight cut from the first clip to the second. You can insert a transition to animate Justine off the screen at the end of the first outgoing clip.

2   In the Timeline, click either side of the edit point to select it. It doesn't matter which side you select.

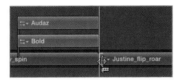

3   In the toolbar, select the Transitions Browser. Then select the Movements category, scroll down, and double-click the Slide transition to apply it to the selected edit point.

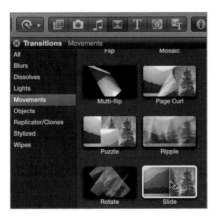

4   Select the transition in the Timeline, and in the Transition Inspector, change Type to
    Slide Push, while leaving Direction as Right. Press the Left and Right Arrow keys to
    step through the transition.

    TIP ▶ When selecting the transition, be careful not to click too close to the middle
    or the edge or you will select an edit point.

The outgoing clip slides off the screen as the incoming clip slides in (and also slides
up because you earlier animated its Y-position with keyframes).

You can apply a variation of this transition to the next edit point.

5   Option-drag the transition from the first edit point to the second to create a copy.

6   In the Transition Inspector, change Direction to Left, and then step through the tran-
    sition. The second clips flies out to the left, and the third clip files in from the right.

    The compound clip above the third video clip does not need the transition because
    you don't see Justine in color until she pulls down the box several frames after the
    transition's end. But for the next edit point, you'll need to place a transition on both
    the primary storyline and on the edit point between the connected clips.

7   Select the first transition in the Timeline (between the first and second video clips),
    and Option-drag it to the edit point between the third and fourth video clips. Step
    through the transition.

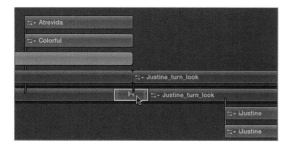

The outgoing clip slides out to the right, and the incoming clip slides in from the left; but because no transition exists between the connected compound clip and the copy of the **Justine_turn_look** clip, you can see offset copies of the video in the Viewer.

In an earlier exercise, you saw that adding a transition from the Transitions Browser to a connected clip automatically places the clip into a storyline. In this case, however, it is more convenient to copy the existing transition in the Timeline to keep the changes intact. Since you can't Option-drag a copy of a transition onto a connected clip that isn't in a storyline, you'll first create the storyline, and then add the transition.

8   Select the compound clip, and then Shift-click the upper **Justine_turn_look** clip next to it.

9   Choose Clip > Create Storyline, or press Command-G.

The clips are now part of a storyline. However, if you try to Option-drag the transition to the edit point, it still won't work because you don't have any extra media, or *handles*, in the compound clip with which to create the transition. Luckily, it's an easy fix.

10   Double-click the compound clip to open it in the Timeline.

11   Trim the end point of all three clips to extend each by seven frames.

The transition is 13 frames, so it needs 6 or 7 frames of handles on each side of the edit point. The dark area into which you are extending the clips indicates that you are creating handles. In other words, you are not changing the overall project duration.

12   Click the left arrow at the upper left of the Timeline to go back in the Timeline history to view the full project. Notice that all the clips and connected clips still end on the same frame.

13   Select the transition below the connected storyline, and then Option-drag it to the edit point between the two clips in the connected storyline. Step through the transition.

The two copies of each side of the transition are now in perfect registration.

14   If necessary, enable the audio clip, and then play the full project.

Great work. In this lesson, you've learned how to create and manipulate keyframes to create animation, and you've employed transitions, blend modes, and compound clips to complete your show open.

Over the course of the preceding three lessons, you've built a complete show open from scratch, employing a great variety of compositing and animation techniques that you can now apply to your own projects.

Lesson Review

1. How many keyframes do you need to create animation?
2. Identify the three locations where you can create and edit transformation keyframes.
3. When does changing a parameter value automatically set a keyframe?
4. Describe three ways to park the playhead directly on a Position keyframe.
5. You have enabled the Transform effect in the Viewer and clicked the Add Keyframe button at the top left of the Viewer. In the Timeline, you've opened the Video Animation Editor for the selected clip, and at the playhead position, you see two diamonds stacked on top of each other for the Transform effect. How many keyframes did you just set?
6. Can some effects parameters be animated without manually adding keyframes?
7. You want to animate a clip to fly onto the screen, stay still for five seconds, and then fly off the screen. What are the minimum number of position keyframes you need to set, and what keyframe interpolation must be chosen for the two keyframes that have the same value?
8. What blend mode, when applied to a connected clip that sits above the primary storyline, will mask the connected clip based on the transparency of the clip beneath it?
9. Connected clips must be part of a storyline in order to accept transitions. How can you create a storyline and add a transition in one operation?

Answers

1. You need at least two keyframes on the same parameter with different parameter values.
2. The Viewer, the Inspector, and the Video Animation Editor in the Timeline
3. When an initial keyframe is already set for a parameter, changing its value at another point in time will automatically create a keyframe.

4. In the Viewer, click the white keyframe indicator on the motion path. In the Inspector, click the arrows on either side of the Add Keyframe button. In the Timeline, move the playhead over the diamond in the Video Animation Editor.

5. You set four keyframes. When you click the Add Keyframe button in the Viewer, it sets keyframes for all the Transform parameters, including Position, Rotation, Scale, and Anchor. The two stacked diamonds in the Video Animation Editor indicate that two or more keyframes exist at the playhead for that effect.

6. Yes, certain effect parameters have fade handles in the Video Animation Editor you can drag to fade the effect on and off.

7. You need four keyframes. The two keyframes with the same value must have Linear interpolation (as opposed to Smooth interpolation) to keep the clip motionless.

8. Stencil Alpha

9. Drag a transition from the Transitions Browser to the start or end point of a connected clip to create a storyline and add the transition in one operation. Alternatively, if the edit point is selected, double-clicking the transition in the Transitions Browser will do the same thing.

Keyboard Shortcuts

Control-V   Open the Video Animation Editor

Finishing Techniques

10

Lesson Files	APTS FCP X ADV Part 3 > Lesson_10
Media	Media > Lesson 10 Media for Relinking
Time	This lesson takes approximately 120 minutes to complete.
Goals	Manage media using preferences and relinking
	Understand color correction workflow
	Explore the color correction interface
	Apply automatic color adjustments
	Use video scopes to identify and manipulate color

Color Correction Basics

Once you complete your final edit, you're ready to polish your project by performing color correction, and preparing the content for the web, broadcast, or disc. This phase of the postproduction process is called *finishing*, and it's the focus of this section of lessons.

In this lesson, you'll acquire a deeper understanding of the color correction tools found in Final Cut Pro X. You'll set up the Final Cut Pro X interface for color correction, use the video scopes to analyze your clips, and apply automatic and manual color adjustments to correct and enhance individual clips, focusing on image contrast. These tools and techniques give you a terrific level of control over the images in your projects.

Getting Ready

For the lessons in this section, you'll need to access the projects and media found on the APTS FCP X ADV Part 3 disk image.

1   CCopy the APTS FCP X ADV Part 3 disk image to your preferred local volume, and double-click it to mount the image.

2   Open Final Cut Pro X. The APTS FCP X ADV Part 3 disk image will appear at the top of the Event Library, containing Events for *Agriculture, Burnt Dinner, Burnt Dinner Finishing, Dining, Hero Scene,* and *In the City,* which are the projects you'll be using within this section.

The APTS FCP X ADV Part 3 disk image should also appear at the top of the Project Library, including individual folders for the projects used in Lessons 10 through 14.

3   If you haven't done so, choose Final Cut Pro > Preferences, click Playback, deselect the "Background render" checkbox, and then close the Preferences window.

By turning off background rendering, you avoid filling the APTS FCP X ADV Part 3 disk image with render files. Most of the operations in the following lessons use real-time effects, so background rendering shouldn't be necessary.

What Is Color Correction?

Color correction was once considered an arcane art that few understood and even fewer practiced. It required hundreds of thousands of dollars of equipment, and as a result, only well-heeled projects benefitted from full-blown color correction sessions.

Fast forward to now. Color correction (or *color grading,* depending on who you ask) is better understood by far more practitioners, and the essential tools for color correction are far more accessible. Final Cut Pro X has a nice collection of high-quality color adjustment controls that let you make subtle or massive adjustments to the color and contrast of the clips in your projects.

But to use these tools to their best advantage, you must first understand the task that lies before you.

Understanding the Essential Tasks of Color Correction

Color correction is a process of evaluating and adjusting the clips in your project to achieve the following general goals:

▶ *Fix problems with individual clips*: Some clips may be too dim, others may have poor color, in still others a particular hue may tint the shot and make the subjects look unattractive. These issues can be fixed, automatically or manually, using the basic Final Cut Pro X color correction toolset.

▶ *Make every shot look its best*: Even clips without clear problems can sometimes be improved by stretching or compressing contrast, increasing or diminishing saturation, or subtly changing the tint of ambient lighting. As you use the color correction tools, you'll also learn techniques for making such overall improvements.

▶ *Make every clip in a scene look like it was shot at the same time in the same place*: Scenes often include clips that were captured at different times of the day, on different days, or in different locations. The Final Cut Pro X color correction tools can help you match shots, regardless of the shooting conditions. Doing so ensures that viewers aren't distracted by differences in lighting and color that call attention to the editing and detract from the flow of a scene. Final Cut Pro X has an automated tool to help with this issue, but in a later lesson, you'll learn manual techniques for matching shots.

▶ *Add style and pizzazz to a scene*: Color correction isn't just about fixing problems. The more creative aspect of color grading is adding a *look*, or a stylized visual treatment, to enhance the mood of a scene, or to expand upon the on-set lighting. Creative color grading can also achieve complicated day-for-night looks, or artificially colored looks for reasons of pure style (such as when creating a music video). Final Cut Pro X has many tools to help you achieve this kind of style, and you can further customize them to best suit your individual needs.

Knowing When to Correct and When to Quit

Color correction is usually treated as part of the finishing process performed when editorial is complete. However, one of the benefits of color correcting within your NLE is that the corrections are attached to your shots, so you can rearrange or trim shots without losing your adjustments.

In any case, even dedicated editors should understand the basics of color correction. Inevitably, a particular shot sticks out during the creative editing process or it doesn't look right because it doesn't match other clips in the scene. As a result, most projects have some color corrections performed long before the finishing phase begins. Due to the power and accessibility of modern editing/grading tools, the line separating creative editorial from finishing blurs more every year.

Those tools conceal a potential pitfall, however. It's often said that "films are never completed, they're simply abandoned." This is especially true in the finishing process. Although the tools permit almost unlimited changes, at a certain point, it's good practice to know when to stop noodling with your project, lock the edit, and focus on polishing and completing your project.

Often, project audio is exported, sweetened, and mixed elsewhere while color correction takes place. In these instances, it's even more important to resist the temptation to alter the edit, as it will throw off the audio/video sync of your project when it's time to remarry the mix to the final visuals.

Using an Appropriate Display

When you're color correcting projects destined for Internet distribution, grading on your computer's display is an acceptable practice—so long as your computer display is of high quality, and you calibrated it using the manual calibration routine in the Displays option of System Preferences, or an automated calibration device.

When you work on a project destined for broadcast, it's essential to color correct while viewing your clips on a dedicated broadcast display that shows true video output.

You can choose from a number of suitable broadcast displays, including flat-panel LCD-based displays, OLED-based displays, plasma screens, and high-end video projectors. No matter which type of display you choose, they should meet the following characteristics for critical color evaluation:

▶   Compatibility with the resolution and video signal output from your video output interface, such as $Y'P_BP_R$, HDMI, or HD-SDI

▶   Suitable black levels (in other words, solid black shouldn't look like gray)

▶   Appropriate brightness for the environment where the display will be used

▶   User-selectable color temperature (with the default set at D65)

▶ Adherence to the Rec. 601 (SD) or 709 (HD) color space standards, as appropriate

▶ Appropriate gamma (preferably user-adjustable between 2.2 to 2.6)

▶ Professional-level calibration and adjustment controls

For all these reasons, you'll want to research which display is appropriate for the type of work you do. Broadcast displays are evolving at a rapid pace, and new models are available every year.

You'll need a video output device to output a true video signal to your broadcast display. Final Cut Pro X is compatible with a wide variety of video output devices. Some are cards that you install inside a Mac Pro; others are boxes that connect to an iMac, MacBook, or Mac Mini via Thunderbolt.

Whichever video output device you have, make sure the latest Final Cut Pro X-compatible drivers are installed, so you can control video output with a preferences setting and a menu command.

1 Choose Final Cut Pro > Preferences.

2 In the Preferences window, click Playback to reveal the Playback options.

3 Choose your output device from the A/V Output pop-up menu.

   If this pop-up menu displays "None Found," then you need to download and install the appropriate drivers for your device.

4 Close the Preferences window, and choose Window > A/V Output to turn video output on and off.

Using the Highest-Quality Media

The color correction process is your last chance to quality-check your project prior to sending it on its way. No matter what media format you used for the creative edit, always make sure to use the highest-quality media you have available for your final project.

It's still frequently the case where projects are edited using low-quality *offline* media (for example, compressed using ProRes Proxy to save space). You want to make sure your project is using high-quality *online* media before you begin the color correction process, to make sure that you're seeing each clip in its most pristine state and working with all the available image data.

Using Original or Optimized Media

One way that projects can be edited using low-quality proxy media is via the "Use proxy media" option in the Playback Preferences. If you've been using proxy media using the automatic proxy management in Final Cut Pro X, you'll need to readjust these preferences before you start working.

1   Choose Final Cut Pro > Preferences.

2   In the Preferences window, click Playback to reveal the Playback options.

3   If necessary, select "Use original or optimized media."

4   From the Playback Quality pop-up menu, choose High Quality.

Now that Final Cut Pro X is set to use the highest-quality media available, you can continue finishing your project with confidence.

Manually Relinking Offline Clips Throughout a Project

You can also manually manage the media your project uses by *relinking* to alternate media files.

The clips listed in the Final Cut Pro Event Browser are simply pointers to the actual media files located on your hard disk. For the most part, Final Cut Pro manages the clip/media file relationship for you automatically.

However, there are situations, particularly during the finishing process, where you may want to manually override this relationship, forcibly relinking a clip with a specific file on disk. Two common instances are:

▶   If you've been handed a project file with a folder of media that's different than the original media path name used by that project.

▶   If you're replacing offline-quality media (such as clips compressed using ProRes Proxy to save space during an offline edit) with higher-quality media archived from the original shoot.

There are other instances where Final Cut Pro simply can't find the file associated with a particular clip. In this case, it will display the Missing File image in place of the thumbnails in the Event Browser and Timeline as well as the preview in the Viewer. Such files are referred to as *offline* files. This can happen for a variety of reasons, such as renaming the source media on disk, moving the source media file to another location, or moving the source media file to the Trash.

If an Event or project has an offline file somewhere within, a warning flag appears on that Event or project's icon in the Event or Project Library.

TIP ▶ A frequent cause of this situation is when a removable hard drive containing the media is unmounted or disconnected from the computer. In that Event, simply mount the hard drive and Final Cut Pro will automatically see it, relink all the offline files and the warning flags go away.

When examining the contents of an Event, each unlinked media file appears with the same warning flag.

Finally, unlinked clips are highlighted in the Timeline with similar red graphics.

When you have offline media in your project, the Relink Media command makes it easy to repair a clip's relationship to its corresponding source media on disk. The command can also save you the hassle of re-editing clips into your project when you substitute one version of a media file for another.

In the following two exercises, you'll learn the two methods of relinking media in Final Cut Pro X.

Relinking Media in the Event Library

Relinking a clip in the Event Browser automatically updates all instances of that file within all events and projects that use that clip. This is especially useful when you've moved a project to another workstation and you need to relink every clip to a new set of media.

In this exercise, you'll relink an offline project to media found in the APTS FCP X ADV Part 3 disk image.

1   In the Project Library, display the contents of the APTS FCP X ADV Part 3 disk image.

2   Open the Lesson 10 and 11 folder in the Project Library. You should see that the *Dining* project is completely offline.

3   In the Event Library, click the *Dining* event to display its clips. Seven offline clips appear in the Event Browser.

4   Click anywhere within the Event Browser, and then press Shift-A to select every clip at once.

5   Choose File > Relink Event Files. The Relink Files dialog appears.

By default, in the Relink Files dialog, Relink mode is set to Missing, which will relink all of the selected files that appear in the Original Files list whether they're offline or not. The Missing mode shows only missing clips in the Original Files list.

6   Click Locate All.

7   In the dialog that appears, navigate to the APTS FCP X ADV Part 3 disk image, select the "Lesson 10 Media for Relinking" folder, and click Choose.

All items from the Original Files list are moved to the bottom list, which shows the correspondence between each clip and the matched file that Final Cut Pro X believes is the correct file for linking based on file metadata such as UUID, name, timecode, and reel number.

8   Click Relink Files.

At this point, all media in the Event Library should update and will appear online. Furthermore, all formerly offline clips in the *Dining* project should also be online.

Manually Relinking Individual Clips

You can also relink clips directly in the Timeline. For example, if you're handed one or two clips that were updated, such as a revised effects clip or a higher-quality piece of stock footage that's been purchased to replace a placeholder version, you can select the old version of that clip in the Timeline and use relinking to update it to the new version.

There's an important difference between relinking in the Timeline, and relinking in the Event Library. When you relink clips in the Event Library, you relink every instance of those clips in every project that uses those Events. However, when you relink a clip in the Timeline, you relink only that one instance of the clip within that project. All other instances of the clip in other projects remain unchanged.

> **NOTE** ▶ The new (relinked) files can have a different resolution and codec than the original files, but they must be the same media type. That is, you can't relink a video clip to an audio file. Relinked files must also have the same frame rate and audio channels similar to the original files. The relinked files can also be trimmed versions of the original files, but they must be long enough to cover all the clips that refer to the files.

In the following exercise, you'll use relinking to update a title at the beginning of the *Hero Scene* to new media with a newer version of the title.

1   In the Project Library, open the Lesson 10 and 11 folder, and open *Hero Scene*.

2   Play through the first clip, and stop after the title disappears. This is generic placeholder text—created with the final Motion treatment—waiting for the producers to determine the final title of the show.

3   In the Timeline, select the **Offline Title** clip.

4 Choose File > Relink Project Files. In the Relink Files dialog, select Relink: All.

5 Click Locate All.

6 In the dialog, navigate to the APTS FCP X ADV Part 3 disk image, and open the "Lesson 10 Media for Relinking" folder. Select the **Final Titles.mov** file, and click Choose.

The **Offline Title.mov** item moves to the bottom list, showing the **Final Titles.mov** file in the Matched File column to indicate that the new media will replace the old media.

7 Click Relink Files. The **Offline Title** clip is updated to link to the new media, and the *Harry's Heroes* title appears in the Viewer.

That's the flexibility of the relinking command. Now that you've learned how to make sure you're using the most appropriate media for your project, it's time to dig into the nuts and bolts of color correction.

Learning the Color Correction Interface

In this section, you'll look at the interface for color correction in Final Cut Pro X, discovering where the color correction tools are located, and how to customize your workspace to work most efficiently.

Exploring the Color Correction Interface

Color correction is accomplished by using controls and modifying parameters found in the Inspector, specifically the Video Inspector and the Color Board.

1   In the Project Library, display the contents of the APTS FCP X ADV Part 3 disk image, if necessary, and then click the disclosure triangle next to the Lesson 10 and 11 folder to show its contents.

2   Double-click the *Burnt Dinner* project to open it, and press Shift-Z to expand its clips to the available width of the Timeline.

3   Use the ; (semicolon) and ' (apostrophe) keys to move the playhead to the beginning of the fourth clip, and then press C to select the fourth clip in the project.

4   At the right of the toolbar, click the Inspector button to open the Video Inspector.

NOTE ▸ You can also open the Video Inspector by pressing Command-4, or choosing Window > Show Inspector.

In the Video Inspector you can see the Color control group. The first two controls enable or disable the automatic color correction controls. Under these, a Correction 1 control contains the default manual Color adjustment for the current clip.

Each clip has a blank Color adjustment, ready for you to use.

5   Click the Color Board button to open the Color Board.

The Color Board shows all the color correction controls for that correction.

6   To make an overall color adjustment to tint the entire clip, drag the Global color control up from its default position toward the orange part of the spectrum.

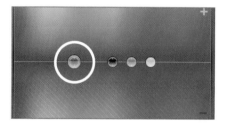

The clip takes on an orange tint that intensifies the farther you drag the control.

7   To return to the Video Inspector, click the back arrow button.

Notice that the Color Board button at the extreme right of Correction 1's row of controls is now colorfully highlighted. This indicates that Correction 1 has been modified.

8   Press ' (apostrophe) to move the playhead to the next edit. Press C to select the fifth clip in the project, and then press Command-6 to reopen the Color Board. Because each clip in a project has individual color adjustments, the controls of the Color Board corresponding to clip 3 are at their default positions.

9   Press ; (semicolon) to move the playhead to the previous edit, and press C to select the previous clip.

The Color Board updates using the tint adjustment you made in step 6. Switching between the Video Inspector and the Color Board is not necessary. Once the Color Board is visible, selecting any clip in a project updates the Color Board with that clip's color adjustment settings.

10   Click the back arrow button to go back to the Inspector, and then click the Reset button corresponding to Correction 1.

The fourth clip now reverts to its original, unadjusted state.

Applying Automatic Color Adjustments

In the preceding exercise, you made a manual adjustment to learn how the interface works. Now, use the automatic Color Balance controls.

1   In the Event Library, select the *Burnt Dinner* Event. Select all the clips contained within that Event, and then Control-click (or right-click) one of the selected clips, and from the shortcut menu, choose Analyze and Fix.

2   In the window that appears, select the "Analyze for balance color" checkbox, and
click OK.

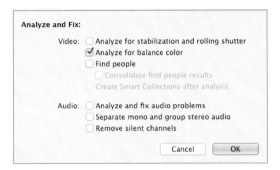

A progress timer appears next to the timecode field to indicate the ongoing progress
of the analysis.

TIP ▸ Click the Background Tasks indicator to open the Background Tasks window.

3   Click anywhere on the fourth clip to select it, if it's not already selected, and review
its parameters in the Video Inspector. The Balance parameter underneath the Color
group should be set to Analyzed.

4   Enable Balance. This turns on the previously analyzed auto color balance adjustment
for this clip.

Before correction   After correction

However, you can easily turn on color balance for all the clips.

5 Select every clip in the Timeline, and then from the Enhancements pop-up menu in the toolbar, choose Balance Color. This turns on the Balance color control for every selected clip in the Timeline.

6 Play through the scene.

Auto color balance does its best to find a pleasing "neutral" correction so that clips appear naturalistic, without tinting or color casts. Auto color balance also adjusts clip contrast so that shadows look deep and highlights appear vivid. This control often works well with decently exposed standard lighting shots, and documentary-type available light shots.

However, auto color balance doesn't necessarily take into account creative lighting. In particular, you can see that the automatic correction applied to clip 2 is a bit over-zealous relative to the original lighting scheme of the scene.

7 Select clip 2, and turn off the Balance parameter. The shot returns to its original color. You can also use this method to turn off auto color balance for multiple selected clips.

8 Press Command-2 to go to the Timeline, and then press Command-A to select all the clips in the project.

9 From the Enhancements pop-up menu in the toolbar, click the Balance Color check-box twice.

If the selected clips all have auto-balance turned on, a checkmark appears to the right of the Balance Color command. Choosing Balance Color will turn off auto-balance for all selected clips.

When only some of the selected clips have auto-balance turned on, a dash appears to the right of the Balance Color command in the Enhancements menu. Choosing Balance Color will turn on auto-balance for all clips.

10 Before continuing with the next exercise, make sure that the Balance checkbox is deselected for all the clips in this project. You won't use the automatic controls in the following exercises.

This exercise illustrated the advantages and drawbacks of the auto-balance controls. In the next few lessons, you'll perform your own analysis of clips using the video scopes to determine which color qualities are desirable, and which are not; and you'll use the manual controls of the Color Board to make custom color adjustments.

▶ **Using "Analyze for Balance Color" During Import**

If you open Final Cut Pro X preferences and click Import, you'll see an "Analyze for balance color" checkbox. This option sets Final Cut Pro X to automatically analyze each imported clip for color balance, and prebalance clips as you start to use them. As you learned, auto-balance can be a double-edged sword, useful for some lighting conditions, and problematic for others; so if you decide to select this option, remember that you can always turn off automatic balance for clips that don't look the way you'd like.

Controlling iMovie Adjustments

Movie has controls for color correction and video effects. When you import an iMovie project, these color corrections and effects are imported along with every other part of the project, which makes it easy to pick up your project where you left off. However, you can disable these effects to perform more precise adjustments using the Final Cut Pro X color correction and effects toolset.

1   In the Event Library, select the APTS FCP X ADV Part 3 disk image. Then, in the Project Library, select the Lesson 10 and 11 folder.

2   Choose File > Import > iMovie Project.

3   When the Import iMovie Project dialog appears, open the iMovie Projects folder within the APTS FCP X ADV Part 3 disk image. Select the *Cooking* project file, and click Import.

The new *Cooking* project appears in the Timeline, and a new Event Library named *Cooking* appears within the APTS FCP X ADV Part 3 disk image.

4   Double-click *Cooking* to open it, and then play through the Timeline. Notice that each of the clips has color and effects that carried over from iMovie to Final Cut Pro X.

5   Click anywhere on the first clip in the Timeline to select it, and open the Inspector, if necessary. Within the Inspector, notice that an iMovie effect was applied to this clip and appears within the Effects group of the Video Inspector.

6   Within the Old World effect, select the Match iMovie checkbox.

When you import a project that uses iMovie effects, Final Cut Pro X defaults to an improved version of each effect designed specifically for Final Cut Pro X. However, the Match iMovie parameter within each iMovie-compatible effect ensures that each effect replicates its original appearance in iMovie. This could be essential if you secured client approval for a clip's appearance in iMovie, or if you simply preferred the iMovie version of the effect.

7   Turn off the Old World effect. With the Old World effect turned off, you still have a color correction applied to the clip, which can be seen in the Color group.

The iMovie color parameter is a single checkbox that controls whether or not the color corrections made in iMovie are used in Final Cut Pro X. No matter how many parameters you modified in iMovie, this one checkbox enables or disables them all at once.

8   Deselect the iMovie color checkbox to disable all iMovie color corrections.

You can also turn off the effects and iMovie color corrections in every clip of your project.

9   Press Command-2 to go to the Timeline, and then press Command-A to select all the project clips. With all the clips selected, the checkbox for effects and iMovie color parameters have three states.

When a subset of selected clips have an effect or iMovie correction turned on, a diagonal split appears in a parameter's checkbox. Clicking a split checkbox turns on that effect or correction for all clips with that effect or correction. Clicking the check-box again to turn off the effect or correction turns off that effect or correction for all selected clips in the Timeline.

The three states of the iMovie color correction checkbox

10 Deselect the checkboxes of the Old World effect and the iMovie color parameter to turn them completely off. The effects and color corrections are now off for all selected clips in the Timeline. Play through the project to verify this.

As you can see, you have several options governing iMovie effects and color corrections. At this point, with iMovie effects and color corrections turned off, you can now redo the color corrections completely from scratch, and introduce your own detailed grading using the original range of color and contrast found in each clip.

Using Video Scopes

In addition to examining your clips on a properly calibrated display, you can consult the video scopes to quantitatively evaluate and compare images you're adjusting.

Final Cut Pro X provides all the necessary video scope displays for color correction. Together, these scopes provide graphic measurements of the luma, chroma, and RGB levels of project clips, helping you to unambiguously evaluate their good and bad qualities, as well as those qualities that differentiate one clip from another.

In this section, you'll view and customize the video scopes, and learn which scopes to use in your everyday work.

Displaying Video Scopes

Video scopes are essential to making careful color adjustments.

1   Open the Project Library and double-click the *Burnt Dinner* project to open it into the Timeline.

   TIP Press Shift-Z to expand every clip in the project to the full width of the Timeline, making it easier to see your entire project.

2 Choose Window > Show Video Scopes, or press Command-7. The video scopes open to the right of the Viewer. If nothing appears inside the video scopes, press Command-2 to go to the Timeline, or select any of the clips in the Timeline.

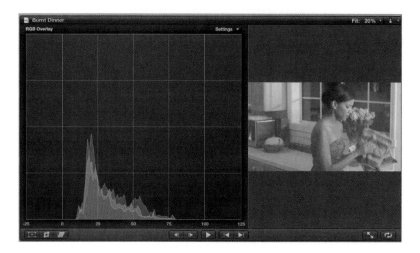

When both the video scopes and Video Inspector are open, the Viewer is reduced to half its size to make room for them. As a result, the Viewer image can be hard to evaluate. If you're monitoring using an external broadcast display, Viewer image size may not be a problem; but if you're monitoring on your computer display, you may want to make more room for a larger Viewer.

3 Drag the border between the Event Browser and the Viewer all the way to the left. This enlarges both the video scopes and the Viewer relative to the Clip Browser and video scopes, and makes it easier to see what you're doing. You can also drag the border dividing the video scopes from the Viewer to the left, shrinking the video scopes and enlarging the Viewer to make it easier to see the image.

NOTE ► If you choose Window > Show Viewer on Second Display, the video scopes appear to the left of the Viewer on your second monitor.

4   Press the ; (semicolon) or ' (apostrophe) keys to navigate to the second clip in the Timeline. Press C to select the clip, which opens it in both the current video scope and the Video Inspector.

NOTE ► You could click any clip to select it, but the playhead would move to whichever portion of the clip you clicked, and you wouldn't necessarily see the same frames used in the following figures. Option-clicking a Timeline clip will select it without moving the playhead.

The video scopes show an analysis of the frame currently appearing in the Viewer.

If you switch focus from the Timeline to the Event Browser, the video scopes will analyze the current frame of the Event being browsed, rather than the frame at the position of the playhead in the Timeline.

5   Turn off skimming by choosing View > Skimming, or pressing S.

Skimming can be an impediment when you want to analyze a specific frame; you don't want the playhead constantly updating position every time you move the pointer.

Using the Histogram

By default, the video scope displays the RGB Overlay histograms. The RGB histogram shows separate red, green, and blue histogram analyses of the image. The three-color channel analyses are overlaid on each other, which allows you to compare the relative distribution of each color channel across the *tonal range* of the image.

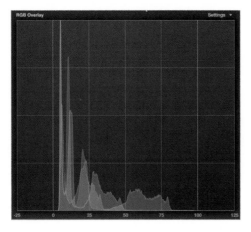

Tonal range is the range of lightness occurring throughout each clip—from the blackest shadows, through the mid-level lightness of the midtones, to the brightest highlights. It's important to learn to distinguish which parts of your image fall into which regions of image tonality. You can use the video scopes to learn these distinctions.

1   Click anywhere on the third clip of the Timeline to move the playhead to a frame of that clip.

Notice that the blue histogram graph is much higher than the red and green histogram graphs. This indicates that the values of the blue channel are much higher than those of the red and green channels, which is intuitive given that the image has a strong blue tint to it.

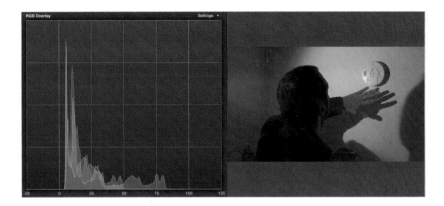

Histograms represent the total number of pixels of each level of luma throughout each color channel of the image by plotting a graph that shows the number of pixels for each percentage of lightness. It's really a bar graph of sorts, in which each increment of the scale from left to right represents a percentage of image tonality on a scale of –25 to +125 (where 0 = absolute black, and 100 represents allowable white), and the height of each histogram bar shows the number of pixels corresponding to that percentage.

Notice also that the red, green, and blue colors of the overlapping histograms mix, so that the overlap of red and green histograms appears yellow, the overlap of green and blue histograms appears cyan, and the overlap of blue and red histograms appears magenta. Finally, the gray portion of the graph shows a histogram of the luma component of the signal.

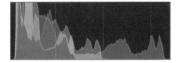

Red, green, and blue histogram overlap can show you where all three color channels "agree" with one another, which can be useful if you're trying to determine if the left- and right-most parts of all three color signals are balanced, or somewhat equal. In the third clip, the left-most part of all three color channels are nearly lined up, which indicates that the colors in the darkest shadows are almost completely neutral.

2   At the upper-right corner of the video scopes, from the Settings pop-up menu, choose RGB Parade.

Each video scope in Final Cut Pro X has several options, some of which represent alternate views of the same information. The RGB Histogram can be switched among the default Overlay view; the Parade view you just chose (which shows each histogram separately, one over another); and individual Luma, Red, Green, and Blue histograms.

3   Click the sixth clip in the Timeline to select it.

In this clip, the RGB Parade view clearly shows that the red channel is strongest (it stretches farthest to the right, peaking at around 65), and the blue channel is weakest (it stretches only to approximately 55). This corresponds to the clearly more neutral (in fact, slightly "warmer," or more orange) color quality of this clip.

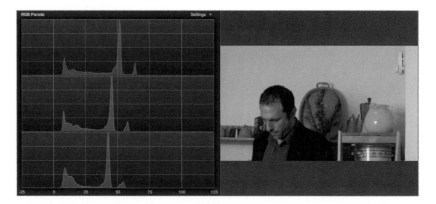

Histograms are good tools for overall analysis because they show you the color balance of an image, as well as how close a clip comes to the darkest and lightest extremes of image lightness that are permissible for broadcast. However, other video scopes can represent even more specific aspects of your clips.

Using the Vectorscope

The Vectorscope shows the overall distribution of color in your image as a "blob" of a graph centered within a circular scale. The blob is actually a collection of individual points (each pixel of the current image corresponds to a connected point in this graph), connected by thin lines that *trace* from point to point.

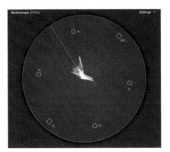

These traces bunch together and appear as "arms" that stretch from the center of the Vectorscope into different directions. The traces of the Vectorscope are colored to reflect the colors that appear in the image, but this coloration is only an approximation of the clip's actual appearance.

The purpose of this graph is to show you how much of which colors are in your clips, and how intense they are.

For each "arm" of the Vectorscope graph, its angle around the circular scale shows the hue (relative to the color targets provided), while its distance from the center of the scale shows the saturation, or intensity, of the color in that part of the image. The center of the Vectorscope represents zero saturation; the farther from the center a point is, the higher its saturation.

In this exercise, you'll learn to "read" images using the Vectorscope.

1   From the Settings pop-up menu of the video scope, choose Vectorscope.

2   Click the eighth clip of the Timeline, move the playhead to frame 01:00:46:13, and examine the Vectorscope graph.

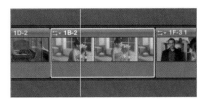

Notice that four main "arms" appear on the Vectorscope graph: a long red one extending toward the R target box, a bluish/pink one extending toward the B target box, a cyan one extending toward the CY target box, and a yellow/orange one extending toward the YL target box.

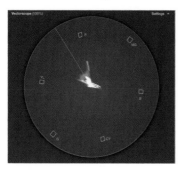

These targets provide a reference to indicate which angles of the Vectorscope correspond to which hues. By noticing which target boxes the arms stretch toward, you can get a sense of how many hues exist within your image.

TIP ▶ Many colorists prefer to work with uncolored video scopes. You can turn off the coloration of the video scope graphs by choosing Monochrome in the video scope Settings pop-up menu. In monochrome mode, the target boxes are even more useful for reference.

The target boxes correspond to the primary and secondary colors of the additive color model upon which video is based. Red, green, and blue are the three primary colors that are added together in varying proportions to create all other visible colors. Magenta, cyan, and yellow are the secondary colors that result by combining any two primary colors: green plus red is yellow, green plus blue is cyan, and blue plus red is magenta.

Notice that the red arm of the graph is longer than the cyan arm of the graph. This shows that the red of the woman's dress is considerably more saturated, or intense, than the cyan of her potholder.

It's useful to know that at the default scale of this graph, these targets also serve as an approximate outer boundary for the acceptable amount of saturation. If any arm of your Vectorscope graph goes beyond these targets, that color is probably too saturated and may later cause problems.

3   From the Settings pop-up menu of the video scope, choose 133%. The Vectorscope enlarges to provide a zoomed-in view of the graph. This can be useful if you're trying

to see the angle of specific portions of the graph that may be small because they're not very saturated.

4   Click the last clip in the *Burnt Dinner* project, and move the playhead to the very beginning of the clip, where the woman is by herself.

Skin tone is one of the most critical colors for adjustment. All viewers have very specific expectations for the hue of human skin, and if that hue is a bit off, it may cause the people in your project to seem unhealthy or unattractive.

For this reason, the Vectorscope has a special target: the Skin Tone Indicator. The Skin Tone Indicator is a diagonal line that falls between the R and YL targets, and it shows the theoretically ideal hue of human skin tone, regardless of the subject's complexion or ethnicity.

To use the Skin Tone Indicator, look for the arm of the Vectorscope graph that comes closest to the indicator. Unless the color of the image is wildly wrong, this should represent the skin tone in the scene. The arm's proximity to the indicator will show you how close the color in your shot approaches the theoretical ideal for skin hue. In the current shot, the skin tone component of the Vectorscope graph is pretty obvious.

5   Click the previous clip in the Timeline (the eleventh clip) to evaluate the closeup of the man.

In this shot, three main arms stick out of the graph, one toward R, one just to the left of the Skin Tone Indicator, and one stretching more toward YL. Looking at the shot, it's probably a good guess that the right-most arm corresponds to the man's skin, since the wood shelving in the background is very similar to human skin tone also, and is less red. Finally, the yellow and orange in the background likely corresponds to the left-most arm of the graph.

6   In the Video Inspector, double-click Crop to view the Crop parameters, and drag the Left, Right, Top, and Bottom sliders until you've cropped to just the man's face.

Cropping a clip limits the analysis performed by the video scope, and isolating the man's face proves our hypothesis about the Vectorscope arms. It also shows that without the distractions of everything else in the shot, the man's face does look pretty red.

This isn't necessarily wrong, but it does demonstrate the value of the Vectorscope in showing a strict numerical representation of which colors really appear in the scene.

This brings up another good point. Be aware that the Skin Tone Indicator is only an *approximation*. Subtle variations of complexion in the population may cause skin tone to fall slightly above (ruddier complexions) or slightly below (olive-skinned complexions) this line. Don't mistakenly think that all people should fall exactly on the Skin Tone Indicator. However, if you keep in mind that the indicator target is merely the center of what's considered ideal, it's a good marker for how close or far different complexions are from where you want them to be.

If the skin tones of your actors are noticeably off, the offset between the most likely nearby area of color in the Vectorscope graph and the skin tone target will give you an idea of the type of correction you should make.

7   In the Video Inspector, click the Crop parameter's Reset button.

8   In the Timeline, click in the last third of the fourth clip.

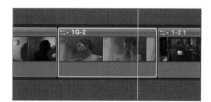

In this shot, a prominent blue arm in the Vectorscope graph indicates how much blue is contained in the scene. You can also see that the red/orange part of the graph is very, very close to the center, which shows that the skin tone and color of the cabinetry in the background are much more desaturated than in the previous shots.

Also notice that the entire graph is off-center relative to the Vectorscope Skin Tone Indicator. Because the outer ring of the Vectorscope represents maximum color saturation, the center of the Vectorscope represents zero saturation, which corresponds to untinted black and white in the scene.

Whenever you see a Vectorscope graph that's off-center like this, it means that the image has no untinted black, gray, or white. This may be the look you want, in the case of an image with extreme tinting, or it may indicate an unwanted "color cast" or color bias in the image that needs to be corrected.

So, if you're interested in examining which hues are in an image, how saturated or intense they are, and how they compare to the hues of other clips, the Vectorscope is your tool of choice.

Using the Waveform Monitor

The Waveform Monitor is yet another tool for analyzing your video signals. In some respects, it works similarly to the Histogram and displays some of the same information. However, while it's a bit more complicated to read, the Waveform Monitor offers advantages that make it very versatile.

1   Press the ' (apostrophe) key to navigate to the eighth clip in the Timeline. Then press C to select the clip and open it in the current video scope and the Video Inspector.

2   From the Settings pop-up menu of the video scope, choose Waveform. The waveform graph appears, showing luma by default. (If it's set to a different waveform display, from the Settings pop-up menu, choose Luma.)

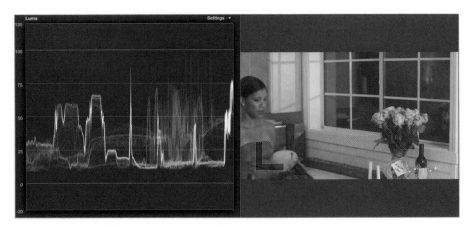

All video clips can be broken down into a *luma* component, which contains all the light and shadow information throughout a clip, and a *chroma* component, which contains all the color information.

In the previous exercise, you used the Vectorscope to analyze the isolated chroma information. Now you'll use the luma waveform graph to analyze the isolated image lightness.

3   In the Video Inspector, double-click Crop to reveal the Crop parameters, if necessary. Then drag the Top slider to the right until its value is 99.

The waveform graph shows an overlapping series of individual waveforms, one for each row of pixels in the clip being analyzed. When you crop the rest of the image, the thin strip of image that remains makes it easy to see how the waveform analysis works.

TIP The graph in the following figure has been intensified using the Brightness slider found at the bottom of the video scope's Settings pop-up menu. This slider increases the visibility of difficult-to-spot video scope features by intensifying lighter areas of the graph.

The vertical scale of the waveform ranges from –20 to +120, which represents the minimum and maximum values a video signal might contain. Practically speaking, 0 represents minimum black, while 100 represents the maximum white that's recommended for media distribution. (Note that the –20 and +120 limits provide room for *undershoots* and *overshoots* that may exist in the source media, but are not meant for distribution.)

To create the waveform graph, each row of pixels in the image is graphed individually from left to right, so that pixels of low lightness levels are graphed closer to the bottom of the graph, and pixels of higher lightness levels are drawn closer to the top.

Consequently, darker areas of the video strip you've cropped appear as dips near the bottom of the graph, and brighter areas of the video strip appear as spikes near the top.

4   Slowly drag the Top slider back to the left, until it's set to 0. As you add more and more rows of pixels to the analysis, additional overlapping waveforms are added to the graph, until a complete analysis appears.

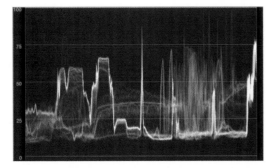

Because the horizontal axis of the waveform graph corresponds to the horizontal dimension of the image being analyzed, there's a correspondence between subjects in the frame and features of the waveform graph. The waveforms are also colored to suggest the colors being analyzed in the image and to help you understand how the waveform corresponds to the frame contents.

5   Press the Spacebar to play the video, and stop playback before reaching the end of the clip.

As the woman walks from left to right, you can see the red dip in the waveform move along with her. You can also see the tall yellow fuzzy portion of the waveform diminish as she walks in front of the flowers.

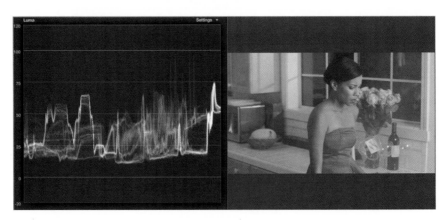

The bright, cool blue highlights of the waveform correspond to the light falling on the cabinets and window sill, and are shown as some of the taller spikes on the graph. Farther to the right, the very tallest spikes in the graph (nearing 100) represent the specular highlights on the wine glasses on the counter.

As you learn how features in the image correspond to spikes and dips on the Waveform Monitor, you will look for three key elements:

Focus on the top of the waveform. The *white point* corresponds to the highest spikes on the graph, which correspond to the lightest features in the image. In the current clip, the specular highlights of the wine glasses are technically the white point (at around 95 relative to the graph's scale), but because so little detail appears in these highlights, they aren't a good way to judge the average highlights of the image. Highlights corresponding to specular highlights, direct light sources, and reflections are often the *peak highlights* of an image.

A more practical white point for evaluating the highlights of our image comes from the light falling on the cabinets and on the windowsill, which are around 60 to 70 relative to the graph's scale. Highlights falling on faces, colored highlights bouncing off objects, and any other bright reflected highlights that are dark enough to contain significant detail can be considered *average highlights*.

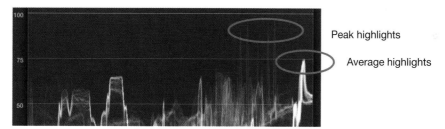

Peak highlights

Average highlights

Whether you choose the peak highlights or the average highlights to define the white point is somewhat subjective, but a good piece of advice is that if the image would look better by raising the average highlights, at the expense of clipping the peak highlights, it's probably safe to do so.

The higher the white point, the brighter your highlights are. The lower the white point, the more subdued your highlights are. When you learn to spot the white point in the Waveform Monitor, you can easily identify how much detail is in the highlights of the image by examining how jagged the highlight graphs are. A jagged graph indicates significant variation between adjacent pixels: in other words, detail within the image.

This scene has a lower, somewhat subdued average white point, which makes sense given that it's a night shot. However, notice that the specular highlights still nearly hit the top of the scale (specular highlights are pinpoint reflections, sun glints, and highlights). Just because a scene happens at night doesn't mean that direct lighting or highlights will diminish along with the reflected highlights elsewhere in the scene.

Turning attention to the bottom of the waveform, the *black point* is the lowest dip in the waveform graph. In the current image, the black point corresponds to the night-time view through the windows, which dips to approximately 10 relative to the wave-form graph's scale.

The black point represents the darkest shadows in the image, and evaluating how jag-ged the black point of the graph is will reveal the amount of shadow detail. A lower black point results in darker shadows, a higher black point results in lighter, milkier shadows. This image has elevated shadows, relative to the 0 of absolute black, which gives the scene a softer, less harsh appearance that is appropriate to the romantic mood of the scene.

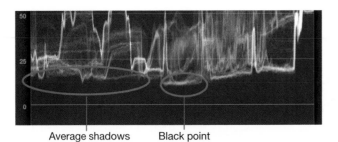
Average shadows   Black point

Now that you've spotted the white and black points, the difference between them represents the *contrast ratio* of the clip. A wider difference between the white and black points indicates a *high-contrast* ratio, while a narrower difference between the two indicates a *low-contrast* ratio. In general, low-contrast clips appear more subdued, while high-contrast clips appear sharper and more vivid.

Finally, the *average midtones* can be seen in the densest cluster of graphed values found between the black and white points. In the current image, the average mid-tones can be seen in the cluster of values ranging from approximately 20 to 40 relative to the graph's scale.

Lower average midtones indicate a generally darker image with more shadow and fewer highlights. Higher average midtones indicate a brighter, more fully lit image with pools of light and highlighted detail. This image has lower average midtones, which is appropriate for an evening scene.

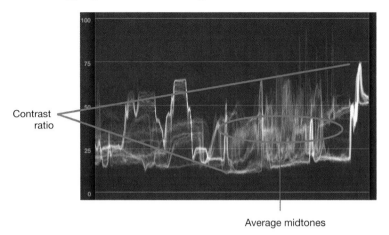

Contrast ratio

Average midtones

6   Click anywhere in the fourth clip in the Timeline.

Now compare the white point, black point, contrast ratio, and average midtones shown in the luma waveform to those of the previous image you evaluated.

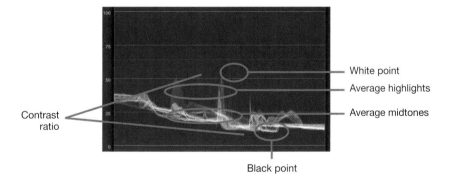

White point

Average highlights

Average midtones

Contrast ratio

Black point

You should immediately spot that the highlights are lower, the shadows are a bit elevated, and the average midtones are quite low. Overall, the contrast ratio (the difference between the highlights and shadows) is much, much lower than in the previous shot. Overall, this is a dimmer, more subdued image, as is indicated by the graph.

The luma waveform is invaluable for evaluating and comparing the relative lightness within a scene. It gives you a precise view of the tonal range of your clip, as well as letting you directly compare the black point, white point, and average midtones of two clips you might later want to match. (You'll learn more about this in Lesson 11.)

7 From the Settings pop-up menu of the video scope, choose Millivolts.

The graph scale changes, now ranging from –140 through 840, with 0 showing absolute black, and 700 showing the maximum allowable white level. Depending on the types of scopes you use, millivolts might be more familiar than the default 0 to 100 IRE scale of the video scope. Also, if you're adjusting your project's color according to quality control (QC) guidelines you've been provided, the maximum and minimum allowable signal strengths may be expressed in mV.

8 Return the scale to IRE, and then from the Settings pop-up menu, choose RGB Parade.

The RGB Parade scope lets you use three waveforms to analyze the color balance of your clips. The video signal is mathematically separated into red, green, and blue color channels, each of which is monochrome. These three monochrome color channels are then analyzed the same way the luma waveform was, and the results are shown side by side.

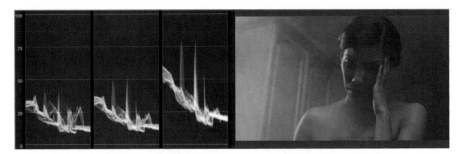

This example shows the relative strength of the red, green, and blue channels. In the current clip, the blue channel is much higher, and is therefore much stronger than the lower red and green channels.

9 Click anywhere in the sixth clip in the Timeline.

In this clip, you can see that the bottoms of the red, green, and blue waveforms are fairly balanced, which indicates that the shadows are relatively neutral.

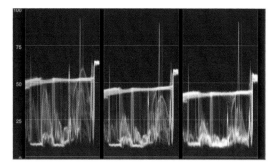

This occurs because red, green, and blue added together in equal measure results in a neutral tone, whether black, gray, or white. This is key information because black shadows and white highlights should always be somewhat balanced with waveforms of roughly equal height at or near the extreme top and bottom of the waveform graph. Color images won't have RGB waveforms that perfectly line up (only desaturated grayscale images have waveforms that do), but the tops and bottoms should roughly line up if the image is not meant to be tinted.

Knowing this, and looking at the tops of the waveforms for the current image, you'll see that the top of the red waveform is higher (not the peak white of the spectral highlights on the pottery, but the practical white point falling within the scene). This shows that a slightly warm, reddish color cast exists in the highlights but isn't in the shadows. This is a valuable detail to know when choosing how to make your upcoming color correction.

10 From the Settings pop-up menu, choose RGB Overlay. The RGB Overlay option shows the same information as the RGB Parade option, except that the three waveforms are overlaid on top of each other.

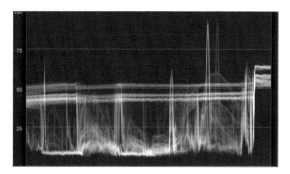

An interesting feature of the RGB Overlay scope is that when parts of the three red, green, and blue waveforms overlap, the colors interact so that neutral parts of the overlay graph appear white. On the other hand, regions where individual color channels are dramatically offset from one another are easy to see as they're distinctly color coded.

Whether you use the Overlay or RGB views is largely a matter of preference, depending on which view makes it easier to find the information you're looking for.

Final Cut Pro has several more waveform viewing modes, but the luma, RGB Parade, and RGB Overlay are the most useful for day-to-day color correction work. In the next section, you'll combine the image analysis you learned here with color adjustments made using the Color Board.

Adjusting Contrast Using the Color Board

All detailed manual color adjustments in Final Cut Pro X are performed within the Color Board, a dedicated color correction interface with controls for the contrast, color, and saturation of overlapping image regions. In other words, you can make separate but overlapping adjustments to the shadows, highlights, and midtones of your images.

All the adjustments you'll make in this section are *primary color corrections*. Primary corrections are adjustments that affect the overall image, and represent the starting point of any color adjustment whether corrective or creative. By learning to make effective primary color adjustments, you'll also learn how to use the Color Board controls to best effect.

Adjusting Contrast Manually

As you learned when using the Waveform Monitor, contrast is the difference between the darkest and lightest parts of an image. It is also the foundation of every adjustment you'll make to your clips.

In this section, you'll manipulate the Final Cut Pro X Exposure controls to modify the shadows, highlights, and midtones, to achieve a specific look.

1   Open the Project Library, if necessary, and double-click the *Burnt Dinner* project to open it into the Timeline. If necessary, open the video scopes (Command-7), narrow the Event Browser, and adjust the video scope and Viewer to a comfortable size.

2   Click in the latter third of the last clip in the Timeline.

Even when the playhead is on the appropriate location, it's vital that you always select the clip you want to adjust—either by clicking it, or pressing C. The Video Inspector always shows the properties of the currently selected clip. If your playhead is on the clip you want to work on, but another clip is selected in the Timeline, you'll make unintended adjustments to the selected clip.

TIP ▶ If the Color Board is already open to a particular set of controls, you can click or otherwise select another clip in the Timeline and the Color Board controls will update to those of the currently selected clip. This feature helps you move more quickly through a group of clips while making adjustments.

3   Use the Settings pop-up menu of the video scope to display the waveform, and choose the Luma option.

As you've learned, the luma waveform is ideal for identifying a clip's contrast ratio. You can immediately see that this clip is fairly dim. However, the luma waveform shows just how much room you have for adjustment.

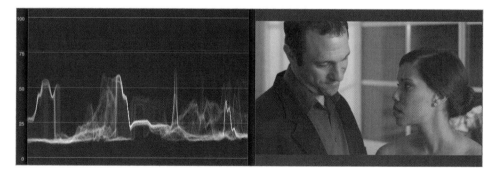

4   In the Video Inspector, click the Color Board button of Correction 1. The Color Board appears and defaults to the Color controls.

5   Click Exposure to open the Exposure controls.

You'll see four specific controls: Global, Shadows, Midtones, and Highlights.

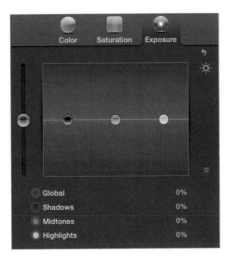

6   Slowly drag down the Shadows control (the black puck) until the faint dips at the very bottom of the luma waveform touch 0 in the graph.

As you do this, notice how the bottom of the waveform moves to match your adjustment. Also notice that the Shadows percentage value updates to reflect your change.

Because the bottom of the waveform represents the darkest shadows within the image, it's a good reference for determining how low the Shadows control can go without going below 0. The faint dips represent subtle details within the shadows: wrinkles, textures, even details within dark hair. Keeping the values above 0 preserves all detail within the image, even though the image is really dark at the moment.

7   Drag up the Highlights control (the white puck) until the waveform spike (corresponding to the highlight on the window sill behind the woman) just touches 100 in the graph.

Some brighter peak highlights—such as those corresponding to the glint reflecting off of her earring—now exceed 100, but those are low-detail highlights you can ignore for now. What's important is to use the Highlights control to adjust any bright, plausible light sources or bright detail-rich reflections up to somewhere between 90 and 100 to maximize the image contrast.

Unfortunately, with the highlights turned up this high, the shine on the man's forehead is a bit too prominent. You don't want to park all highlights at 100 percent.

8   Drag down the Highlights control until the spike corresponding to the man's forehead in the luma waveform falls to approximately 75. The highlights now look a bit more natural.

When you adjusted the highlights, you may have noticed that the shadows were dragged up a bit. These controls are somewhat interactive, such that a large adjustment to one will inevitably affect the other. Think of the Highlights and Shadows exposure controls as two ends of a rubber band with you stretching the video signal between them.

9   Drag down the Shadows control until the bottom of the luma waveform just touches 0 again.

Stretching the contrast, as you've just done, is often the first step toward creating a more vibrant and appealing image. Scenes are frequently shot with deliberately low contrast to avoid "clipping," or eliminating detail in the highlights or shadows and to provide the best possible raw media for later color correction. In those situations, you are expected to make adjustments to realize the final image contrast that was actually intended by the director of photography.

10 Just to see what happens, drag down the Shadows slider so that the portion of the waveform corresponding to the man's jacket falls underneath 0, and the portion of the waveform corresponding to the woman comes to just underneath 0.

Dragging the shadows under 0 is known as "crushing the blacks." Although crushing the blacks just a little bit can increase contrast, you'll also lose the fine shadow details. You can see this in our extreme example, as the man's jacket has lost most of its detail, and each actor's hair has flattened out. Indiscriminately crushed blacks can make hair and shadows on clothing unattractive.

11 Drag up the Shadows control again until the bottom of the waveform rests at 0. Now that you have a "contrastier" image, it's time to set the overall illumination.

12 Slowly drag up the Midtones control (the gray puck) until the top of the average mid-tone falls around 60 to 70 on the waveform.

The Midtone exposure control adjusts all values between the shadows and highlights in such a way that leaves the shadows and highlights "pinned" in place, while stretching everything in-between. To return to the rubber band analogy, if the shadows and highlights set the position of both ends of the rubber band, the Midtones control grabs the middle and stretches and scales those values toward either end.

As you adjust the Midtones control, you can see that the very bottom of the waveform (the part touching 0) remains "stuck" at 0, and the middle portion of the graph has stretched out.

Practically speaking, you might consider the Midtones exposure control to be your "time-of-day" slider. Due to the adjustment you just made, the image has become quite a bit brighter and could plausibly pass for a daytime shot. But that's not what you want.

13 Drag down the Midtones control, until the faces are bright enough to be seen clearly, but dark enough so the scene still looks convincingly like evening.

While the luma waveform can guide you in setting the black and white points of your image, setting an appropriate midtones level is much more a matter of feel and experience. In other words, you'll know the right level when you see it.

14 To compare the corrected image with the original, click the back button to return to the Video Inspector. Then, in the Video Inspector, click the Correction 1 checkbox to turn the correction on and off.

Before   After

Often, it's useful to toggle your correction on and off to see if you're on the right track by comparing what you're doing to the original shot. In this case, the improvement to the image should be immediately clear.

You should be able to see that the "after" image has more definition, crispness, and presence. That's the benefit of making a simple adjustment to contrast.

Comparing Global and Shadows Exposure Adjustments

So far, you've used the Shadows, Highlights, and Midtones controls to stretch and adjust image contrast, but the Global control has remained untouched. The Global control works similarly to the Shadows control, but with one key difference that's hard to appreciate without trying it out. In this exercise, you'll learn the difference between the two controls, and when to choose one or the other.

1   Click anywhere in the eighth clip in the Timeline. Then in the Video Inspector, click the Color Board button, and click Exposure.

2   Drag up the Highlights control until the average highlights of the luma waveform just touch 100. The image is a bit bright, but don't worry about that just yet. The next few adjustments will compensate.

3   With the highlights turned up, drag down the Shadows control until the black point of the luma waveform just touches 0.

As in the previous exercise, the overall luma waveform has stretched out so that the highlights remain near where they were, while the graph between the shadows and highlights has become taller. That's how the Shadows control works: It leaves the highlights where they are, and stretches the graph between the shadows and the highlights.

4   With the Shadows control selected, press Delete to return the control to 0.

5   Drag down the Global control (the vertical slider to the left of the Exposure controls) until the bottom of the luma waveform just touches 0, and watch what happens to the graph.

As you adjust the Global control, the luma waveform doesn't stretch. Instead, the entire waveform simply moves down so that everything is darkened equally, including the peak and average highlights.

In other applications, this type of control is sometimes referred to as *lift* because it equally lifts (or lowers) the luma of the entire video signal. You can think of the Global exposure control as a shortcut to use when you want to adjust every part of the signal, either lightening the shadows through the highlights, or darkening them. Once you've set the overall levels in this way, you can perform more specific adjustments using the Shadows, Midtones, and Highlights controls.

Or, you can ignore the Global control altogether, simply using the other controls to adjust the signal. There is no right or wrong way to work, simply what's fastest and most comfortable for you.

Take 2

Try making your own contrast adjustment to the seventh clip in this sequence. Use all the Exposure controls to maximize the contrast from the darkest shadows to the brightest highlights without clipping detail. Then set the midtones for a well-lit look that still looks like evening. If you want to experiment further, try adjusting all three exposure controls to create the impression of different times of day.

> **TIP** ▶ Additionally, it's often important to play through a clip before you start making adjustments because a clip's color and contrast can change as people move through a location, and the camera pans to different angles. Choose a frame that best represents the average color and contrast of the clip before you start your corrections.

Lesson Review

1. What are the four essential tasks of color correction?
2. Should you use proxy or original/optimized media for color correction?
3. How do you open the video scope using the keyboard?
4. What does the Vectorscope show you?
5. How do you alter the lightness of the brightest part of an image?
6. What contrast control can be described as controlling mood or time of day?
7. What does the luma waveform show you?
8. What does it mean if the graph in the Vectorscope is off-center?
9. How can you see if the skin tone in an image is correct?

Answers

1. Fixing problems, making each clip look its best, matching clips, and adding style
2. Original or optimized media
3. Press Command-7.
4. An analysis of the hue and saturation appearing in a clip
5. Using the Highlights exposure control of the Color Board
6. The midtones

7. The ranges of image contrast

8. There's a color cast, or tint, in the image.

9. From the proximity of the nearest "arm" of the Vectorscope graph to the Skin Tone Indicator

Keyboard Shortcuts

Command-4	Show Video Inspector
Command-6	Go to the Color Board
Command-7	Show video scopes

11

Lesson Files
: APTS FCP X ADV Part 3 > Lesson_11

Time
: This lesson takes approximately 120 minutes to complete.

Goals
: Understand how multiple color controls work together

Work with the Color Board to manually correct color casts

Learn to use color temperature to make creative adjustments

Analyze specific color issues using different video scopes

Transition between color corrections

Adjusting Color and Saturation

In the previous lesson, you learned how to read video scopes and adjust the contrast of clips in your program. In this chapter, you'll use the Color Board to adjust clip color and saturation.

At the end of the lesson, you'll also learn how to create smooth transitions between two different color adjustments in the same clip.

Using the Color Controls

The Final Cut Pro X color controls introduce a new method of color balancing that seeks to combine the specific control over which parts of the image you're correcting, with an easier to understand way of making the necessary changes to either add or remove color casts, or tints, in the image. In this exercise, you'll learn how each of the four color controls affects the image differently.

1   From the Project Library, open the *Test Pattern* project into the Timeline. If necessary, press Command-7 to open the video scopes. From the Settings pop-up menu, choose RGB Parade. Then close the Event Library and adjust the video scope and Viewer to a comfortable size.

This project consists of a single clip: a ramp gradient from black to white. This test pattern will help you see exactly how the color controls affect specific areas of your clips.

2   In the Timeline, click the **Gradient** clip to select it. Click the Color Board button of Correction 1 and click Color, if necessary.

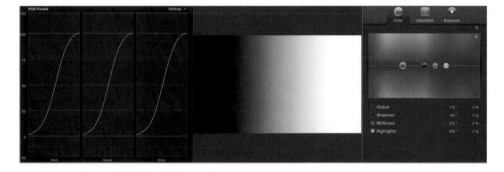

The gradient is completely without color. As a result, the red, green, and blue waveforms in the RGB Parade scope are exactly equal because equal amounts of the three primary colors combine to a completely neutral shade of black, gray, or white.

3   Drag up the Highlights color control toward blue.

Dragging up any of the controls adds the hue shown in the background of the Color Board to the tonal range influenced by that control. In this case, you've altered the highlights, *rebalancing* all three color channels simultaneously in that range. You can see that the tops of all three RGB waveforms have become unequal, while the bottoms of the waveforms remain neutral.

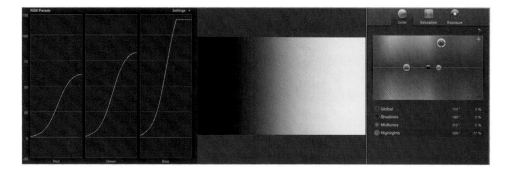

The brightest two-thirds of the gradient are tinted blue, while the darkest one-third remains neutral. Furthermore, the blue tint gradually decreases as the gradient transitions from the highlights into the shadows, so that the exact point where the hue added by your adjustment falls off is difficult to perceive.

4   Drag up the Shadows color control into the green region.

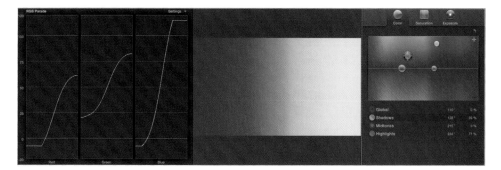

The darkest area of the gradient turns green. In the middle of the gradient, where the two color controls overlap, you see a smooth transition from green to blue. The interaction has also turned the blue a bit cyan.

The magic of the color controls is that each one affects a specific tonal region of your image. The Highlights control rebalances color in the brightest parts of your clips, while leaving the darker shadows unchanged. The Shadows control rebalances color in the darkest parts of your clips, while leaving the highlights unchanged. Meanwhile, both adjustments gradually fall off so that it's impossible to see where one correction ends and another begins, and multiple control adjustments interact smoothly.

This means that you can target your adjustments where they're most needed, either rebalancing the highlights or rebalancing the shadows. More to the point, you can create multiple adjustments of varying levels that affect different regions of the image.

5   Click the Reset button, located above the upper-right corner of the Color Board, to return the gradient to its neutral state.

6   Drag up the Midtones color control toward red.

You can see that the Midtones control affects the middle region of grays—leaving the darkest and lightest part of the image unaffected—even though the red you've added falls off gently into both the shadows and highlights.

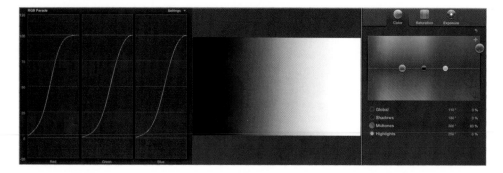

The Midtones control is effective for extending a highlights correction down even further when the peak highlights are already neutral. It's also a good control to use when you want to push a slight tint to an image without muddying neutral shadows and highlights.

In the next exercise, you'll use these controls to make a variety of real-world corrections.

Manually Eliminating Color Casts

In general, you want to adjust color balance *after* you've corrected contrast because the available tonal range of a clip will determine how the color balance controls work. In other words, if a clip has no highlights above 75 in the luma waveform, the Highlights color control won't be able to do as much to alter the image. In that case, you might want to use the Midtones color control.

Although the automatic color balance control often does a good job, the results may not always realize your expectations for the scene. For this reason, it's valuable to know how to manually adjust clip color.

In this exercise, you'll combine exposure and color adjustments, use the Vectorscope and RGB Parade scope to spot unbalanced color (a color cast), and use the color controls to correct the problem.

1   From the Project Library, open the *Burnt Dinner* project into the Timeline. If necessary, open the video scopes, close the Event Library, and adjust the scope and Viewer to a comfortable size.

2   Click anywhere in the fourth clip in the Timeline.

    Before you make any color adjustments, you need to adjust contrast.

3   From the Settings pop-up menu of the video scope, choose Waveform and Luma.

4   In the Video Inspector, click the Color Board button of Correction 1, if necessary, and then click Exposure.

    Even though this is a night scene, highlights within the picture can still be bright. In this shot, some elements would benefit from even more brightness: the light falling through the window onto the cabinet and the highlights on the woman's face and hands.

5   Drag up the Highlights control until the peak highlights of the image hit 75, and then drag down the Shadows control until the black point of the graph hits approximately 10.

In this image, it wouldn't do to drop the shadows all the way down to 0 because you'd turn the room into an inky black cave. Leaving the shadows a bit elevated preserves the detail in the woman's face, and leaves the room behind her with the impression of greater spaciousness.

Now that you've adjusted the contrast, you'll look at the color.

6   From the Settings pop-up menu of the video scope, choose Vectorscope. You should immediately notice that the graph is offset from the center point of the Skin Tone Indicator in the Vectorscope. As you learned previously, this shows that the image has a blue bias.

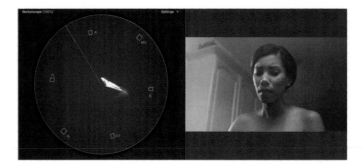

The cinematographer decided on a "midnight blue" lighting scheme, which is a bold take on a traditional choice. However, in postproduction you may decide that a more neutral treatment would be better. You'll use the color controls to reduce the amount of blue and bring more of the true color back into the image.

But which of the controls to choose first? Each of the three main color controls affects a different tonal region of the image.

When you examine the image, you notice that the main volume of blue is caused by the lighting, specifically the blue highlights that fall throughout the image. Conveniently, Final Cut Pro has the exact control you need.

7   To reduce some of the blue in the highlights, select the Color button of the Color Board, and then drag the Highlights color control down into the "negative" blue area.

To reduce or eliminate a colored tint from a particular tonal range, you drag the corresponding control down in the Color Board, under the middle line, until it's on top of the hue you're trying to reduce. The farther down you drag, the greater the amount of hue you eliminate.

That's the fundamental way the color controls work. In short, dragging one of the color controls to a color *above* the middle line *adds* a tint-particular hue to the image; dragging to a color *below* the line *removes* a tint of that hue from the image.

Next, you'll more precisely adjust the color while using the Vectorscope as a guide.

8   Once again, drag the highlights within the negative blue region of the Color Board, but this time watch the Vectorscope and try to move the control so that the graph moves closer to the center of the Skin Tone Indicator. While you do so, pay attention to the arm of the graph that stretches closest to the Skin Tone Indicator. There's an abundance of skin tone in the shot.

As you make this adjustment, it pays to keep one eye on the Vectorscope, and the other on your image. In general, if you trust your display, the important thing is that the image looks right. The video scopes are valuable guides for showing how you need to adjust your images, but ultimately the amount of correction you make is a subjective decision.

In any case, you should find that when the Vectorscope graph is more centered, and the orange/red arm of the graph falls somewhat along the diagonal Skin Tone Indicator, the image looks more neutral. If you return to the Video Inspector and turn Correction 1 off and on, you'll see a clear difference before and after this adjustment.

Before correction   After correction

The Vectorscope is a valuable tool for general analysis, but sometimes a clip will have more problems than the Highlights control can solve. In this case, the RGB Parade scope can provide a more precise color analysis of your image and give you specific guidance in choosing the color controls to use.

9   Click anywhere in the third clip in the Timeline. The color controls were already open, so the Color Board updates to reflect the settings of clip 1A-2.

Again, before making any adjustments to color, you need to adjust contrast.

10   Choose Waveform, and then from the Settings pop-up menu of the video scope, choose Luma. In this shot, the light falling through the window onto the wall could be brighter, which would make the overall shot less murky.

11   Click Exposure, and drag up the Highlights control until the average highlights corresponding to the smoke detector just touch 100.

Some of the small, faint spikes corresponding to the peak highlights now fall above 100; but those are not significant details. It's OK if they are clipped (or cut off) by a subsequent adjustment or effect that you apply, such as the Broadcast Safe effect (more on that later).

As it is, the shadows have a pleasing, soft quality; but if you wanted to create a harder, starker image with more contrast, you could drop the shadows down even lower.

12 Drag down the Shadows control until the bottom of the graph is at the equivalent of 5 on the waveform scale.

NOTE ▶ You may be wondering why the values on the scale are printed in increments of 25. With most grades, the only values that really matter are the outer boundaries of 0 and 100. Everything in the middle is relative. What's important is how things look, rather than the precise number values of the signal. As a result, these exercises have a lot of wiggle room.

Now that you've achieved a pleasing level of contrast in the image, it's time to consider the color.

13 In the Color Board, click Color, and then from the Settings pop-up menu of the video scope, choose RGB Parade.

The RGB Parade scope shows the relative strengths of each of the three primary color channels of an image. For the current clip, the tops of the three color waveforms are wildly imbalanced, and the bottoms are almost perfectly balanced. This shows that the highlights and midtones have a significant color cast, and the shadows are neutral.

14 To reduce some of the blue in the highlights, drag the Highlights color control down into the "negative" blue area.

Simply dragging over the color you want to eliminate is good for making small changes, but if you want to make larger, more precise changes, you need to make adjustments while watching the RGB Parade scope.

15 Drag the Highlights control down around the "negative" blue area of the Color Board until the top of the average highlights of the blue waveform just touches 75, and the top of the average highlights of the green waveform lies perfectly between the red and blue waveforms.

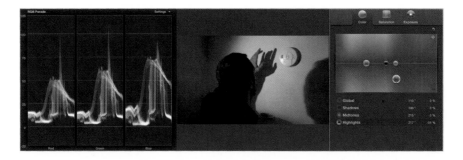

The image is still a cool blue, but the blue is now much more subtle than it was originally. However, in making such an extreme adjustment, you've turned the shadows a bit orange. It's subtle, but if you look at the bottoms of the waveforms in the RGB Parade, you should notice that the red channel is elevated and the blue channel is depressed.

16 Drag the Shadows color control toward negative orange, until the bottoms of the RGB Parade waveforms are level.

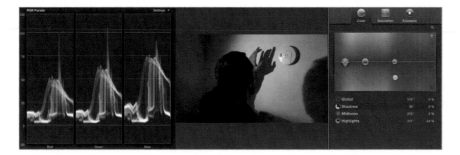

Now that the bottoms of the three waveforms line up, the shadows are nicely neutral. If you return to the Video Inspector and turn Correction 1 off and on, you'll see a dramatic before-and-after of this adjustment.

The RGB Parade scope is not only a terrific tool for showing that a color cast exists, it also helps you select the color adjustment control needed to make an exact correction.

Take 2

Try making your own contrast and color adjustments to the ninth clip in this sequence. Maximize the contrast from the darkest shadows to the brightest highlights while keeping the evening character of the shot, and then correct for the slight reddish tinge.

TIP ▶ Sometimes, a Vectorscope graph will look perfectly centered, even though you suspect the image has a very slight color cast. In these cases, the RGB Parade scope can be a better indicator of the highlights and shadows balance. In particular, slight imbalances in the shadows can create barely perceptible color problems. They're hard to spot, but cause the image to "feel" wrong. These problems are much easier to see using either the RGB Parade or RGB Overlay scopes.

Adjusting Color Temperature Creatively

Color casts aren't always bad. Another way of looking at the quality or coloration of lighting in your clips is to consider the color temperature of the dominant lighting in the scene.

Probably the most succinct example of the differences in color temperature would be the quality of light you get from an incandescent light (say, a 60-watt bulb), compared to the quality of light from an ordinary fluorescent or CFL bulb. Light from the incandescent bulb will appear more orange compared to a fluorescent light, which usually appears bluer.

When the lighting in a scene is completely neutral, the colors throughout the scene are at their most "true," and you shouldn't find any atmospheric tint in the image. However, many times a clip is too neutral, and the visuals appear clinical and less appealing than they should.

At other times a distinct color cast in the image will be desirable. For example, sunset lighting is dramatically warm, and it tints subjects with a distinct orange lighting. This is a perfect example of when you would not want to eliminate a color cast.

In other cases, the lighting of the scene may be neutral, but you want to create the illusion of a dominant color temperature. "Warm" and "cool" lighting can influence the emotional feel of your images. Saying that "warm lighting is romantic" and "cool lighting is distancing" is tremendously simplistic, but there's truth in the idea that the dominant color temperature of the lighting will affect audience response to what's happening.

In the next exercise, you'll carefully insert a subtle color cast to add visual character to some otherwise neutrally lit scenes.

1   Click anywhere in the fourth clip to select it, and click Color in the Color Board.

The original color cast in this clip had already been neutralized. While the dominant "blueishness" is gone, the image remains cool, which is a reasonable look for an evening scene.

However, with one color tint visibly eliminated, you have the option of subtly pushing the color of the scene in other directions to give the image a different feeling.

2   Drag up the Midtones control slightly into the positive orange area of the Color Board, above the center line. You want to add a slight amount of orange to the scene, but not too much.

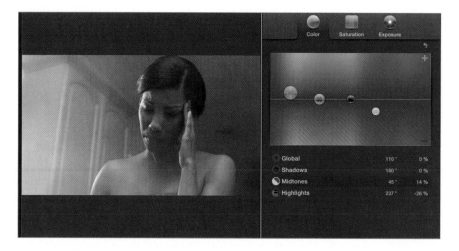

As you drag the Midtones control, you add orange throughout the middle area of image tonality. You might also refer to this as "warming up" the image. When working with color, orange tints are generally considered "warm," and blue tints are considered "cool."

The original "cool" treatment with blue in the highlights

A "warmer" treatment with more orange in the midtones

The advantage of creating color casts with the Midtones control is that you can keep nice, solid-looking blacks and bright, pure white highlights while altering everything in-between.

However, another, bolder technique is to use the Highlights color control to alter the color temperature of a scene.

3   Click anywhere in the last clip to select it.

4   Drag the Highlights control up slightly into the positive blue-cyan area of the Color Board, above the center line. You want to add a slight amount of blue to the scene (a "silvery" quality), but not too much.

This last adjustment cooled off the scene, but it also pulled the shadows—which weren't quite at 0—into the same quality of cool, which may make the shot look a bit more tinted than it should be. Look at the uneven bottoms of the three graphs in the RGB Parade scope. This change also requires a compensating adjustment using the Shadows color control.

5   Drag down the Shadows control slightly into the negative blue-cyan area of the Color Board, until the bottoms of the three waveforms of the RGB Parade scope are roughly level with one another.

While you might not have been aware of the tint in the shadows, you should now notice that it's gone. The entire image looks considerably more naturalistic.

As you can see, color correction isn't just about correcting problems. Sometimes it's about creating a warm, cool, or neutral quality of light that should have been in the original media, but for whatever reason wasn't.

For this reason, it's important to be able to control subtle shifts in color quality within specific tonal regions of your images using the color controls.

Image with original color

Image with cooler highlights

Image with cooler highlights and neutralized shadows

Take 2

Try adjusting contrast and color in the tenth and eleventh clips in this sequence. Adjust the contrast, and then experiment with adding stylistic tints to the images, warming or cooling them off. If you want to try something really different, try adding a greenish tint to the highlights to simulate bad fluorescent lighting.

> **NOTE ▶** Consumer fluorescent bulbs often emit a spike in the green part of the spectrum that is invisible to the eye but easily recorded by film or digital cameras.

Using the Global Color Control

As you've seen, the Highlights, Shadows, and Midtones controls can adjust extremely specific regions of image lightness. The Global color control, as its name implies, lets you make larger adjustments that affect every tonal region of the image at once.

Now you'll use the Global color control to produce overall corrective adjustments and bold stylistic changes.

1   From the Project Library, open the *Cooking* project into the Timeline. In a previous exercise, you turned off iMovie effects and color adjustments, leaving these clips in a completely uncorrected state. Verify that iMovie effects and adjustment are still disabled.

2   Click the first clip of the project to select it and display its parameters in the Video Inspector or Color Board. If the Video Inspector is open, click the Color Board button of Correction 1 to open the Color Board.

With the video scope set to the RGB Parade view of the waveform, you should notice that the red channel is a bit higher than the green channel, and the blue channel is a bit lower. While difficult to see within the shot, this situation creates a subtle coloration you can correct using the Global control.

3 Drag the Global color control (the bigger control with crosshairs) to negative orange in the Color Board until the bottoms of the three color channel waveforms are level. (This will be a very small adjustment.)

TIP ▶ To make fine adjustments, click a control to select it, and then press the Up, Down, Left, or Right Arrow key to move it.

As you make this adjustment, notice that all three color channels are simultaneously rebalanced in this operation, but the waveform of each color channel is lifted or lowered in its entirety, rather than being stretched. In this way, the Global color control is similar to the Global exposure control in that it lifts affected image components, rather than stretching them.

4 Return to the Video Inspector and turn Correction 1 off and on. You can see that your adjustment was subtle, but the neutralizing effect on the image is clearly discernable.

In this way, the Global color control can also be one of the first color adjustments you make to level out the shadows while simultaneously adjusting the rest of the image. This technique is appropriate for images in which a color cast is equally strong in the shadows, midtones, and highlights. You can then use the other color controls to make further color adjustments as necessary.

Another use of the Global color control is to create large, image-wide tints for creative effect.

5   Open the Color Board again, if necessary, and drag the Global color control up into the positive orange region of the Color Board, until the entire image has a strong, orange tint.

This kind of strong tint is often called a color wash, and can be useful as the basis for bold stylistic treatments, such as when using video within a title sequence, as a background, or creating a video montage with a wholly separate visual quality.

Here, you can see even more clearly that the Global color control lifts or lowers each of the three color channels in their entirety.

Take 2

Try making similar global color corrections to other clips in this sequence. Combine them with high- and low-contrast adjustments to achieve different looks.

Adjusting Saturation

So far, you've manipulated both the contrast and color control, but you've yet to explore a third set of controls: saturation.

Saturation refers to the intensity of a particular color or group of colors. A highly saturated red is more vivid and intense than a less saturated red of identical hue. In many applications, a single saturation control lets you adjust the overall saturation of all colors throughout the image.

Final Cut Pro X provides considerably more detailed saturation adjustments then previous versions of Final Cut Pro, with a total of four controls. In this exercise, you'll make global and targeted saturation adjustments, and learn how to affect different parts of the image.

1   From the Project Library, open the *Burnt Dinner* project into the Timeline. If necessary, open the video scopes, close the Event Library, and adjust the video scope and Viewer to a comfortable size.

2   Click anywhere in the last third of the last clip in the Timeline to select it and display its parameters in the Video Inspector or Color Board. If the Video Inspector is open, click the Color Board button of Correction 1 to open the Color Board.

You adjusted this clip in a previous exercise to achieve a higher-contrast look with cool highlights and neutral shadows. Now, you're going to adjust the saturation of different parts of the image.

3   In the Color Board , click saturation to open the saturation controls.

4   Set the video scope to display the Vectorscope.

5   Drag the Global saturation control (the leftmost slider) down to the bottom of the slider's range. As you drag the Global saturation control down, notice that the Vectorscope graph shrinks and completely disappears when the image is grayscale.

As shown earlier, the size of the Vectorscope graph, or each graph arm's distance from the center, indicates the amount of saturation in the clip. When you completely remove color from a shot, the Vectorscope graph disappears because the image has no color to analyze.

6   Slowly drag the Global saturation control back up, and watch the Vectorscope graph grow as the image becomes more colorful. Continue dragging the Global saturation control up past the neutral halfway point to the top of the slider.

The Vectorscope graph has gotten considerably larger, showing how much the saturation has increased. Additionally, you can see that the entire image has grown more colorful and intense with a strange, artificial look.

Since the Global slider increases saturation throughout the image, it increases the colorfulness of the image even where you might not expect to see it, such as in shadows and darker regions of the image that are typically desaturated in real life. For this reason, increasing Global saturation too much is rarely advisable.

7   Click the Reset button, or press Delete.

TIP ▶ The Reset buttons in the Color, Saturation, and Exposure areas of the Color Board reset those parameters exclusively. They do not reset the entire color adjustment. In other words, you can reset Saturation while leaving the Color and Exposure controls unaltered.

The Global slider is extremely useful for increasing image saturation when a clip looks lackluster, or for decreasing overall image saturation when you want a clip to have a more muted look.

8   Drag the Global saturation control down about halfway between the neutral center position and the bottom of the slider's range.

At this diminished state, you can still see color throughout the image, but it's very faint and muted. This is the basis for any look using muted color, and can allow you to create more colorfully tinted looks that don't appear excessive.

9 Click Color to open the color controls, and drag the Midtones color control up into the blue region to add a cool tone to the desaturated image.

In its desaturated state, the image takes on an interesting cool tone; but because it's so desaturated, the color cast you introduced isn't as distracting as it would be if the image were at full saturation.

10 Click Saturation to reopen the saturation controls, and click the Reset button to return saturation to the default neutral position.

Returning to the original saturation value of the image, you can see that the blue tint you added now takes on a vivid, undesirable character.

11 Press Command-Z to undo the saturation increase and return image saturation to its previously muted level.

In this case, you might find that a tonally specific, targeted saturation increase would give you a more sophisticated look. That's where the Shadows, Midtones, and Highlights saturation controls come in. These controls let you make targeted adjustments to image saturation within each range of image tonality.

12 Drag the Midtones saturation control up to the top of its range.

With this adjustment, you significantly increased image saturation, but it doesn't affect the shadows (which ordinarily should be less saturated) or the highlights (where the whites of the image reside), so the increase doesn't look quite as artificial.

For this reason, the Midtone saturation control can be a useful way to increase image saturation without putting unwanted color in the shadows and highlights where it might look strange.

13 As an experiment, try raising and lowering the Shadows and Highlights saturation controls to see how these adjustments affect the image.

You should notice that, as with the color controls, broad overlap exists between each of the three tonal ranges affected by these controls, so that excessive adjustment of shadows or highlights saturation inevitably affects midtone saturation. This is the way these controls have been designed, and with time you'll learn to control and use these interactions to your advantage.

Take 2

Try making targeted saturation adjustments to the eighth and ninth clips in this sequence. Add warm and cool color tints of your own in conjunction with saturation increases and decreases to get a feel for how the color and saturation controls interact.

Changing Saturation with Contrast Adjustments

Now that you're exploring the interaction of the color, saturation, and contrast controls, you should be aware of one more interaction. Because of the way Final Cut Pro X processes color, changes to image contrast using the exposure controls also affect image saturation. In this brief exercise, you'll see the results of that interaction.

1   With the *Burnt Dinner* project open and the video scope displaying the Vectorscope, click anywhere in the last third of the first clip in the Timeline to select it and display its parameters in the Color Board. Then, in the Color Board, click Exposure.

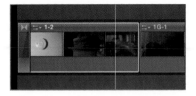

In its uncorrected state, this clip has a dark, muted blue look.

2   Drag up the Highlights exposure control to raise the white point, lightening the image by stretching this clip's contrast.

As you raise the contrast of this clip, notice that the Vectorscope graph grows larger, and the blue of the image becomes more saturated. This is by design. Even if you make no adjustments to the saturation controls, using the exposure controls to raise contrast also increases image saturation. Conversely, lowering image contrast also lowers saturation.

In general, this is a good thing because low-contrast images can usually benefit from a bit of increased saturation and increased contrast. However, you must be aware of this interaction so that you can control it, depending on the look you need to create in your clips.

For example, if you want muted color but need to raise image contrast, you can always later lower saturation using the Global saturation control.

Dissolving Between Two Grades

So far, you've made a variety of adjustments designed to affect an entire clip, from beginning to end. However, the lighting within a clip sometimes changes so drastically that you'll need to grade the first half differently from the second half. For that reason, it's always a good idea to play a clip completely through, before you start to grade it.

In this exercise, you'll see how to create transitions between different grades applied to the same clip.

1   Open the Project Library and double-click the *Burnt Dinner* project to open it into the Timeline. If necessary, open the video scopes, close the Event Library, and adjust the video scope and Viewer to a comfortable size.

2   Press the ; (semicolon) and ' (apostrophe) keys to move the playhead to the fifth clip in the Timeline. Press C to select the clip and display its parameters in the Video Inspector or Color Board. If the Video Inspector is open, click the Color Board button of Correction 1 to open the Color Board.

3   Play through the clip, and return the playhead to the beginning of the clip when you're done.

When the light in the room is turned on, about halfway through the clip, the character of the room predictably changes, such that a grade successfully applied to the beginning of the clip might not work so well at the end. Let's try it.

4   With the fifth clip selected, move the playhead anywhere over the first half, when the room is still dark. Drag the Timeline Zoom slider to the right, or move the pointer into the Timeline area, and press Command-= (equal sign) to zoom into the Timeline, so it's easier to navigate to specific clip frames.

5   Set the video scope to display the luma waveform, and then click Exposure. Adjust the Shadows exposure control so that the bottom of the waveform just sits on 0, and adjust the Midtones exposure control so the average highlights just touch 50. You're lightening the image while keeping the shadows dark.

6   Click Color, and drag the Highlights color control up into positive blue, to "blue up" the highlights even more.

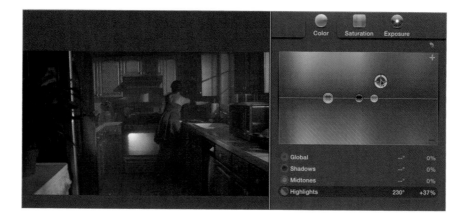

7 Click Saturation, and lower the Shadows saturation control to reduce saturation in the darkest shadows, and raise the Highlights saturation control to increase saturation in the brighter portion of the image to compensate.

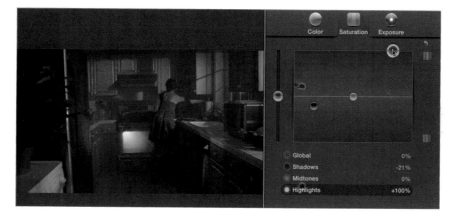

8 Play the clip. If you like, go back to the Video Inspector and turn Correction 1 off and on to see a before/after of the correction you just made, but be sure to reopen the Color Board when you're done.

Notice that, with this initial adjustment, the night portion of the clip looks the way you want it, but now the "lit" portion of the clip looks washed out and unflattering. This is a perfect instance of needing to create a transition between two different adjustments.

In Final Cut Pro X, you cannot animate color adjustments. However, you can split a clip into two halves, grade each half separately, and then dissolve from the first grade to the second to create a seamless transition.

9   Press the Left and Right Arrow keys to move the playhead over the clip and identify the range of frames over which the lighting is raised. In this clip, the room lighting is on a dimmer, so it takes approximately 12 frames to go from "night" to "lit," from approximately 01:00:33:21 to 01:00:34:09.

> **TIP** ▶ Even when room lighting is changed using a switch, bulbs often need time to warm up, so there's usually at least two or three frames of transition from "unlit" to "lit" practical lighting.

10 Move the playhead to the middle of the transition (around 01:00:34:03), and choose Edit > Blade (or press Command-B) to "blade" or split the clip into two at the position of the playhead.

11 Click the edit you just created at the position of the playhead, and choose Edit > Add Cross Dissolve (or press Command-T) to add a cross dissolve at the selected edit point.

12 Control-click the Cross Dissolve transition in the Timeline. From the shortcut menu, choose Change Duration, and in the timecode entry field, type *12* and press Return to change the duration to 12 frames.

You've now created a situation where the "night" portion of the shot dissolves to the "lit" portion of the same shot, and the transition covers the duration of the practical change in lighting.

Now that you've set up this artificial transition, you can grade the second half of the clip for the best possible "lit" look.

13 Click anywhere on the "lit" second half of the clip, and open the Color Board for Correction 1.

14 Click Exposure, and adjust the Highlights exposure control so that the average highlights just hit 75. Adjust the Midtones exposure control so that the average midtones fall between approximately 15 and 50. Adjust the Shadows exposure control so that the very bottom of the left of the luma graph falls just below 0.

15 Click Color, and drag the Highlights color control from blue to orange (not much, only around 15 percent more according to the Highlights parameter shown below the Color Board).

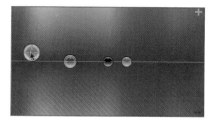

16 Click Saturation, click the Reset button, and then raise the Midtones saturation control to make the middle region of tonality more colorful, without making it look radioactive.

You've created a distinct, warm, and well-lit grade that's more appropriate for the second half of the clip.

17 Play through both halves of the clip. As you can see, the "night" grade transitions cleanly into the "lit" grade, with both halves of the shot adjusted for optimal appearance.

The "cool night" treatment   The "tungsten-lit warm" treatment

In clips with changing lighting, it's worth taking the time to create custom grades for each part of the clip to ensure that you have the look your project needs at all times.

Take 2

Now that you've set up the transition from one part of the shot to the next, try creating different types of adjustments—low contrast, high contrast, colorful, muted—to see how different scenic treatments segue into one another.

Lesson Review

1. What is a color cast?

2. If an unwanted orange tint is in the brightest parts of the image, what adjustment might you make in the Color Board?

3. Which Color Board control alters color throughout the entire tonal range of the image?

4. Will changes to exposure alter which parts of the image the color controls will affect?

5. What happens to image saturation when you increase image contrast by lowering the Shadows and raising the Highlights exposure controls?

6. Which two color controls can you use to align the bottoms of the red, green, and blue color channels as viewed in the RGB Parade scope?

7. What does color temperature describe?

8. What does it mean if the bottoms of the red, green, and blue waveforms in the RGB Parade waveform don't align?

Answers

1. An unwanted tint in the image

2. Move the Highlights color control to negative orange.

3. The Global color control

4. Yes

5. Saturation increases.

6. The Global and Shadows color controls

7. The "color" of the lighting, seen primarily as a tint to the image

8. A color cast, or tint, exists in the shadows of the image.

Keyboard Shortcuts

Command-7	Open the video scopes
Command-B	Split (or blade) a clip into two parts
Command-T	Add a cross dissolve

12

Lesson Files	APTS FCP X ADV Part 3 > Lesson_12
Time	This lesson takes approximately 90 minutes to complete.
Goals	Learn how to automatically balance two clips
	Master the process of breaking a scene down for balancing
	Understand how to use video scopes to compare different aspects of two clips
	Use different commands to copy corrections among similar clips in a scene
	See how to properly apply the Broadcast Safe effect

Color Matching

Matching the color and contrast of one shot to another is one of the most fundamental aspects of the color correction process, and dates back to the photochemical color timing process used for decades in film.

Of course, it's no longer necessary to time a film, develop an answer print, and develop it prior to making your next pass. You can simply adjust the Final Cut Pro X Color Board controls and see how your scene improves, all in real time.

With Final Cut Pro X, you can automatically or manually match one shot to another. Each method has its advantages and disadvantages, and in this chapter you'll learn both. Furthermore, you'll also apply a single correction to multiple shots, and combine multiple corrections to streamline your workflow.

Understanding Shot Matching

Shot matching (sometimes referred to as *scene-to-scene correction*) is key to ensuring that your edit plays seamlessly to your audience. In a narrative project, a five-minute scene may consist of shots photographed over an entire day, or if the material is ambitious, shots made over several days or weeks. You may even be expected to match insert shots taken *months* later during reshoots.

Subtle variations in lighting, shadow, and color temperature make cuts more obvious than they ought to be. For example, cutting from a brighter shot to a darker shot within an evenly lit room will call attention to that edit point, even if an audience member might not identify the exact problem.

Shot-to-shot variation can also be a problem in documentary filmmaking. A camera operator may "ride" the exposure on the fly, adjusting for rapidly changing conditions. A cinematographer might make a mid-interview adjustment to a room's lighting to improve the visuals. Or, an available-light field shoot may simply have so many different angles that, after editing, the lighting appears chaotic.

All of these conditions necessitate matching one shot to another, also referred to as *scene balancing*. The idea is to adjust the contrast and color within every shot to create the illusion that a scene was photographed at one time and in one place.

Matching Clips Automatically

There's no shame in admitting that scene balancing is not going to be the most exciting part of your day. As fun as grading can be, once you've defined the look of a shot, adjusting the rest of the shots in that scene to match your grade can be tedious.

To make your day more enjoyable, Final Cut Pro X has an automatic Match Color tool you can use to quickly match one clip to another. As with all automatic tools, the result is not always perfect, and you give up a certain degree of control. However, this tool can be effective with the right type of footage, and can certainly speed things up when it produces the results you desire.

Performing Simple Clip Matching

In the following exercise, you'll use the Match Color tool to automatically balance all the shots in a documentary scene.

1   In the Project Library, display the contents of the APTS FCP X ADV Part 3 disk image, and then click the disclosure triangle next to the Lesson_12 folder to show its contents.

2   Double-click the *Agriculture* project to open it, and press Shift-Z to expand its clips to the available width of the Timeline. Then press Command-4 to open the Inspector.

3   Click the first and fourth clips in the project, and compare how they look.

The first and fourth clips compared

Notice that the first shot is considerably yellower than the fourth shot. In fact, by clicking each of the five clips in this project, you should notice that each has a slightly different color cast.

4   Click the first clip to select it, and then in the Color group of the Inspector, click the Match Color checkbox.

When you select the Match Color checkbox, the Viewer changes to a two-up display titled Match Color. At the bottom of the Viewer you are directed to "Skim to a frame you want to match, and click to preview."

5   Move the pointer over the fourth clip in the Timeline, and then click the clip. As you move the pointer over the fourth clip, the frames you're skimming are displayed on the left, and the current frame of the clip you want to adjust is on the right. When you click, the frame on the right is automatically adjusted to match the frame on the left.

However, clicking only previews what that match will be like using the frame you clicked on.

6   Click a different frame within the fourth clip. Notice that the automatic adjustment is subtly different. As you can see, choosing different frames yields different results. For this reason, the interface encourages experimentation before you decide on a match.

7   Click the fourth clip a few more times until you find a match you like. Then, click Apply Match, or press Return.

When you click Apply Match, an adjustment is made and stored within the Match Color parameter of the Color group in the Inspector. The Viewer once again displays just the frame at the position of the playhead. The Correction 1 settings are not affected. If necessary, you can always change the Match Color adjustment.

8   With the first clip still selected, in the Inspector, click the Match Color parameter's Choose button.

The 2-up display reappears in the Viewer, ready to match another clip.

9   Click a variety of frames of the last clip in the Timeline, and click Apply Match (or press Return) when you're finished.

There's considerably more variation when choosing different frames from the last clip, so make sure that you preview several sections of the clip before making a final choice.

Matching Corrected Clips

In the previous exercise, you matched the first clip to an uncorrected clip elsewhere in the Timeline. You can also match clips to other clips that are already color corrected.

1   Click the middle of the third clip to select it, and in the Video Inspector, click the Correction 1 Color Board button to open the Color Board.

2   Press Command-7 to open the video scopes. If necessary, set the video scopes to display the RGB Overlay and Histogram.

3   Click Exposure. Drag the Global slider down until the left side of the shared gray portion of the Histogram is just to the left of 0. Then drag the Midtones slider up until the tallest green and red spikes in the Histogram touch 75.

4   From the video scope Settings pop-up menu, choose Vectorscope. In the Color Board, click Color, and drag the Highlights color control up toward a blue/cyan split until the Vectorscope graph is somewhat centered and a large blue arm points toward the B target.

5 Click Saturation, and drag the Midtones saturation control up to approximately +36%. At this point, you should have a contrasty, cool version of the image.

6 Click the first clip in the Timeline to select it, and in the Color Board, click the back arrow button to return to the Video Inspector.

7 Click the Match Color parameter's Choose button, and click any frame of the third clip (the one you just adjusted). Click Apply Match. The Match Color preview updates to match the color treatment you created in the third clip.

This technique provides you with a bit more control than simply matching uncorrected clips. If you want to impose a particular look on a scene, you can first make a primary adjustment to a clip that's most representative of the scene, and then use Match Color to match the rest of the clips in the scene to it.

Take 2

Use the Match Color tool to match the rest of the clips in the *Agriculture* project to the third clip. Next, reset the color controls of all the clips in the project, and try creating a different look using a different clip, using the Match Color controls to match the other clips in the project to your new look.

Matching Clips Manually

It's tempting to think that the Match Color tool will solve all of your problems. The truth is, it often works well, but sometimes the results are not quite what you would prefer. You can see this situation in the following exercise.

1   Open the Project Library, and double-click the *Hero Scene* project to open it in the Timeline.

2   Select the fourth clip in the Timeline to open it in the Video Inspector.

3   In the Video Inspector, select the Match Color checkbox, and click the fifth clip in the Timeline to preview the resulting match.

While the general quality of shot 4 now approximates that of shot 5, you should immediately see that the skin tone and highlights of the image are considerably flat-tened and blown out. The automatic choices made to match these two shots are too brute force for the material. In this situation, manual matching will allow a more deft adjustment.

4   Click Cancel to skip the operation.

Breaking Down a Scene

Successful scene balancing requires organization. Before you do anything, you need to watch the entire scene to get a sense of what you're starting with, and where you need to take it, grading-wise.

After watching the scene, pick a single clip that best represents the location of the scene and the people within it. This might be a long shot; it might be a medium two-shot; or it could be a close-up, if it's a tightly photographed scene. Whichever clip you use, it should be representative of the color, contrast, and content found throughout that scene.

This is important because you'll be making your first adjustments to this *reference* clip, and then comparing every other shot in the scene to that reference as you match every other clip to it.

This method prevents you from chasing your tail in an unending, overlapping series of undisciplined revisions. For example, you would grade shot 1, and play around with it for a while until you're sure you like the result. Then match shots 2, 3, and 4 to shot 1, and you're finished.

However, if you grade shot 1, and then match shot 2 to shot 1, and then match shot 3 to shot 2, the comparative color balance might work for that cut, but could be noticeably different from shot 1. Then you match shot 4 to shot 3, introducing more inadvertent variation. In the end, shot 4 doesn't really match shot 1, and you need to start all over again.

For the next exercise, see if you can choose a good image to use as a reference from the following series of clips:

If you chose the first clip, that is, in fact, a very good reference candidate for the scene. It's a nice wide shot that shows the overall location, its lighting is representative of all the angles within the scene (including the sunlit patio and the shaded doorway), and the main character can be seen clearly.

Here's something else to keep in mind. Sometimes a scene is a mixed bag of clips from a qualitative point of view. Half of the clips may be wonderfully lit and noise free, while the other half may be compromised as a result of changing lighting conditions or a problem during the shoot.

In situations when some of the clips might be difficult to correct, you may need to choose a reference clip from one of the problem clips to determine the best adjustment to make under the circumstances. By so doing, you'll have a far easier time matching higher-quality to lower-quality clips, than taking on the (perhaps impossible) task of matching the poor-quality clips to the high-quality.

In the following series of exercises, you'll match clips within a scene with one another to achieve good continuity of color and contrast.

Grading the First Clip

Once again, your first order of business is to choose a reference clip, and make a correction that best suits the scene.

1   If necessary, open the Project Library, and double-click the *Hero Scene* project to open it in the Timeline.

2   Click in the last third of the first clip in the Timeline to select it and open it in the Video Inspector. The Viewer shows the black-suited man crouched in front of the door.

3   Click the Color Board button of Correction 1, and press Command-7 to open the video scopes, if necessary.

4   From the video scope Settings pop-up menu, choose Waveform (make sure it's set to Luma), and then in the Color Board, click Exposure.

5   Drag the Shadows exposure control down until the bottom of the waveform graph just touches 0, and drag the Midtones control up to around +9%. This raises the contrast of the image, while lightening the midtones a bit to make sure that you can clearly see the details within the man's black suit.

6   From the Settings pop-up menu, choose RGB Parade. In the Color Board, click Color.

7   Drag the Highlights color control up just a bit into the orange part of the spectrum (around 46°, +18%) to warm up the image. Drag the Shadows color control down to negative orange until the very bottoms of the red, green, and blue waveforms line up again. This warms up the environment to give some heat to the day, while keeping the black of the man's suit deep and untinted.

8   Click Saturation, and drag the Midtones saturation control down to around –15% to mute the skin tones and greens of the shot just a bit.

9   For one last check, set the video scope to display the luma waveform. The luma waveform is over 100, so click Exposure, and lower the Highlights exposure control so that
the top of the graph just touches 100.

In general, the luma levels of a video signal should never go above 100 because you
risk clipping out detail you might want to keep. You may also get into level trouble if
you're handing your program off for broadcast playback.

If you'd like to compare the corrected clip with the original, click the back arrow
button to return to the Video Inspector, and select and deselect the Correction 1
checkbox to turn the correction on and off.

Before correction

After correction

Match Other Clips to the Reference Clip

Now that you've set a grade for the initial clip, it's time to start matching other clips to
clip 1. In this exercise, you'll compare two clips in the Timeline, and learn how to spot
differences quickly using video scopes to guide your corrections.

1   Return to the Timeline. Press ; (semicolon) and ' (apostrophe) to jump back and forth
between the beginning of the first clip and the beginning of the second clip.

Using these keyboard commands is the easiest way to compare two clips and see their
visual differences. You'll see both full-frame shots in rapid succession, which helps
overcome your eye's built-in ability to adapt to the ambient color within a scene.

For example, after staring at the grade from the previous exercise for a few minutes, you
may have thought that the adjustments you made were fairly subtle; but jumping back
and forth between it and the next ungraded clip reveals just how big the difference is.

Using these keys, while convenient, has one shortcoming: You can't choose the frames
you're comparing. To compare two specific frames, you need to use markers.

2 Drag the playhead to the frame you were viewing while adjusting the shot in the previous exercise (somewhere in the last third of the first clip). Press M to place a marker.

3 Drag the playhead to an appropriate frame of the second clip. (There's a lot of motion, so you'll want to choose the frame with the least amount of motion blur.) Press M to place another marker.

4 With both markers placed, press Control-; (semicolon) and Control-' (apostrophe) to jump between the clips at these two adjacent markers. By looking at the black-suited man's face in both shots, you'll clearly see the differences between the two clips; but if you also use the video scopes, you'll be able identify the kinds of adjustments needed to make the second clip match the first.

5 If necessary, move the playhead over the second clip, and press C to select it.

6 From the Settings pop-up menu of the video scope, choose Luma (make sure it's set to Waveform). Then press the Control-; (semicolon) and Control-' (apostrophe) to compare the waveform graphs of the first and second clips.

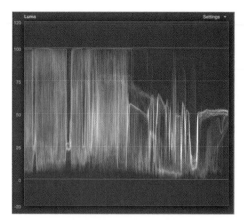
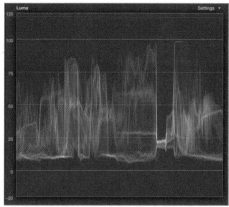

Clip 1 luma waveform   Clip 2 luma waveform

Examining both clips, you can see how the waveform graph really shines. Knowing where the man's suit corresponds to the waveform in each clip, you can directly compare the black points of the luma graphs to compare the heights. Similarly, you can see where the highlights of the sky peak in each graph, as well as how the average midtones compare within each graph. Using these graphs as guides, you can adjust exposure as necessary to match the contrast of the second clip to the first.

7   Select the second clip in the Timeline. In the Color Board, click Exposure, and drag the Shadows, Highlights, and Midtones exposure controls so that the bottom, top, and middle of the luma graph of the second clip matches as closely as possible that of the first clip.

> **TIP**▸ Use the values shown in the following figure as a guide.

Keep one eye on the video scopes and the other on the image. When the extremities and averages of the waveform graphs more or less line up, use the image as your final guide. Keep in mind that you're evaluating image lightness, not color.

8   With exposure adjusted, from the Settings pop-up menu of the video scope, choose RGB Parade; and in the Color Board, click Color.

9   Use the keyboard shortcuts to compare the two clips.

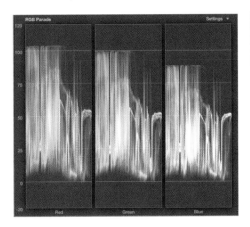

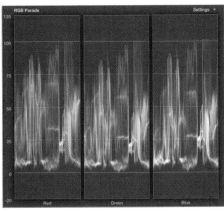

Clip 1 RGB Parade waveform   Clip 2 RGB Parade waveform

10   Drag the Highlights color control up toward orange until the tops of the red, green, and blue waveforms corresponding to the second clip are offset to match those of the first. The results won't be exact, just similar, with red highest, green lower, and blue lowest.

11   Continue to flip between both clips, and drag the Shadows control down toward negative orange so that the bottoms of the red, green, and blue waveforms of clip 2 line up similarly to those of clip 1.

12   Apply whatever small tweaks are necessary to make the tops and bottoms of the RGB Parade scope line up as closely as possible.

Again, the results at this point won't be identical. You'll want to keep an eye on the image to ensure that the general hue and quality of the highlights match, but don't spend too much time on it. At this point, it's more important that the shadows, rather than the highlights, are well adjusted.

13   From the Settings pop-up of the video scope, choose Vectorscope, and flip between the two clips to compare the Vectorscope graphs.

The Vectorscope graphs won't be identical no matter what you do—both shots have different distributions of color—but the orientation and centering of both graphs should be recognizably similar. If not, a small adjustment to the Highlights color control might improve the match.

If you're satisfied that the waveforms of both clips are oriented approximately the same, and that they're both centered similarly, it's time to adjust saturation.

14   From the Settings pop-up menu of the video scope, choose 133%, and flip back and forth to compare the graphs of both clips.

Clip 1 Vectorscope close-up   Clip 2 Vectorscope close-up

In both clips, notice a small arm of the Vectorscope graph stretching out along the Skin Tone Indicator. This represents the man's face, and if your color matching is good, this segment should be along the same angle in both graphs. On the other hand, this segment should also be smaller in the first clip (which you deliberately desaturated) than in the second clip. Next, you'll adjust to correct this.

15 Click Saturation, and while flipping between clips, lower the Midtones saturation control until the segments of each Vectorscope graph corresponding to the Skin Tone Indicator are approximately of equal length.

At this point, the color quality of both the first and second clips should be looking similar, if not identical.

16 Set the video scope to display the luma waveform. With all these adjustments, you should notice that the top of the waveform is over 100.

17 Click Exposure, and lower the Highlights exposure control so that the top of the graph just touches 100.

NOTE ▶ If you take the time to look at the RGB Parade waveform before and after making this last adjustment to the highlights exposure, notice that in addition to bringing the highlight exposure of the second clip in line with that of the first, the RGB levels are now of equal height.

The first and second clips compared after matching

This may seem like a lengthy process, but with practice (after you've matched several hundred clips), you'll get faster, and matching one clip to another will become second nature.

Eventually, you'll find you no longer have to examine the video scopes so closely every time, but matching using scopes will continue to be a valuable skill for those difficult-to-match shots in which it's hard to spot the exact differences.

Copying Grades

Now that you have two balanced corrections, you might want to see if one of them might make a good starting point for adjusting another clip in the scene. When copying adjustments from one clip to another unrelated clip, the chances are it won't work perfectly; but if it comes close, you may spare yourself from completely reinventing the wheel. In the next exercise, you'll learn how to paste effects from one clip to another, and fine-tune the result to match yet another clip to the your reference.

1   Select the second clip in the Timeline, and press Command-C to copy it.

2   Select the fourth clip, and choose Edit > Paste Effects, or press Command-Option-V.

When using the Paste Effects command, all effects, including color adjustments, are duplicated from the clip you copied and pasted to the target clip. This is an all-or-nothing operation. You cannot select which effects are pasted and which are not.

The fourth clip before and after copying and pasting effects from the second

The result is pretty good, but a few more adjustments will make a more perfect match. First, you need to relocate the markers to better compare this clip to the reference clip.

TIP Starting with a copied correction that's close and tailoring it to a new clip is often faster than starting anew, but not always. If you can't make a copied correction match within four or five tweaks, you might want to consider resetting the correction and starting over.

3   With the playhead over the fourth clip, press M to place a marker at the current frame.

4   Press Control-; (semicolon) to move the playhead to the previous marker on the second clip, and press Control-M to delete the marker.

5   Open the Waveform Monitor, and in the video scope, set it to Luma. Press Control-; (semicolon) and Control-' (apostrophe) to flip between the first and fourth clips and compare their waveform graphs.

Notice that the black point of the fourth clip isn't quite as low as that of the first clip. Also, the brightest highlights of the fourth clip aren't as bright as in the first clip; but that's all right, the man's shirt probably shouldn't be as bright as the sunlit sky in the reference. In this situation, you need to make a judgment call based on the content of the image, and not simply make the waveforms match.

6   To make the black point match, make sure the fourth clip is selected, and then open the Color Board, if necessary. Click Exposure, and drag the Shadows control down so that the lowest point of the waveform just touches 0.

This is a small change, but notice that the shadows within the scene become denser, providing a better match to the reference clip.

7   Use the shortcut keys to flip between the two clips and compare them.

Using Hidden Commands to Apply Corrections

At this point in the process, a few angles of coverage are adjusted and matched. Now is a good time to see if you can simply apply any other corrections from one graded clip to other clips with the same angle of coverage.

This is an important technique for working faster, especially when correcting narrative programs with well-defined angles of coverage; or documentary shows with a variety of interview subject headshots that each have a single correction you can use over and over again.

Three commands in Final Cut Pro X are somewhat hidden. They're not in any menu, and they're not assigned default keyboard shortcuts. These commands are for applying corrections from one, two, or three clips back, and are incredibly useful for scene balancing. In this lesson, you'll expose these commands, and use them to continue matching more of this scene to the reference clip.

1   Choose Final Cut Pro > Commands > Customize.

2   In the search field at the top right of the Command Editor, type *apply*.

   Three commands appear at the top of the list of found commands: "Apply Color Correction from Previous Edit," "…from Three Edits Prior," and "…from Two Edits Prior." These commands have no keyboard modifiers applied to them.

3   Choose "Apply Color Correction from Previous Edit," and press Shift-Control-1 to assign that keyboard shortcut to the command.

4 In the dialog that appears, click Make Copy, type a name for your command set, and click OK.

5 Choose "Apply Color Correction from Three Edits Prior," and press Shift-Control-3 to apply a shortcut.

6 Choose "Apply Color Correction from Two Edits Prior," and press Shift-Control-2 to apply a shortcut.

7 Click Save, and close the Command Editor. Now that you've assigned keyboard short-cuts to these three commands, you can use them to copy color corrections in the Timeline.

8 Click the fifth clip in the Timeline to select it. Notice that the fifth clip (in which the man is lying down) is from the same angle as the second clip (in which the man stands up). Chances are good that the same adjustment may work for both.

9 Press Shift-Control-3 (three edits prior) to copy the adjustment from the second clip to the fifth clip.

10 Select the sixth clip. This shot is from the same angle, so press Shift-Control-1 (previous edit) to copy the adjustment from the fifth to the sixth clip.

11 Play through the fourth through sixth clips to see how well they match. You may notice that the fourth and sixth clips match well, but the fifth clip seems a bit bright and a bit yellow.

12 Select the fifth clip, set the video scopes to display the luma waveform, and open the Color Board of Correction 1, if necessary.

13 Click Exposure, and lower the Highlights exposure control until the top of the wave-form graph just touches 100.

14 To evaluate the color, set the video scope to display the RGB Parade waveform.

15 Remove the marker from the fourth clip, add a marker to the fifth clip, and press the keyboard shortcuts to jump between the first and sixth clips while comparing the two images.

Even though a comparison of clips four through six revealed a discrepancy, you still want to match them to the reference clip (in this case the first clip) to make sure that you're doing a consistent and accurate match.

Comparing the RGB Parade graph of the fifth clip to the first, notice that the bottoms of the red, green, and blue graphs are offset, lending more of a color cast in the shadows of the clip than is desirable.

16 Click Color, and drag the Shadows color control toward negative orange until the bottoms of all three graphs align (somewhere around 23°, –2%).

At this point, flipping between the two clip markers should reveal a reasonably good match, with one exception. You may notice that the man's face seems less saturated in the fifth clip than in the first. This can be verified using the Vectorscope.

17 Set the video scope to show the Vectorscope, and flip between the first and fifth clip markers. Sure enough, the Vectorscope of the fifth clip is smaller than the first, indicating that it's less saturated.

18 With the fifth clip selected, click Saturation, and drag the Midtones saturation control up until the arm of the Vectorscope graph running along the Skin Tone Indicator is equal to the length of the arm in the first clip's Vectorscope graph.

At this point, you should have a convincing match between the first and fifth clips, and you shouldn't see a distracting difference between shots when playing the fourth through sixth clips. With this done, you can continue copying grades.

19 Click the seventh clip, which is identical to the fifth clip, and press Shift-Control-2 (two edits prior) to copy the adjustment from the fifth clip to the seventh clip.

20 Select the eighth clip. This clip is clearly from the same angle as the fourth clip, but it's too far away to be able to use the Apply Color Correction commands. In this case, you'll once again have to use the Paste Effects commands.

21 Select the fourth clip, and press Command-C. Then select the eighth clip, and press Command-Option-V.

22 Use Paste Effects to copy the correction from the second clip to the ninth clip, and from the first clip to the eleventh clip.

23 Select the tenth clip, and press Shift-Control-2 to apply the correction from the eighth clip. You can see that once you've graded at least one representative clip from each angle of coverage, you can quickly copy and apply those corrections to similar clips throughout a scene.

TIP Of all the Apply Color Correction commands, "Apply Color Correction from Two Edits Prior" is the most useful in situations where an edit takes the form of A-B-A-B-A, cutting between two angles of coverage.

Matching Insert Clips

So far, you've matched all the clips to the reference of the first clip in the scene. Of the first 11 clips, only the third clip remains ungraded. If you play the third and fourth clips together, you'll see that this is a push-in sequence because the fourth clip is a closer take of the third. For this reason, it is even more critical to achieve a good match.

1   Select and copy the fourth clip. Select the third clip, and press Command-Option-V to paste the effects.

2   Set the video scope to display the Vectorscope, and click Color to reveal the color controls.

3   Flip between the third and fourth clips using shortcut keys (the clips are right next to one another, so you needn't set markers), and compare their Vectorscope graphs.

Clip 3

Clip 4

When matching two clips in which one is a tighter version of the other, you always want to compare them to achieve the closest match possible.

In this case, as you flip back and forth, notice that the Vectorscope graph moves down and to the left in the third clip compared to the fourth clip. This movement, and the fact that the third clip is yellower then the fourth clip, is a clue to the kind of adjustment you need to make.

4   Click Color, and with the third clip selected, drag the Highlights color control up and to the left (toward a redder orange). Flip between the clips as you continue adjusting the Highlights color. Ultimately, the arm of the Vectorscope that most closely aligns with the Skin Tone Indicator should be roughly in the same position for both clips, and the lighting of both clips should visually match (possibly at around 27°, +24%).

5   When you believe you've achieved a good match, view the entire scene to see how well it plays.

At this point, you should have a well-balanced scene, in which no one clip stands out as noticeably different in color or contrast. However, you won't always get things right on the first pass, so if you see anything that sticks out, go ahead and continue tweaking.

▶ **Some Tips on Shot Matching**

Scene balancing is an iterative process. Colorists commonly continue making small tweaks and adjustments each time a scene is played to account for slight changes in lighting as the camera angles change, or some aspect of the clip becomes more noticeable than when grading began.

When playing through a scene you've already graded, take a few minutes to tweak anything you think needs it. And remember, no matter what the video scopes show, at the end of the process the most important thing is achieving a *visual match*. If two images look like they match but the scope graphs seem subtly at odds, go with the look.

Also important is knowing when you've made a reasonable match, and moving on so you don't lose time. (Every project always has a lot more clips that need adjusting.) Your goal is to create a *plausible* match between all the clips in a scene. The audience's ability to overlook continuity errors provides a small bit of wiggle room when it comes to shot matching, so absolute perfection is not required (nor will it be attainable, depending on how different two clips are).

Focus on the audience's overall impression of each shot. One small element that doesn't exactly match may not be that important if the overall tone and feel of the shots are consistent. Furthermore, be mindful of which parts of an image the audience will be most focused on.

For example, if you have people in the scene, you'll want to make sure to match the skin tones of a particular actor appearing in multiple clips because the audience is going to be looking right at her. On the other hand, that small newspaper in the corner of the frame is not likely to be an object of attention; so if it's slightly off, but the rest of the scene seems to match, then it can probably be overlooked.

Take 2

Now that you've balanced the first half of this scene, balance the last eight shots using the same techniques.

Using Additional Corrections and Effects in a Scene

Having balanced a scene in the previous exercises, you'll now learn how to build upon a base correction, adding more adjustments and effects to create ever more sophisticated looks.

Adding Corrections to Individual Shots

Although every clip edited into a project starts out with one default color correction (named Correction 1), you can add more corrections to apply more adjustments. These adjustments can modify the base look of a clip or add an additional "style" change on top of an underlying correction. In this exercise, you'll apply additional color corrections to contribute a bit of style to the *Hero Scene* project.

1   If necessary, open the *Hero Scene* project into the Timeline. This exercise assumes that you matched the first 11 clips of this sequence in the previous exercises.

2   Select the first clip in the Timeline, and open its parameters into the Video Inspector. If the Color Board is currently open, click the back arrow button to return to the Inspector.

3   To add a new correction, click the Add Correction button at the top of the Color group in the Video Inspector.

A new correction appears, Correction 2, and it's stacked underneath Correction 1. Its Color Board button is still dimmed, indicating that it has not yet been modified.

4   Click Correction 2's Color Board button to open the Color Board. Although the base grade you've already created is a nice, warm look, additional corrections will let you experiment with other looks while keeping what you've already done. If you don't like your experiments, there's no harm. You can simply disable or remove the additional correction and recover your original corrections.

5   Drag the Highlights color control towards positive blue, to cool down the image and add a very subtle bluish tinge to the bright areas. (The example uses Highlights color values of 224°, +36%.)

6   Click Exposure, and drag the Midtones exposure control down to darken the inside shadows of the clip, thereby creating a more subdued look. (The example uses a Midtones exposure value of –9.)

7   Click Saturation, and drag the Midtones saturation control all the way up to boost the intensity of color. Then lower the Shadows saturation to reduce color intensity in the

darkest parts of the image, while leaving the lighter parts of the image more saturated than they were before (–45% should be good).

The result is very a cool, overcast day type of lighting.

8   Click the back arrow button, and deselect and select the Correction 2 checkbox to compare your change to the original.

The original correction   With an additional cool blue correction

Because your "overcast look" has been applied in a separate correction, disabling it lets you return to the previous, underlying look you created. Because all color calculations are done at extremely high quality behind the scenes, pushing and pulling the color and contrast of a clip like this does nothing to reduce its quality.

Saving and Applying Correction Presets

Now that you've created a new look, you can apply it to the other clips. In this exercise, you'll learn to save individual correction settings for future use.

1   Select the first clip in the Timeline. Make sure that Correction 2 (the new "overcast" look) is turned on, and click its Color Board button.

2   From the Color Board's Action pop-up menu, choose Save Preset.

3   When the New Preset dialog appears, type *Overcast Day*, and click OK. The Action menu contains a variety of Color Board presets to create stylized looks. When you save your own preset, you store the settings from the currently open correction to this menu. If you reopen the Action menu, you'll see your Overcast Day preset at the bottom of the list. Now, you need to apply this look to other clips in the project.

4   Select the second clip in the Timeline. Click the back arrow button to open the Video Inspector, and click the Add Correction button.

5   Click the Color Board button for Correction 2, and from the Action menu, choose your Overcast Day preset.

The second clip now has the overcast look. If you play the first two clips together, they should match. Because the settings you've added to them are identical, if the underlying corrections create a good match, they should continue to match.

This is one way to apply a consistent overlying look to a series of previously graded clips. Furthermore, all the presets you store in this menu are available for future projects, so you can develop a library of frequently used looks to create a series of "secret sauce" adjustments for the future.

Adding Corrections to an Entire Scene Using Compound Clips

Preset adjustments are powerful, but when you have long scenes, separately applying additional corrections to every clip can be cumbersome. Another way is to turn your balanced scene into a compound clip and then apply a single grade to all the clips at once.

1   Remove Correction 2 from the first and second clips in the Timeline by selecting each clip, selecting Correction 2 in the Video Inspector, and pressing Delete.

2 Select the first 11 clips in the Timeline by dragging a selection rectangle around all of them, or by clicking the first clip and Shift-clicking the eleventh clip.

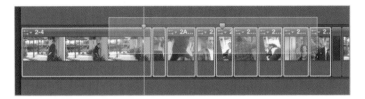

3 Choose File > New Compound Clip, or press Option-G, to turn the selected clips into a single compound clip.

Compound clips share a single group of effects settings, which is extremely useful for applying one set of color corrections to an entire scene worth of clips. If you examine Correction 1 in the Video Inspector, you'll see that the default correction for the compound clip is empty, ready to be used to affect the entire sequence of clips found within.

4 With the new compound clip selected in the Timeline, click the Color Board button.

5 From the Action menu, choose the Overcast Day preset.

6 Play through the compound clip to see how all the clips are equally affected by this preset. Not only is this an effective way to quickly apply a single set of corrections to multiple clips, it's also very convenient when you need to make revisions.

7 From the Action menu, choose Sewer.

Immediately, the entire scene is graded to this new look. You can try applying several presets to see how they look, but don't expect all of them to work well. The effect of each preset is highly dependent on the range of contrast and color found in your clips. A very bright clip will respond differently to a preset than will a very dark clip.

> **TIP** Several presets boost image highlights. When you apply these to an image that already has bright highlights, the result might be an extremely clipped image with flat, detail-less pools of white. Although this may be what you're going for, when it becomes a problem you can add another correction to the compound clip to readjust the highlights and midtones and recover the detail you need in the image.

Changing to Compound Clips

Remember that compound clips can be opened by double-clicking them to reveal the individual clips within. Individual clips in an open compound clip can be adjusted just as in any project, so you can easily make individual tweaks and adjustments to single clips within a compound clip.

After you've opened a compound clip, click the left arrow (at the upper-left corner of the Timeline) to return to the full Timeline of your project.

Finally, if you start creating a lot of compound clips to adjust your scenes, renaming them might help you keep track of which compound clip corresponds to which scene. To rename a compound clip, select it in the Timeline, click Info in the Inspector, and then choose Edit Compound Clip Settings from the Action pop-up menu at the bottom right of the Inspector. Type a new name for the clip, and click OK.

Adding Other Effects to a Grade

Final Cut Pro X has many other effects you can use to stylize your project's images. You can apply these effects to a balanced scene to achieve a creative effect, just as you previously applied presets. Also, like color corrections, effects can be applied to individual clips and to compound clips.

1   Using the *Hero Scene* project from the previous exercise, select the compound clip. If the Color Board is open, click the back arrow button to open the Video Inspector.

2   Press Command-5 to open the Effects Browser, and select the Stylize video category. Scroll through the thumbnails until you find the Projector effect, and double-click it to apply it to the compound clip.

3   Play through the compound clip. In conjunction with the Sewer preset you added to Correction 1, the Projector effect gives this part of the scene a rough, "grindhouse cinema" feel. Because the underlying clips match, any effects you apply to this scene will affect each clip in the same way. You can use effects to apply looks that are simply not achievable using color correction.

Using Broadcast Safe

Effects can have a dramatic impact on the video signal levels of a clip, so it's important to understand the Final Cut Pro X *order of operations* when it comes to video processing. You'll see what this means in the following exercise.

Understand that whatever an effect does to the video signal takes place before any corrections you apply. This is significant when you're trying to respect the outer boundaries of 0 to 100 (as measured by the Histogram and waveform video scopes) required when submitting a program for broadcast and some other types of distribution.

1   With the compound clip still selected, delete the Projector effect, and click the Reset button for Correction 1 to return the scene to its previously graded state.

2   Double-click the compound clip to open it up, and then select the first clip of the series. When you first graded this clip, you capped the highlights at 100 to avoid any excess clipping. Now, you're going to boost these highlights to blow them out.

3   If necessary, open the video scope (press Command-7), and set it to display the luma waveform.

4   Click the Color Board button for Correction 1, click Exposure, and drag the Highlights exposure control up until the highlights are at around 110.

The highlights get white hot, creating harsh, bright patches of light. Assuming you like the results of clipping out the highlight detail, you can apply the Broadcast Safe effect to limit the maximum signal to 100, thereby avoiding a QC (quality control) violation with the broadcaster.

5   Click the back arrow button to return to the Video Inspector, and then open the Effects Browser. Select the Basics video category, and double-click Broadcast Safe to add it to the current clip.

In the Waveform Monitor, notice that absolutely nothing happens to the video signal. Broadcast Safe is supposed to clip the video signal at the outer boundaries of 0 and

100, but in this case nothing happened because video effects are applied *before* color corrections. Your color adjustment is applied after the Broadcast Safe effect.

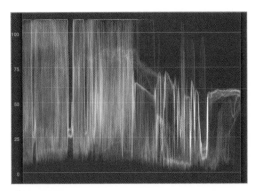

6   In the Video Inspector, delete the Broadcast Safe effect. Click the left arrow button to go back in Timeline history, and click the beginning of the compound clip to select it again.

7   Double-click the Broadcast Safe effect to add it to the compound clip. You should now notice that the highlights are capped at around 95.

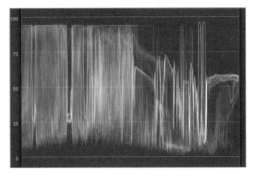

Effects applied to compound clips are processed *after* the color corrections are applied to its individual clips. This is how you can get around the limitation of effects applied before corrections and manually change the order of operations.

Now, knowing that 0 and 100 are the outer boundaries of broadcast safe for the luma component of a video signal, the automatic adjustment made by the Broadcast Safe effect seems excessive. In fact, you can reduce the Amount parameter to lessen the amount of the signal that is clipped. However, before you do that, take a look at another aspect of the video signal.

8   From the Settings pop-up menu of the video scope, choose RGB Parade.

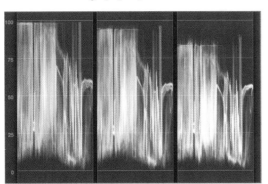

In most cases, 0 and 100 are also the outer allowable boundaries for a video signal decoded to RGB. Notice that if you turn off the Broadcast Safe effect in the Video Inspector, the red and green channels are well above 100. The Broadcast Safe effect is limiting the RGB components of the signal as well, and the result is a reduced luma level. However, the current effect is a bit conservative, so you can minimize it.

9   In the Broadcast Safe effect, drag the Amount slider to the left, reducing how much the signal is attenuated, until the top of the red channel just touches 100. At this point, the signal is probably fine, and you're ready to move on with other adjustments.

In general, it's better to limit your signal between 0 and 100 manually—using corrections of your own that are tailored to each clip—than it is to arbitrarily reduce overly bright detail using the Broadcast Safe effect. However, if you're deliberately looking to blow out highlights or crush shadows as part of the look you're trying to achieve, the Broadcast Safe effect is the right tool for the job.

▶ Broadcast Safe and Quality Control

Networks impose QC standards for the minimum and maximum allowable signal levels you can use when submitting a program for terrestrial or satellite broadcast. If your program's levels fall outside of these limits, even just a little, the network may reject it, resulting in missed deadlines, fines, and very unhappy clients. When finishing any program destined for commercial distribution or broadcast, make sure you ask for the relevant QC guidelines, and use these to "legalize" your program to adhere to the necessary standards.

Lesson Review

1. Where is the Match Color control?
2. What's the best way to specify two frames for comparison?
3. What's the first thing you should do when starting to balance a scene?
4. What's an ideal scope for comparing color balance in the highlights or shadows?
5. What's an ideal scope for comparing saturation?
6. Which two scopes are good for comparing image contrast?
7. Which video scope can you zoom into?
8. How do you copy effects from one clip to another?
9. What three commands aren't initially assigned but useful for copying color corrections in the Timeline?
10. Can you use the Broadcast Safe effect to limit the results of a correction made to the same clip?

Answers

1. In the Color group of the Video Inspector
2. Use markers.
3. Choose a reference clip to compare all other clips in the scene to.
4. The RGB Parade scope
5. The Vectorscope
6. The waveform set to Luma and Histogram set to Luma
7. The Vectorscope
8. Copy a clip, and then select another clip and use Command-Option-V to paste effects.
9. The Apply Color Correction from Previous Edit, …from Two Edits Prior, and …from Three Edits Prior commands.
10. No

Keyboard Shortcuts

Option-G	Turn selected clips into a compound clip
M	Place a marker
Command-Option-V	Paste effects
Command-5	Open the Effects Browser
Command-7	Open the video scopes

13

Lesson Files   APTS FCP X ADV Part 3 > Lesson_13

Time   This lesson takes approximately 90 minutes to complete.

Goals   Understand the purpose of secondary corrections

Use the color mask controls to isolate colors

Use shape masks to adjust different parts of the picture

Apply combinations of color and shape masks to create specific corrections

Use keyframe shape masks to create animated corrections

Lesson 13

Making Isolated Color Adjustments

In this lesson, you'll learn how to make *secondary corrections* to bring some finesse to your grades. Secondary color corrections are targeted adjustments to specific elements within a scene and have literally hundreds of uses. They allow you to:

- ▶ Adjust the color of the sky
- ▶ Fix troublesome skin tones
- ▶ Brighten a face that's not distinct enough from the background
- ▶ Desaturate a shirt that's distractingly colorful
- ▶ Intensify the color of foliage in an exterior shot
- ▶ Legalize a single oversaturated color without desaturating everything

Final Cut Pro X provides two ways to isolate subjects for secondary correction: Using masks that you create by keying specific colors, and using shapes that surround areas of the image.

In the following exercises, you'll use both techniques, individually and in combination, to isolate aspects of images and perform subject-specific corrections.

Using Color Masks

One of the most flexible tools for making targeted corrections is the color mask. Essentially a chroma keying operation, color masks let you turn any hue of the spectrum into a mask for isolating a subject.

In the following exercise, you'll use color masks to target specifically colored features within multiple clips and address a variety of creative issues.

1   In the Project Library, display the contents of the APTS FCP X ADV Part 3 disk image, and then click the disclosure triangle next to the Lesson_13 folder to show its contents.

2   Open the *In the City* project, and press Shift-Z to expand its clips to the available width of the Timeline.

3   If necessary, open the video scope (press Command-7), and set it to display the luma waveform.

4   Select the first clip. The image of the woman sitting in front of her house has a lovely variation of color that is ideal for showing off what you can do with the Final Cut Pro X mask effect.

Before beginning secondary color correction, always make sure you've exhausted the creative possibilities of a primary correction using Correction 1. A single primary correction can save you several secondary corrections. Diving into a secondary correction is usually a mistake, unless you have a specific task that requires it.

5   Click the Color Board button to open the Color Board. Click Exposure, and drag the Global exposure control down until the bottom of the waveform just touches 0.

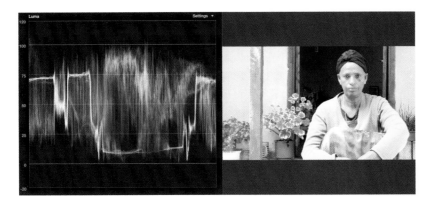

This creates nice, dense shadows in the image and also lowers the white point so that the highlights fall under 100, which is ultimately ideal. At this point, you're done. Although the image has a somewhat warm color cast, it's desirable for most of this image, and you'll later adjust specific colors that shouldn't be so warm.

6   Click the back arrow button to return to the Video Inspector, and set the video scope to show the Vectorscope.

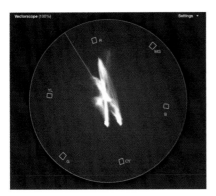

Now that you've made a primary correction, you need to create another correction in the Color group to perform a secondary adjustment. If you used the mask effect with Correction 1 for this task, you'd inadvertently limit the effect of Correction 1, which is not what you want.

7   Click the Add Correction button to create Correction 2. You'll use Correction 2 to adjust the woman's blue sweater, without altering anything else in the scene. As you can see in the Vectorscope, there is excellent separation between the various pools of different hues throughout this image—an ideal situation for color masks.

8   Click the Add Color Mask button of Correction 2, but don't do anything just yet.

Underneath Correction 2, a Color Mask control appears with a color swatch, a slider, and a color picker, which is turned on (highlighted in blue) and ready to pick a color.

9   In the Viewer, move the pointer to the blue-green wall, click the portion of the wall to the right of the doorway, and drag slowly outward.

As you drag away from the pixel you clicked, a circle appears to define how much of the image is being sampled for the mask. The mask you're creating is shown as the saturated portion of the image, while everything not included in the mask appears as a desaturated gray. Dragging outward enlarges the sample area and expands the mask; dragging inward shrinks the sample area and reduces the amount of the image that's masked.

10   Continue dragging outward until you've masked the majority of the wall without including the woman's sleeve or other parts of the image. When you've isolated as much of the wall as you can—while omitting everything else—release the mouse button.

You should have been able to mask the entire wall except for the bottom portion to the left of the doorway and beneath the potted plant. Fortunately, you can expand the mask to include this area, too.

NOTE ▶ If you're dissatisfied with your sampled region, click again somewhere else in the Viewer to clear the current mask, and drag a new sample circle to redefine the mask.

11 With the Correction 2 mask eyedropper button still highlighted, Shift-drag in the section of the wall beneath the plant to add that part of the image to the mask. Release the mouse button when you're finished.

When you Shift-click with the eyedropper, a + (plus sign) appears next to the eyedropper, and the saturated/desaturated mask selection view shows that you are adding to the previously sampled region of the image rather then resampling from scratch.

Be careful not to include the leaves or wood in the selection, although the edge of the woman's right sleeve is unavoidable.

TIP ▶ You may get a better result with a series of small selections made by Shift-clicking multiple areas.

Now that you've sampled the maximum amount of wall along with the woman's sleeve, you'll use the Option key to remove that sleeve from the selection.

12 With the Correction 2 mask eyedropper still highlighted, Option-drag to create a sample circle over the woman's sleeve. As you drag, the mask shrinks to omit that portion of the image. Continue dragging until you've omitted as much of the sleeve as possible while retaining the maximum amount of the wall in the mask. Release the mouse button when you're finished.

When you Option-click with the eyedropper, a – (minus sign) appears next to the eyedropper, and the saturated/desaturated mask selection view shows that you are subtracting from the previously sampled region of the image.

Using this method, you can add to and subtract from several parts of the sampled mask to fine-tune the mask area as much as possible.

13 When you're satisfied with your mask's isolation of the wall, click the eyedropper button to deselect it. At this point, you've defined the region you want included in the mask. Next, you'll further refine the mask using the Softness slider, located between the color patch showing the currently sampled hue and the eyedropper button.

14 Option-drag the Softness slider slowly to the left.

Option-dragging the slider forces the Viewer to show you the mask in black and white. White indicates the portion of the image in the mask, and black indicates the omitted parts of the image.

15 Keep Option-dragging the Softness slider to the left until the fringing on the woman's sleeve is almost gone, and then release the mouse button. At this point, you have a good mask and are ready to make an adjustment.

16 Click the Color Board button for Correction 2 to open the Color Board.

With the Color Board open, you'll know you're making an adjustment that's limited by a mask because the Inside Mask and Outside Mask buttons appear next to the Action pop-up menu.

These buttons appear only when you're limiting a correction using a mask or shape, and they let you apply different settings to the inside and outside of the mask. This effectively gives you two corrections in one.

17 With Inside Mask turned on by default, drag the Midtones color control up toward positive green.

As you make this adjustment, watch what happens in the Vectorscope. The distinct arm of color stretching between the CY (cyan) and G (green) targets is moving toward green. The Vectorscope is an excellent tool for viewing how color-limited masks affect the video signal.

18 Drag the Midtones color control until the wall is distinctly greenish, but don't drag it too high or the level of saturation will be distractingly vivid.

> **NOTE ▸** If you're worried that your mask isn't quite perfect, don't be. As long as the color adjustment you're making is in the same general families of hue and saturation as the original color, you can get away with imperfect masks so long as the holes and edges don't move or call attention to themselves by being in an awkward part of the image.

19 When you're done, click the back arrow button to return to the Video Inspector.

20 Turn Correction 2 off and on to see a before-and-after comparison of this adjustment.

Before correction

After correction

Now that the wall is a more vivid and distinct color, the woman is not competing so well with the background. Because you're going for a vivid, colorful look in this example, she could stand out more if you make one of her garments more colorful. Let's target her blue/cyan sweater.

In this exercise, you'll discover that masking a color need not be a multistep process.

21 Click the Add Correction button to add Correction 3.

22 Click the Add Color Mask button, and then start dragging somewhere around the woman's left shoulder to sample her blue sweater. Expand the sample until you've masked most of the sweater, while masking as little of the surrounding scene as possible. You won't be able to include the darkest shadows of the sweater, but that's OK.

NOTE ▶ As you're masking, remember that some colors are meant to mimic pools of light and shadow. This means, so long as you're not completely changing the hue of a subject (which does require a perfect mask), it may be fine to exclude shadows or highlights in the mask.

23 Click the eyedropper button to disable sampling, and Option-drag the Correction 3 Softness slider to the left until you've eliminated as much of the non-sweater fringing as you can.

TIP ▶ If you make a sample selection you don't like, you can press Command-Z to undo the last sample.

24 Click the Color Board button for Correction 3 to open the Color Board.

25 Drag the Midtones color control up into positive blue to make the sweater a bit less cyan and a bit more saturated. Stop when you've achieved a nice balance between the green of the wall and the blue of the sweater.

So that's all there is to it. By adding additional color corrections and using the mask tool, you can isolate colors and manipulate the color, saturation, and exposure as necessary to make highly specific changes.

TIP If you leave a color mask's eyedropper button turned on when you open the Color Board, you can modify the mask while making color adjustments, without having to return to the Video Inspector.

Working Inside and Outside of Masks

Once you've created a color mask (any type of mask, actually), you have the added flexibility of making separate adjustments to the inside and outside of the mask within the same color correction. It's like having two corrections in one.

In this exercise, you'll use inside and outside masks to create an early morning look for a clip, while keeping the skin tones in the shot healthy and naturalistic.

1   Click anywhere within the second clip of the project.

2   Open the Color Board for Correction 1, and set the video scope to the luma waveform.

3   Click Exposure, and drag the Shadows control down until the black point of the waveform dips just below 0. This stretches contrast and adds some visual weight to the image.

4   Set the video scope to display the Vectorscope to examine the color distribution.

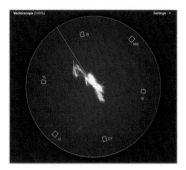

The Vectorscope graph is fairly well centered. However, all the dark-complexioned skin tones are angled toward the orange side of the Skin Tone Indicator, indicating warmth.

5   To alter the atmosphere, click Color, and drag the Highlights control up into the positive blue/cyan area of the Color Board to cool off the image.

Because you're working to simulate a change in color temperature due to lighting, the Highlights control is a logical tool to make this adjustment. However, while the environment is certainly cooled off, the highlights in the children's faces have turned a bit blue. You can address this unflattering situation using a mask.

6   Click the color Reset button, and then click the back arrow button to open the Video Inspector.

7   Click the Add Correction button to add Correction 2, and then click its Add Color Mask button and sample one of the children's faces to create a mask for only the skin tones. (The lower facial area of the second child from the right works well.)

8   For this adjustment, it's important to eliminate as much background fringing in the mask as possible. Option-click to subtract any bits of mask appearing on the tree or the corrugated wall behind the children.

9   When you're satisfied with the mask, turn off the color mask, and click the Correction 2 Color Board button.

   You've created the necessary mask to isolate the faces. Now you want to make the same cool-blue adjustment you made in step 5, but apply it to everything except the children's faces.

10   Click the Outside Mask button, located at the bottom of the Color Board.

11   Drag the Highlights color control up into the cyan/blue area of the Color Board to cool down everything outside the mask.

As you can see, this technique is extremely effective; however by cooling down the environment this much, the protected faces look unnatural. This occurs because, in reality, the quality of light of the *illuminant*, or dominant light source in a scene, typically affects everything within that scene. By excluding the faces, you've created an unnatural color contrast. The solution is to make a small adjustment to the faces to bring them into the scene.

12 Click the Inside Mask button. Notice that the color controls all move to their default positions. Because the settings for Inside Mask and Outside Mask are completely independent, changes made in one mode have no effect on the controls of the other.

13 Drag the Midtones color control up very slightly, toward blue/cyan. The goal is to take a bit of the edge off of the intensely warm skin tones without turning the faces blue. With the exception of specular highlights on shiny skin, skin tone generally falls within the midtones of the scale.

14 Click Saturation, and drag the Midtones saturation control down just a little so that the faces aren't quite so intensely colorful.

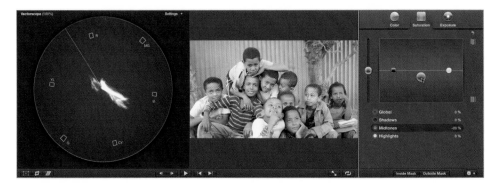

You're finished. If you return to the Video Inspector and click the Color checkbox to turn the entire grade off and on, you can compare the difference.

Original image

Stylized image using inside and outside mask adjustments

You'll often manipulate the inside and outside portions of a mask to control how a particular adjustment affects various subjects in the frame. It's a common technique and useful for a wide variety of situations.

▶ Masks Always Sample the Source Image

When you're applying multiple color corrections to a single clip, each new adjustment operates on the output of the previous color correction. For example, if Correction 1 desaturates an image quite a bit, it's the desaturated state of that image that Correction 2 modifies.

However, masks are an exception to this. The original source of the clip is always sampled, regardless of how many color corrections came before it. So, no matter how extremely you adjust the color and contrast of a clip, you'll be able to create color masks based on its original colors.

Using Shapes to Target Frame Regions

Color masks are flexible and have dozens of uses, but you'll still find many situations in which the feature or region you want to adjust is either too complicated to key on or so simple that it's not worth the trouble.

For example, if you wanted to darken the wall of a hallway to create a region of more intense shadow, various multicolored features—such as artwork, wallpaper, and doors—could make using a color mask difficult. This is an excellent situation in which to use a shape mask.

On the other hand, if you just want to brighten someone's face or adjust the contrast of a sign by a road, creating a shape that surrounds the thing you want to manipulate might be easiest, rather than meticulously sampling and isolating the area.

Using a Shape to Create a Vignette

Vignettes are a darkening around the edges of the frame, typically produced by an optical filter that cuts off light coming into the lens or by a mechanical defect of the lens structure, a matte box, or other obstruction that infringes on the corners of the scene being imaged.

Vignettes are artificially created all the time for creative effect, and are also useful for directing audience attention and darkening elements at the edge of the screen that you may not want seen.

In this exercise, you'll use a shape in the simplest possible way: to create a darkening vignette.

1   If necessary, open the *In the City* project you've been working on in the last few exercises.

2   Open the second clip into the Video Inspector.

3   Click the Add Correction button to add Correction 3, and then click the Add Shape Mask button.

A circular onscreen control (OSC) appears with handles you can use to move, resize, rectangularize, soften, and rotate it.

4   Drag one of the side handles toward the edge of the frame to widen the shape.

5 Drag the top handle up to make a taller oval that just encompasses the top and bottom child of the group.

6 Click the Correction 3 Color Board button to open the Color Board. At the bottom of the color board, you'll see the same Inside Mask/Outside Mask buttons that were available for color masks, letting you know that you're working on a secondary operation.

What you want to do is create a darkening around the edges of the frame, so you'll adjust everything that's outside of the shape OSC.

7 Click Outside Mask. Click Exposure, and drag the Highlights exposure control down to darken the edges.

Dropping down the highlights or midtones mutes the lighting without crushing the blacks. If you instead lowered the Shadows control, you would end up with a harsher, less smooth vignette with really dense, clipped blacks.

8   Now that you can see the darkening effect, click anywhere along the outer edge and drag the shape OSC farther from the center, increasing the softening of the vignette and making the effect more subtle.

9   Move down the shape by dragging the center handle so that there's more darkening at the top edge than at the bottom. This prevents too much of the vignette from appearing on top of the kids.

You now have a nice, soft, subtle vignette surrounding the kids, but it may be too subtle. Stretching the softness away from the center as you did resulted in a very gradual falloff. Although that's good, it also results in the darkest part of the vignette being well off the side of the screen. You can fix this by reducing the overall size of the shape, and then stretching out the softness border even farther.

10   Shift-drag the top handle of the shape OSC down to shrink it overall until it bisects the faces of the top and bottom child. When you Shift-drag the resizing handles, you constrain the shape proportions, resizing it overall without squeezing or stretching it. At this point, you have a nice vignette.

11 To see the effect without the shape OSC in the way, click the back arrow button to return to the Video Inspector, and turn off the shape mask for Correction 3.

Combining Shapes

Using shapes to selectively lighten or darken different parts of an image is sometimes referred to as *digital relighting*. The vignette in the previous exercise was an extremely simple example of this, but you can make much more subtle adjustments that fit invisibly into the lighting scheme of a clip.

Specific, shaped shadows can do much to add depth and dimension to an otherwise flat lighting scheme. However, certain situations often call for including or excluding scene elements that intersect the shape you're using to perform digital relighting.

In the next exercise, you'll create some subtle shadows, and in the process, use multiple intersecting shapes to make sure that foreground subjects don't also fall into background shadows.

1 With the *In the City* project open, select the first clip to open it into the Video Inspector.

2   Click the Add Correction button to add Correction 4, and then click the Add Shape Mask button.

3   Reposition, resize, and soften the shape so that the bottom size and softness boundaries encompass only the bottom half of the frame from the bottom of the woman's neck to her wrists.

4   Drag the rectangular handle (to the left of the top resize handle) to flatten the curve of the shape and make the shape more of a strip running along the bottom.

5   Click the Correction 4 Color Board button. Click the Outside Mask button, and then click Exposure and drag the Midtones control down to darken the bottom of the image.

Dragging the Midtones exposure slider darkens the floor and plants behind the woman, but leaves some of the brightest highlights alone, creating more naturalistic darkening shadows behind her.

Unfortunately, this operation has also darkened the woman, which doesn't quite serve our goal of bringing her out from the background. Fortunately, you can create another shape to exclude her from the darkening operation.

6   Click the back arrow button to reopen the Video Inspector, and click the Add Shape Mask button for Correction 4 to create a second shape OSC.

7   Reposition and resize the second shape so that it conforms to the woman and intersects the first shape. Notice that the Shape Mask button for Shape Mask 2 is highlighted to indicate which shape OSC is currently active.

All shapes are added together automatically, which means that any Outside Mask operation you create affects only those areas outside *all* the shapes you create. This makes it easy to create many additional shapes to exclude the features you don't want affected by a particular correction.

Before adding shadow

After adding shadow to the floor in the background

Similarly, any Inside Mask operations will affect whatever is inside every shape you've created for that correction.

Combining Shapes and Masks

Masks and shapes have different strengths. For example, masks are essentially chroma keys, so they automatically follow a subject in motion without the need for keyframing or manual animation.

On the other hand, when you want to adjust a region that is not easily defined by a single color, a shape can more quickly and easily limit your correction.

However, you can combine shapes and masks in a variety of ways to create highly flexible and very specific corrections. In the next two exercises, you'll combine shapes and masks to address two common correction issues.

Masking Difficult-to-Isolate Skin Tones

In this exercise, you'll mask the woman's face in the first clip, and then use a shape to exclude similarly colored elements of the scene from this mask.

1   With the *In the City* project open, select the first clip to open it in the Video Inspector.

2   Click the Add Correction button to add Correction 5, and then click the Add Color Mask button.

3   With the eyedropper chosen, sample the woman's face by dragging from her nose outward until you've included her face and neck. In the process, many other parts of the scene may also be included, but you can ignore everything except the doorway behind her, which should remain excluded.

It should be easy to create a solid mask that includes both the highlights and shadows of the woman's face, but to do so you'll end up including other elements such as the post, some fringing on her dress, and a number of unwanted edges. However, instead of adding and subtracting from the mask using the Shift and Option keyboard modifiers, you can create a shape to exclude what you don't want.

4   Click the Add Shape Mask button to add a shape to Correction 5, and then reposition and resize the shape as an oval that closely surrounds the woman's face and neck. Reduce softness to exclude as much of her red dress as possible.

TIP ▶ You can Option-drag the Softness slider a bit to view the mask in black and white.

5   Click Correction 5's Color Board button to open the Color Board. By default, when a shape mask's Inside Mask button is turned on at the same time a color mask is applied, the final mask includes only the region where the color mask and shape mask intersect. This important feature lets you work more quickly when isolating hard-to-separate subjects with colors that are very similar to other elements in the frame.

6   Click Exposure, and then raise the Highlights exposure control and lower the Shadows exposure control to stretch the contrast in the woman's face, making her a bit brighter and giving her more definition.

As you make this adjustment, you can see that it is successfully limited to just her face and neck. By lightening the woman's face by adjusting the midtones, you avoid blowing out her highlights, which would be unflattering. By also dropping her shadows to increase the overall contrast of her face, you give her more definition and keep the adjustment looking natural and consistent with the rest of the image.

NOTE ▶ As you can see, grades often consist of many separate corrections working together, and Final Cut Pro X makes this easy. However, these exercises represent an unusually detailed treatment for this clip. While they're representative of the kind of detail work you might be able to put into a thirty-second spot or a music video, long-form work such as broadcast or feature documentaries might not allow the time or budget for such elaborate corrections. As you work, make sure you keep your schedule and not get lost in a grade to the point where the day is almost over and you've corrected only fifty of the six hundred clips you needed to correct.

Masking Corrections to the Sky

In this exercise, you'll combine shapes and masks in a different way to make a correction to the sky, while omitting subjects passing in front of it.

1   With the *In the City* project open, click near the very beginning of the third clip to open it into the Video Inspector.

2   Open the Color Board for Correction 1, and use the exposure controls to drop the shadows a bit and raise the midtones, thereby stretching the contrast of the darker portion of the image. Then, open the color controls, and drag the Midtones color control up into positive orange just a little to warm up the overall clip.

3   Click the back arrow button to return to the Video Inspector. Click the Add Correction button to add Correction 2, and click the Add Shape Mask button.

4   Reposition, resize, and soften the shape to isolate the sky, locating the inner region of the shape at the top part of the sky and the outer softness ring near the tops of the buildings and trees.

TIP Drag the rectangular control to the left of the top resize handle to square off the shape, making it easier to isolate the sky with a long rounded rectangle.

5   Click the Correction 2 Color Board button. Click Color, and drag the Highlights color
    control up into the positive blue/cyan to put some blue into the sky.

> **NOTE ▶** When adding blue to a sky, subtlety is key, although to make this change
> more visible in print, the correction shown here was exaggerated. Experiment with
> different shades to see what looks best to you.

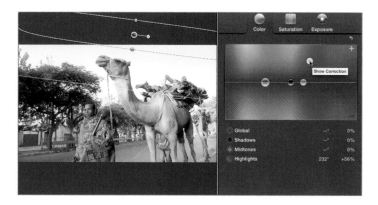

Using shapes to add a blue gradient to the sky is a long-used technique, and in many
instances, it may be all you need to do. Because of the way sunlight scatters in the atmosphere, skies are usually a gradient of color which helps the illusion. Adding only colors
somewhere between blue and cyan is helpful also. However, in this clip, the camel is tall
enough to poke its head into your clever illusion. Since camels aren't typically blue, you'll
need to fix this.

6   Click the back arrow button, and then click the Add Color Mask for Correction 2.

7   Drag a large sample circle near the upper-right corner to mask most of the sky,
    excluding the camel and treetops.

8   Shift-click a much smaller sample circle at the upper-left corner of the sky to expand
    the mask a bit more in that area. Immediately, the blue you added to the sky is limited

to the intersection of the color mask you just created and the shape you made. The camel's head and the treetops return to their natural colors, and you're finished.

Before correction

After sky enhancement with intersecting color and shape masks

Incidentally, some additional camera movement occurs in this clip. Fortunately, the sky correction you've made is amorphous enough so that you don't have to animate the shape to move with the camera. The blue of the sky makes enough sense on its own.

In the next exercise, however, you'll learn how to animate shapes for situations when your correction does need to move.

Animating Shapes

When you create a shape that must adjust to a subject that's moving, or you isolate a region of a clip in which the camera is in motion, you may need to animate the shape to follow the movement. Shape animation uses keyframes, and animates much like other parameters and effects in Final Cut Pro X.

In this lesson, you'll use shape animation to highlight a car in a documentary-style clip.

1   With the *In the City* project open, click near the beginning of the fourth clip to open it into the Video Inspector.

2   Click the Add Shape Mask button, then resize and reposition the OSC shape to surround the white van that's just passing the intersection.

TIP   Shift-dragging one of the repositioning handles is the fastest way to resize the entire shape to hug the van.

In this case, you're creating a special effect to highlight one particular van to the viewers—as one might do in a documentary or forensic project—and no primary correction is necessary.

3   Click the Correction 1 Color Board button. Click the Outside Mask button, and click Exposure to drag the Highlights exposure control down to darken everything except the van inside the shape.

4   Click the back arrow button to return to the Video Inspector. At this point, you've created the highlighting effect you need, and you can animate the shape to follow the van as it drives.

5 In the Video Inspector, click the Keyframe button for the Shape Mask 1 parameter to add a shape keyframe at the current position of the playhead.

The Keyframe button turns orange to indicate that a keyframe is present at the current position of the playhead.

6 Move the playhead forward to the end of the clip, and then drag the shape to the current position of the car.

Another keyframe is automatically added at the current frame as indicated by an orange Keyframe button.

The arrow to the left of the Keyframe button indicates that a keyframe exists to the left of the playhead. You can click these left (or right) arrows to jump the playhead to the next keyframe in that direction.

Play the clip. The shape, and your correction, moves to follow the car.

The animated shape follows the van.

You can also click the upper-left corner of any clip in the Timeline to open its Adjustments pop-up menu and choose Show Video Animation. This opens the Video Animation Editor in the Timeline, within which you'll see a "Color: Correction 1: Shape Mask 1" item with the two keyframes you've created. In this editor, you can add keyframes (Option-click the keyframe track), remove keyframes (select a keyframe, and press Delete), or move keyframes (drag them left or right). (For more information on using keyframes, see Lesson 9.)

Animating shapes is necessary whenever you're using a shape to adjust a region in motion, such as a moving subject or as in a roving camera shot. However, shape animation can also be a way to use color corrections creatively.

Lesson Review

1.   What's a secondary correction?
2.   What's the difference between a color mask and a shape mask?
3.   How do you add to a color mask?
4.   How do you subtract from a color mask?
5.   What does the color mask's Softness slider do?
6.   Can you apply separate color adjustments to the inside and outside of any mask?
7.   What happens when you add more than one shape mask to a correction?
8.   If you add a shape mask to a correction with a color mask to create three masked areas—one with the color mask only, one with the shape mask only, and one where they intersect—which area will be adjusted if you use the Color Board?
9.   How do you animate a shape mask?

Answers

1.   A correction that's limited to a specific area of the image
2.   Color masks let you isolate a color, while shape masks isolate a portion of the frame using a shape.
3.   Shift-drag in the Viewer to add to the sampled area.
4.   Option-drag in the Viewer to subtract from the sampled area.

5. It adjusts the edge softness of the sampled range of color.

6. Yes

7. All masks are added together.

8. The area where the shape and color masks intersect

9. Add keyframes to the Shape Mask parameter in the Video Inspector, or use the Adjustments pop-up menu in the Timeline.

14

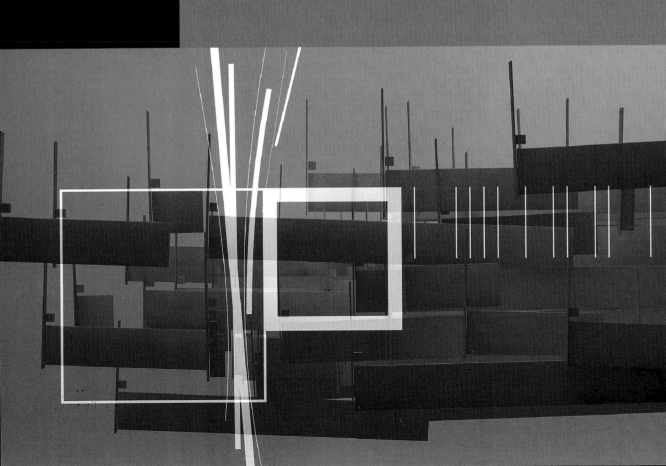

Advanced Sharing and Sending to Compressor

In this final lesson, you'll discover some of the advanced sharing options available in Final Cut Pro X. In particular, you'll learn about exporting XML, exporting media using roles, and sending your projects to Compressor for customized output in a wide variety of formats.

Additionally, you'll use Compressor to perform other essential tasks such as inserting closed captioning and creating surround sound assets—both of which are common deliverables in professional workflows.

You'll find the content for Lesson 14 at the root level of the companion disc Apple Pro Training Series: Final Cut Pro X Advanced Editing, Disc One.

> **MORE INFO** ▶ Basic sharing techniques are covered extensively in *Apple Pro Training Series: Final Cut Pro X* by Diana Weynand (Peachpit Press). You're encouraged to consult that book for additional information on sharing to disc, to the web, to Apple devices, or to other formats.

Appendix **A**

Using DSLR Footage

One of the most exciting and growing groups of filmmakers are those using digital SLR cameras (such as the *Canon 7D*, *Nikon D90*, and *Panasonic XL-1*) instead of traditional video cameras.

Editing footage shot with a DSLR (sometimes called *HDSLR* or *video DSLR*) is no different than editing footage shot with any other device, but Final Cut Pro X has a few features specifically designed to smooth the DSLR workflow and improve the editing experience.

This appendix covers several aspects of Final Cut Pro X that will particularly appeal to DSLR users, including the ability to edit video files without transcoding, the ability to begin editing immediately without waiting for media to be copied (or transcoded, if you choose to transcode), and an extremely easy method for syncing audio and video recorded on separate devices.

Importing DSLR Footage

DSLR cameras record footage in various formats and to a variety of storage media such as secure digital (SD), compact flash (CF), SxS memory cards, and others. In most cases, you can import files into Final Cut Pro X using the Import Files command.

1   Connect your camera to your computer using the cable that came with the camera, and turn it on.

    If your camera doesn't appear as an icon in the Finder, remove the camera's memory card and insert it into the card slot on your Mac (if it has one) or into an external card reader. The card appears in the Finder as a new volume.

    TIP Because most users will record over the memory card in the camera, it is wise to copy the entire memory card onto a hard disk to create a backup. See "Backing Up Your Media" in this appendix for more information.

2   In Final Cut Pro X, choose File > Import > Import Files to open the Import Files window.

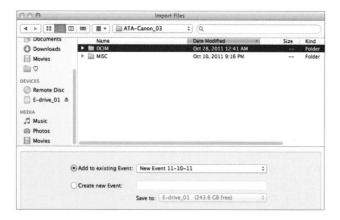

3   Locate the DCIM folder inside the camera folder, and then locate the still image or video files you want to import. The files may be in the root of the DCIM folder or in a folder one or two levels down. File structures vary by camera model and manufacturer.

4   Select the files you want to import. Command-click to choose multiple files.

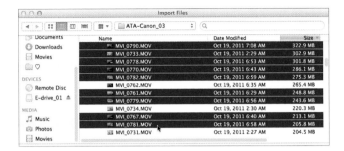

5   Choose the appropriate settings in the Import Files window.

If you're importing directly from the camera or memory card, be sure to select the "Copy files to Final Cut Events folder" checkbox.

You probably do not want to select "Import folders as Keyword Collections" because it will assign keywords—such as DCIM and other folder names—to all of your clips.

MORE INFO ▶ For more about the transcoding options, see the "No Transcoding Necessary!" sidebar in this appendix.

The Video and Audio analysis options can all be performed during the import or at any point later in the editing process. For more about clip analysis, see Lesson 1.

6   Click Import to add the selected clips to the current event.

▶ No Transcoding Necessary!

One advantage Final Cut Pro X offers of particular interest to DSLR users: the ability to edit footage in the native format in which it was shot. For most DSLRs this means a long GOP compression method such as H.264.

Final Cut Pro can play and edit files in these native formats without first performing a time-consuming con-

| Transcoding: | ☐ Create optimized media |
| | ☐ Create proxy media |

version to a different format. To skip the transcoding process, deselect the "Create optimized media" and "Create proxy media" checkboxes in the Transcoding section of the Import Files window.

> **TIP** ▶ You can always choose to transcode the imported files at a later time using the Transcode Media command.

As you add titles or other effects, any rendering that occurs will use the Apple ProRes 422 codec to ensure that the video always looks its best.

Optionally, you may choose to transcode your camera originals, either into an optimized format (usually Apple ProRes 422) and/or into the proxy format. These transcoded clips may provide improved playback performance compared to the camera originals on some Mac computers and will be more compatible with other software outside Final Cut Pro X.

Transcoding can be performed during the import process, or at any time thereafter by choosing File > Transcode Media, and then choosing "Create optimized media," "Create proxy media," or both.

> **NOTE** ▶ If either conversion has already been performed, that option is dimmed in the Transcode Media sheet.

Transcoding may also improve playback performance of multicam clips. When you select the "Create optimized media for multicam clips" setting in the Playback pane of Final Cut Pro Preferences, Final Cut Pro X will transcode your files in the background and create optimized versions when you add them to a multicam clip.

If you do choose to transcode on import or by using the Transcode Media function at any time, the conversion will be performed in the background and won't interrupt or interfere with your work. Be aware that converted files may require significantly more disk space than the long GOP originals.

Backing Up Your Media

Always make backup copies of your camera-original footage. Ideally, you should create a minimum of two copies stored on separate hard disks in case one drive unexpectedly fails.

> **TIP ▶** If your production was particularly expensive to produce or was a one-of-a-kind event, you might consider creating a third backup archive and storing it at a separate physical location.

Final Cut Pro cannot create a camera archive from most DSLR memory cards, so your best bet is to simply duplicate the entire memory card by dragging its icon from the Finder to your backup hard disk.

Alternatively, you could use Disk Utility (found in Macintosh HD > Applications > Utilities) to create a new disk image containing the contents of your memory card.

Be sure to name your backups in a very clear, easy-to-identify way. Although immediately after shooting you may believe that you'll never forget which backup is which, in a few months or years you'll be very thankful your naming convention left nothing to chance.

A wise naming scheme is to label the backup folder with the full date, camera name, and reel number for the card being backed up. If you produce many programs with overlapping shoot dates, you might also add the name of the show or project, or store the backups in an appropriately named parent folder.

Editing During Import

Another feature that benefits DSLR users is the ability to begin editing immediately after importing the footage into an event.

You can begin viewing and editing your footage even *while* Final Cut Pro X imports the files from the camera memory card. You can watch the clips, and add metadata, markers, clip ratings, and keywords. You can make selections and add them to projects. The only thing you can't do is move or delete clips because, technically, those clips don't exist yet.

During importing, Final Cut Pro will access the files directly from the memory card (or from the folder containing the backup you're importing) until they're successfully copied; and then as each clip is fully imported, Final Cut Pro will transparently switch to using the versions in the Event folder.

If you choose to transcode into optimized versions, you can continue to work while the computer generates the new files in the background. As the optimized files are successfully created, Final Cut Pro uses those versions instead of the camera originals.

Synching Audio and Video

One of the few disadvantages of DSLRs is that they are primarily still-image cameras, so they lack professional audio recording capabilities. Because of this, many DSLR video producers record sound to a separate audio recorder.

As long as you record scratch audio on the DSLR camera, Final Cut Pro X can sync up the audio and the video and generate a compound clip, allowing you to edit with one file that contains both the video and the high-quality audio (even though they exist as separate files on your hard disk).

1   Use the Import Files command to import your audio files and video files into a single event.

You may need to add metadata to the clips or change the clip names so you can identify which audio and video clips belong together. In this example, the clip names include the scene and take number, making it very easy to find the corresponding clips.

2   Select a video clip and its companion audio clip.

3   Choose Clip > Synchronize Clips, or press Command-Option-G.

A new synchronized clip—containing the perfectly synchronized content of the two clips—appears in the Event Browser.

NOTE ▶ If the audio clip begins before, or ends after the video clip, you will see black frames at the start or end of the compound clip.

4   Repeat steps 2 and 3 for each clip you want to sync.

5   Select all the compound clips and add a keyword (such as *Synced*) so they will be easy to locate without wading through all the original files.

Choosing Audio Channels

When you create synced clips, each clip contains the scratch audio from the camera as well as the high-quality audio from the audio recorder.

Before editing these clips, you should silence the scratch audio, so you hear only the high-quality audio when editing the clips into a project.

1   Select a synced clip.

2   Open the Audio Inspector and expand the Channel Configuration section.

Each of the channels is labeled, and you can skim them individually to verify which is the high-quality audio and which is the scratch audio.

3   Deselect the scratch audio channel.

4   Repeat these steps for each synchronized clip.

Editing with DSLR Footage

That's all you have to do to work with DSLR source footage. You can take advantage of all the features and powerful editing options in Final Cut Pro X just as you can when using footage shot with any other type of camera.

Index

Apple Certification
Fuel your mind.
Reach your potential.

Stand out from the crowd. Differentiate yourself and gain recognition for your expertise by earning Apple Pro certification to validate your Final Cut Pro X skills.

This book prepares you to earn Apple Certified Pro—Final Cut Pro X Level Two status. Level Two certification attests to a deeper understanding and mastery of advanced features of the application. You can only take Level Two exams after you earn Level One certification.

Three Steps to Certification

1   Choose your certification path.
    More info: training.apple.com/certification.

2   All Apple Authorized Training Centers (AATCs) offer all OS X and Pro Apps exams, even if they don't offer the corresponding course. To find the closest AATC, please visit training.apple.com/locations.

3   Register for and take your exam(s).

"Certification is important because it proves to employers, peers, and faculty that you have mastered the software and are ready to take on creative challenges."

— Jonathan Blake Huer,
Director of Emerging Technologies,
Ball State University

Reasons to Become an Apple Certified Pro

- **Raise your earning potential.** Studies show that certified professionals can earn more than their non-certified peers.

- **Distinguish yourself from others in your industry.** Proven mastery of an application helps you stand out from the crowd.

- **Display your Apple Certification logo.** Each certification provides a logo to display on business cards, resumes and websites.

- **Publicize your Certifications.** Publish your certifications on the Apple Certified Professionals Registry to connect with schools, clients and employers.

Training Options

Apple's comprehensive curriculum is available in many formats. How do you like to learn?

- Hands-on classroom training at Apple Authorized Training Centers worldwide

- Apple Pro Training Series books in both print and digital format

- Apple Video Training Series and video training apps for select titles

- New Test Yourself iPhone/iPad apps from Peachpit help you prepare with confidence

Visit training.apple.com to view all your learning options.

training.apple.com/certification

WATCH
READ
CREATE

Meet Creative Edge.

A new resource of unlimited books, videos and tutorials for creatives from the world's leading experts.

Creative Edge is your one stop for inspiration, answers to technical questions and ways to stay at the top of your game so you can focus on what you do best—being creative.

All for only $24.99 per month for access—any day any time you need it.

creativeedge.com